CLIVE JAMES

THE BOOK OF MY ENEMY

COLLECTED VERSE 1958–2003

PICADOR

First published 2003 by Picador
an imprint of Pan Macmillan Ltd
Pan Macmillan, 20 New Wharf Road, London N1 9RR
Basingstoke and Oxford
Associated companies throughout the world
www.panmacmillan.com

ISBN 0 330 42004 6

Clive James and the publishers wish to thank Westminster Music Ltd
and Onward Music Ltd for permission to use copyright song lyrics.

The right of Clive James to be identified as the
author of this work has been asserted by him in accordance
with the Copyright, Designs and Patents Act 1988.

Some material previously published as *Other Passports: Poems 1958–1985*,
first published 1986 by Jonathan Cape Ltd.
Peregrine Prykke's Pilgrimage through the London Literary World
first published 1974 by Jonathan Cape Ltd,
revised version first published 1976 by Jonathan Cape Ltd.

5 7 9 8 6

A CIP catalogue record for this book is available from
the British Library.

Typeset by Intype London Ltd
Printed and bound in Great Britain by
Mackays of Chatham plc, Chatham, Kent

To the memory of my mother

MINORA MAY JAMES

1910–2003

Contents

ix

EARLIER VERSE

Acknowledgements

Acknowledgements are due to the editors of the *Australian Book Review*, the *Australian's Review of Books*, *Encounter*, the *Listener*, the *London Review of Books*, the *New Review*, the *New Statesman*, the *New Yorker*, the *Observer*, the *Spectator*, the *Guardian* and the *Times Literary Supplement*, in which some of these poems first appeared.

Some of the earlier poems appeared in the Sydney University magazines *Arna*, *Hermes* and *Pluralist*; *Melbourne University Magazine*; and the Cambridge University magazines *Cambridge Review*, *Carcanet*, *Inverse*, *Granta*, *Pawn* and *Solstice*.

Some poems have been anthologized in *Young Commonwealth Poets '65*, edited by P. L. Brent; *New Poems 1971–1972*, edited by Peter Porter; *New Poems 1972–1973*, edited by Douglas Dunn; *Anthology of Contemporary Poetry*, edited by John Wain; *Brand X Poetry*, edited by William Zaranka; *The Faber Book of Parodies*, edited by Simon Brett; the *Oxford Book of Satirical Verse*, edited by Geoffrey Grigson; the *New Oxford Book of Australian Verse* and the *Oxford Book of Australian Religious Verse*, both edited by Les Murray; and the *Faber Book of Australian Verse*, edited by Peter Porter.

Some of the occasional poems first appeared in celebratory collections for Dame Leonie Kramer, Margaret Olley, Peter Porter and Anthony Thwaite. My gratitude to their various editors for the invitation. My gratitude also to Westminster Music and Essex Music, for their generous agreement to the use of some of the earlier song lyrics.

The *ur*-Version of *Peregrine Prykke's Pilgrimage through the London Literary World* was first performed at the Institute of Contemporary Arts on the night of June 3rd, 1974, under the auspices of the Poetry International Festival. It was later printed in the *New Review* for August 1974 and was also made available in a signed, limited edition of 200 copies. For the Improved Version, published in 1976, the versification was modified extensively throughout the poem, and characters, scenes, speeches, vignettes and atmospherics were added to the tune of some 350 lines.

Special thanks should go to Alan Jenkins, Karl Miller, Anthony

Thwaite, Claire Tomalin, John Gross, Mary-Kay Wilmers and the late Ian Hamilton, all of whom, at various times, played uncomplaining host to the kind of guest who not only moves in, but spreads himself out. I should also, on a point of national pride, acknowledge the generosity of Shelley Gare, Les Murray, Peter Porter (again and always), Peter Rose and Luke Slattery, for their gratifying conviction that some of my work in verse should be brought home to the land that somehow inspired it all, even when I was so long away.

I should also thank my book editors, Tom Maschler, Peter Straus and Andrew Kidd, for their generosity in countenancing the sort of publishing venture that joins the bottom line to the far horizon.

Introduction

When, in 1986, I decided it might be worth trying to keep some of my poems alive under the all-embracing title *Other Passports*, I gave that book an introduction which breathed intermittent fire. Behind the pyrotechnics, it was really a form of apology for blundering into territory already well marked out by figures whose credentials I knew to be in better shape. If the introduction to this volume turns out to sound less embattled, that will be because, although I have quite a few subsequently written poems to add, I feel less need to crack hardy about why I should want to do so. *Other Passports* surprised me by getting away with it. As the first paperback collection of contemporary verse that Picador ever published, it appeared in the airport bookshop spinners like any of my other books, or any books by any author sharing the same imprint. In such a context it had all the marks of a misjudged venture simply begging to be overlooked. But somehow it made its way, and eventually, over the course of about fifteen years, it sold out, leaving a gratifying space in the warehouse where there might well have been a hulking tumulus of printed paper slated for the pulp machine. The original Jonathan Cape hardback edition even got some favourable reviews, although all but the very best ones took it for granted that I was expressing myself in verse form only as a sideline to my other activities, most of them pretty reprehensible. I still had my face on screen a lot in those days, so it was axiomatic that the mind behind the face could only be playing with serious matters as a supplementary strand of entertainment.

I was ready to go along with that, and still am. I still think that a career as a poet is the wrong idea for most people who write verse, because it can lead to a concern for the reputation, and hence to that unedifying process – be it ever so sedulous and even sacrificial – by which the output is kept up when a real inner need is lacking, and the Muse doubles as an inflatable doll. But the writer who confines himself to never writing a poem except to answer a specific impulse might have to resign himself to having no reputation at all, because he looks like a part-timer. His best course, I now think, is to take it on the chin. He should forget his pride and remember his privilege. With no established apparatus to speak for them, his poems will speak for themselves. If they don't, he will have no ground to recoup before he tries again. If they do, it might be partly because nobody was expecting him to speak at all. At the pool table, the first weapon of the hustler is to look as if he does not belong.

Sceptics will assuredly spot that a book called *The Book of My Enemy* is a naked attempt to co-opt the notoriety that accrued to my poem 'The Book of My Enemy has Been Remaindered'. No doubt because of the intensities of cynicism, envy and hatred that it allegedly revealed, that poem was much anthologized in both Britain and Australia, and there is a German version appropriately rephrased for the nation that invented *Schadenfreude*. Needing whatever help I can get on the bookshop shelves, I would be a fool not to capitalize on an established brand. But in its truncated form, and transferred to the spine of a book, the title has another meaning. The urge to write in verse has always been my financial enemy, and I have always done my best to resist it, right from the beginning of my professional career. I had a family to feed, and prose paid. For poetry, the established magazines have always paid something, but when you measure the income against the time taken to compose in verse, it falls a long way behind fossicking for gold on Hampstead Heath. Like the ward sister who wants her nurses kept on short commons so as to freeze out any misfits who might secretly dream of auditioning for the Spice Girls, I persist in seeing some virtue in this wedding of the vocation to a vow of poverty. My great Australian contemporary Les Murray has argued convincingly for how a lifetime poet should get a better share of the revenue he will eventually generate, but not even he much likes the idea of subsidized poetry. He doesn't think the world owes him a living: he just thinks the publishing industry owes him a fair shake. I agree with that, but on the understanding that a fair shake must work out at not much more than a token payment for an expenditure of time, effort and concentration that can never be rewarded at its true cash value. If it could, any dullard who put in the graft would be on easy street. In that sense, my poems are my best claim to seriousness. Everything else I wrote paid me for my time. My poems never did, and still don't. But they still keep coming. The enemy is still with me.

Most of what he has made me do since the publication of *Other Passports* has here been added to the section called Recent Verse, a classification I have felt worth retaining because the date when I began feeling more confident about speaking in my own voice still feels recent to me even as the distance stretches to half a lifetime. Among the many additions are the handful of poems included in my essay book *The Dreaming Swimmer*, now out of print and probably fated to remain so. All the other Recent Verse additions, however, have not previously appeared in book form. The rest of the classifications from *Other Passports* can be retained without quibble, although one of them needs, like Recent Verse, to be substantially expanded. To the section called Verse Letters and Occasional Verse extra, mainly longer, poems written in later years have been added. In the section called Verse Diaries, I have restored the preface to the first, book-form publication of *Poem of the Year*, a preface I deleted from *Other Passports* on the principle that poems should proceed to their fate unaccompanied by explanations. But the preface, I have since decided, is something other than an explanation, and anyway it contains a tribute to Louis MacNeice's wonderful long poem *Autumn Journal* that it is only fitting to record here, because nothing else in the twentieth century so affected my idea of what public verse should aim to do. MacNeice's name is not heard as often now as it ought to be, but some younger readers might catch from the preface the urge to read his masterpiece themselves, and thus be taken back to a point in time when a lavishly gifted poet invented a whole new possibility – a possibility that he fulfilled with a candid dignity, a wealth of invention, and a mastery of rhythmically propelled colloquial eloquence that not even his more famous friend W. H. Auden could ever quite match.

Two new sections have been added. One of them is called Song Lyrics. For almost a decade in the late 1960s and the early 1970s I regularly wrote song lyrics for the music of Pete Atkin, who performed our songs on half a dozen commercial albums which eventually proved not quite commercial enough, the English chanson tradition being at that time short of a market from the viewpoint of the recording industry. It still is now, but now the A&R departments of the record companies are no longer the sole arbiter, because the World Wide Web can circumvent them and assemble a niche market out of enthusiasts. It turned out, as the Web expanded, that our own early enthusiasts had reproduced themselves, and now all the original Pete Atkin vinyl albums are available on CD to meet the demand, which can satisfy itself directly through the shop at the exemplary website www.peteatkin.com without going near a high-street record store: a very satisfactory development from our angle, because the music business in its unreconstructed form found it all too easy to lose our work in the shuffle. One consequence of this encouraging rebirth is that Atkin and I are back on the road at the eleventh hour, touring a song show in both Britain and Australia. After thirty years I am once again choking on the nosh in motorway cafes, and writing song lyrics in my down time between gigs. (As you can gather, I have dusted off the old vocabulary, if not the old flared trousers and polyester paisley shirts.) Already there is a whole new album, called *Winter Spring*. Many of the song fans have shown an encouraging interest in my other work in verse, and it doesn't seem impossible that the same interest might operate in the other direction. Not many poems are really lyrics in the sense that they can be set to music, but the idea is at least five hundred years old that there are lyrics which are really poems, give or take the odd stretch where only the melody can make sense of the scansion. The connection suits my prejudices and indeed my practice. In poetry I try not to write anything that can't be said, and it is a short step from saying to singing, although a tricky enjambement will often turn the step into a limp. But with due allowance for the necessity to keep a lyric clear line by line and not too compressed, I try just as hard with a lyric as with a poem to say as much as possible in a short space, and the two superficially different enterprises belong together deep down: so deep down, in fact, that I often don't know, when the first phrase comes, whether the finished piece will end up on stage or on the page.

Another section, at the end of the book, is formed from a single poem, my mock epic *Peregrine Prykke's Pilgrimage through the London Literary World*. The opus was written for performance at the ICA in June 1974, with myself as the narrator, Martin Amis in the role of the eponymous hero and Russell Davies brilliantly incarnating all the other roles, the models for which, in many cases, were sitting, and sometimes writhing, in the auditorium. The text was subsequently published as a limited-edition pamphlet by the *New Review*, and later as a book by Jonathan Cape, with illustrations by the aforesaid, omnicompetent Davies. It did well enough as a publication to tempt me into *folie de grandeur*, and over the next three years I published annual mock epics on different subjects. In the introduction to *Other Passports* I could be heard still harbouring the illusion that the four long poems might one day be reprinted as an integral work. Since then it has become clear even to me that only the first poem has a right to life. Its three sequels have all dated incurably, so I must let them go, with due anguish for the effort they took and the ambitions I rested in them. In this form as in any other, including the television script, I have always written everything as carefully as if it was meant to last forever, and in the full knowledge that I would be lucky if even a few things did. If you could tell in advance which project had the wings to dodge oblivion, you could go easy on all the others. Alas, it doesn't work that way. As Peter Cook once said, the BBC is full of transvestites, but we can't tell which ones they are.

Peregrine's quest, however, goes on, and always will. There is always someone like him: goggle-eyed at the splendour of the literary world and aching to be part of it. (I can remember when he was me.) But if the bedazzled young Perry was wrong about the glamour of it all, he was right in his capacity for admiration, and especially in his admiration for the poets. Even among the careerists and the poetasters, there are few who have ever made a name without writing at least one stanza that got into the common memory, and they could not have done that without sacrificing, at least for a short time, their ordinary pleasures to the stringent demands of the enemy. His modus operandi is to invade the mind with a single phrase, and then take over your life until you find all the other phrases that belong with it in a tight perimeter that excludes the ones that don't. Should you succeed, he retreats, and you may return to your other responsibilities. The surest mark of the incurable poet, the lifer, is to fear, rather than hope, that the enemy might not attack again. By that measure, and for what it is worth to say so, this book is not a supplement to my writing life, but at the heart of it. Poetry as a career, perhaps not: but as a mental condition, certainly. What kind of treatment might be appropriate for the mental condition is for the reader to decide. There were critics who recommended a straitjacket, but I have heard less from them as time goes by. If he lives long enough, the patient takes over the asylum.

London, 2003

Original Introduction to

Other Passports: Poems 1958–1985

During thirty years of writing verse, one hopes to have improved, but can only have done so by becoming more self-critical, a development which tends to winnow the crop in advance of the harvest. Therefore I am pleased to find some things asking to be kept even from early on. If it does not sound too grand to say that there was an initial phase, it was the ten-year period in which I wrote what were meant to be lyric poems. These mainly went into university magazines and newspapers either in Sydney or in Cambridge, and in the pages of those publications most of them demand to lie undisturbed. Though I never had what it took to be obscure, clarity still had to be worked for. Local outbreaks of straightforwardness from the early part of this struggle are here preserved under the title Earlier Verse, not because I want to disown them but because even at their most transparent they try so hard to disown me. To write in his own voice is every poet's object, and my voice, I have since realized, was the prosaic one I speak with. It was so close to hand that it took an age to reach.

A big help along the way was a second phase, not represented here. At Cambridge I began writing song lyrics for the music of my fellow undergraduate, Pete Atkin. In the next eight years we published half a dozen record albums. I never wrote from a surer instinct. But there came a point, while I was still writing song lyrics, when another instinct awkwardly insisted that I was not yet quite through with writing verse. The awkwardness lay in the fact that the new urge was theatrical. Having my song lyrics performed had given me a taste for going public. My mock epic poem *Peregrine Prykke's Pilgrimage* was the brazen outcome. Eventually it had three successors, and all four mock epics might one day appear together in a single volume suitably annotated, but here I need only say that before attempting that first, long, parodic poem-for-performance I wrote a number of isolated parodies, imitations and lampoons, most of which were first published under the name of Edward Pygge.

Hard news about Edward Pygge might prove useful to those scholars who concern themselves with the London Literary World in its more subterranean aspects. Pygge's activities were designedly shrouded in mystery, but by now there is a new generation of literati on the scene to whom the mystery looks like a conspiracy. It never was. Pygge simply happened. In his heyday he was three people. Ian Hamilton invented him, and composed, mainly for the pages of that astringent little magazine the *Review*, his first withering attacks on current poetic fashion. My own additions to the swinish canon were made in order to generate more material for a one-night literary spectacular presented at the ICA in the Mall. Rehearsed irregularly at the Pillars of Hercules in Greek Street, Soho, and unofficially known as the Edward Pygge Revue, the show was produced by Hamilton and myself but stolen outright by Russell Davies, who made a dramatic, unheralded appearance in the role of Pygge. Seemingly just off a plane from Chicago, Davies wore a dark suit, darker shirt, white tie, pointed shoes, and a black fedora with the brim pulled low over the eyes. He carried a violin case under his arm as if it contained a Thompson sub-machine gun loaded ready for action. He read our Pygge poems in a variety of voices to stunning effect. It should also be said that his own Pygge poems, when he could be persuaded to write them, were of deadly accuracy and unmatched inventiveness. He had that flair. The last two lines of 'The Wasted Land', for example, were supplied by Davies *sotto voce*, or perhaps *blotto voce*, as he sipped a pint at rehearsal. I appropriated them without compunction.

A man to respect, a back-room boy, an itinerant torpedo whose power depended on the obscurity of his turned-up coat collar, Edward Pygge found his reputation turning into fame, with all of its attendant dangers. On two occasions there were double-page spreads of Pygge poems in the *New Statesman*. Pygge started showing up in the same paper's weekly competition. He became a handy sobriquet for anyone who had a spoof to launch. The feminist termagant Edwina Pygge put in an appearance. Obviously it would have been only a matter of time before Edward and Edwina were joined by Kedward Pygge and their Nordic cousin, Hedwig Pygge. The star having gone nova, he duly dissipated into a nebula. Occupied by long confections far out of scale with Pygge's pinpoint focus, I forgot that I had ever been part of the collective brain beneath that dangerously angled black hat.

As well as the mock epics which are not here, I wrote verse letters which are. The first seven of these were published in book form under the title *Fan-Mail*, a term which Philip Larkin, in a letter, correctly pointed out should not have a hyphen. A slim volume verging on the flimsy, it was reviewed like the plague but did me good. The different verse forms I adopted were identical in their salutary discipline. It sounds like masochism and sometimes felt like it, but in the long run the exigencies of rhyme and metre made plainness mandatory by revealing would-be profundities as fudge. Here I have felt bound to discard only the first verse letter I wrote. Addressed to John Fuller, it was too clumsy to keep, in view of the high standards of craftsmanship he has set for those poets of his generation who have followed his example in producing, or trying to produce, urbane and entertaining public verse.

The only other things I have subtracted from the *Fan-Mail* verse letters are the italicization, extra capital letters and cognate olde worlde furniture which excused them as a deliberate throwback, when I should have admitted that I meant every word of them. I have included two verse letters written less apologetically later on, the ones to Michael Frayn and Craig Raine, and in the same section put two birthday poems, for Anthony Thwaite and Gore Vidal. This whole intermediate phase of extended rhyme-scheming was rounded out, symbolically if not chronologically, by my fourth mock epic *Charles Charming's Challenges*, for which the West End critics demanded that its perpetrator be transported to Botany Bay, and were not to be mollified by the information that he was born there. Adopting a new disguise as a novelist, I discreetly vacated the poetic scene.

While hiding out through a long winter, I remembered Pygge. Having found a legitimate freedom of language through strict form, I was ready to recapture, *in propria persona* this time, my share of Pygge's laconic anarchy, his mimetic disdain, his heroic disinclination to be impressed. It occurred to me that the poems I had written under his name were the first that had been entirely mine – the reason that I reproduce them here, minus the porcine pseudonym. A strange characteristic of parody is that by tightening your grip on someone else's throat you can loosen your own tongue. Pygge would pitch his voice at any level that suited the case, shade it to any tone. Either he trusted his own personality to come through anyway or else he simply didn't give a damn. Now that he had finished copying everybody else, I resolved to copy him.

The shorter pieces grouped under the heading Recent Verse were composed in the euphoria of this very elementary breakthrough.

Taking strict form from my longer poems and polyphonic courage from Pygge, I wrote them in matching stanzas when the occasion demanded, and free verse when it did not. But the freedom would not have been the same without the discipline, nor the discipline without the freedom. In the compound of those two elements resides the only concept of the modern that I am willing to understand. Recent verse is a category which I hope I will go on adding to for the rest of my life. It turned out, however, that the urge to write longer poems was not extinct, merely dormant. They rose again in the form of verse diaries. 'An Address to the Nation' was the rehearsal for *Poem of the Year*. I include them both here, without the author's note attached to the latter when it was first printed in book form. If these two verse diaries seem to take up a disproportionate space, it doesn't mean that I value long poems more than short ones. But I don't value them less, either. At any length, the aim is brevity.

London, 1986

RECENT VERSE

The Book of My Enemy Has Been Remaindered

The book of my enemy has been remaindered
And I am pleased.
In vast quantities it has been remaindered.
Like a van-load of counterfeit that has been seized
And sits in piles in a police warehouse,
My enemy's much-praised effort sits in piles
In the kind of bookshop where remaindering occurs.
Great, square stacks of rejected books and, between them, aisles
One passes down reflecting on life's vanities,
Pausing to remember all those thoughtful reviews
Lavished to no avail upon one's enemy's book –
For behold, here is that book
Among these ranks and banks of duds,
These ponderous and seemingly irreducible cairns
Of complete stiffs.

The book of my enemy has been remaindered
And I rejoice.
It has gone with bowed head like a defeated legion
Beneath the yoke.
What avail him now his awards and prizes,
The praise expended upon his meticulous technique,
His individual new voice?
Knocked into the middle of next week
His brainchild now consorts with the bad buys,
The sinkers, clinkers, dogs and dregs,
The Edsels of the world of movable type,
The bummers that no amount of hype could shift,
The unbudgeable turkeys.

Yea, his slim volume with its understated wrapper
Bathes in the glare of the brightly jacketed *Hitler's War Machine*,
His unmistakably individual new voice
Shares the same scrapyard with a forlorn skyscraper
Of *The Kung-Fu Cookbook*,
His honesty, proclaimed by himself and believed in by others,

His renowned abhorrence of all posturing and pretence,
Is there with *Pertwee's Promenades and Pierrots* –
One Hundred Years of Seaside Entertainment,
And (oh, this above all) his sensibility,
His sensibility and its hair-like filaments,
His delicate, quivering sensibility is now as one
With *Barbara Windsor's Book of Boobs,*
A volume graced by the descriptive rubric
'My boobs will give everyone hours of fun.'

Soon now a book of mine could be remaindered also,
Though not to the monumental extent
In which the chastisement of remaindering has been meted out
To the book of my enemy,
Since in the case of my own book it will be due
To a miscalculated print run, a marketing error –
Nothing to do with merit.
But just supposing that such an event should hold
Some slight element of sadness, it will be offset
By the memory of this sweet moment.
Chill the champagne and polish the crystal goblets!
The book of my enemy has been remaindered
And I am glad.

Sack Artist

Reeling between the redhead and the blonde
Don Juan caught the eye of the brunette.
He had no special mission like James Bond.
He didn't play the lute or read *Le Monde*.
Why was it he on whom their sights were set?

For let's make no mistake, the women pick
Which men go down in history as avid
Tail-chasers with the enviable trick
Of barely needing to chat up the chick –
From Warren Beatty back to ruddy David.

But why the broads latch on to the one bloke
Remains what it has always been, a riddle.
Byron though famous was both fat and broke
While Casanova was a standing joke,
His wig awry, forever on the fiddle.

Mozart made Juan warble but so what?
In *Don Giovanni* everybody sings.
The show would fall flat if the star did not
And clearly he's not meant to sound so hot:
His women praise him, but for other things.

They trill of his indifference and disdain
But might have liked his loyalty still more.
We can't, from how they lyrically complain,
Conclude that when he left they liked the pain
As much as they enjoyed the bliss before.

Bad treatment doesn't do it: not from him,
Still less from us, who find out when we try it
That far from looking tickled they turn grim,
Leaving us at a loss out on a limb,
Instructed to obtain a kite and fly it.

Which doesn't make the chap of whom we speak
Some gigolo devoted to their pleasure.
The fancy man turns no strong woman weak
But merely pumps out what was up the creek.
Plundering hulks he lays up little treasure.

Good looks don't hurt but rate low on their own.
The teenage girls who fall for Richard Gere
Admit his face is random flesh and bone
Beside Mel Gibson's, that his skin lacks tone
And when he smiles his pin eyes disappear.

They go bananas when he bares his chest
But torsos that outstrip his leave them cold.
One bit of you might well be the world's best
But women won't take that and leave the rest:
The man entire is what they would enfold.

The phallus fallacy thus shows its roots
Afloat in the pornographer's wet dream
By which a synechdochic puss in boots
Strides forward frantic to be in cahoots
With his shy mote grown into a great beam.

A shame to be without the wherewithal
But all the wherewith you might have down there
Won't get the ladies queuing in the hall –
Not if you let it loose at a masked ball,
Not if you advertise it on the air.

None of which means that lust takes a back seat.
Contrariwise, it is the main event.
The grandest *grandes dames* cease to be discreet.
Their souls shine through their bodies with the heat.
They dream of more to come as they lie spent.

The sort of women who don't do such things
Do them for him, wherein might lie the clue.
The smell of transcendental sanction clings
Like injured ozone to angelic wings –
An envoy, and he's only passing through.

In triumph's moment he must hit the trail.
However warm the welcome, he can't stay.
Lest those fine fingers read his back like braille
He has to pull out early without fail –
Preserve his mystery with a getaway.

He is the perfect stranger. Humbler grades
Of female don't get even a brief taste –
With Errol Flynn fenced in by flashing blades
And Steve McQueen in aviator shades
It always was a dream that they embraced.

Sheer fantasy makes drama from the drab,
Sweet reverie a slow blues from the bleak:
How Cary Grant would not pick up the tab,
Omar Sharif sent roses in a cab,
Those little lumps in Robert Redford's cheek.

Where Don's concerned the first glance is enough:
For certain he takes soon what we might late.
The rest of us may talk seductive guff
Unendingly and not come up to snuff,
Whereat we most obscenely fulminate.

We say of her that she can't pass a prick.
We call him cunt-struck, stick-man, power tool,
Muff-diver, stud, sack artist, motor dick,
Getting his end away, dipping his wick,
A stoat, a goat, a freak, a fucking fool.

So we stand mesmerized by our own fuss,
Aware that any woman, heaped with grief,
Will give herself to him instead of us
Because there is so little to discuss –
And cry *perfido mostro!* in relief.

Her true desires at long last understood,
She ponders, as she holds him locked above her,
The living definition of the good –
Her blind faith in mankind and womanhood
Restored by the dumb smile of the great lover.

The Supreme Farewell of Handkerchiefs

With acknowledgements to Arthur Gold and
Robert Fizdale, authors of *Misia*

'I've left that great page blank,' said Mallarmé
When asked why he'd not written of his boat.
There are such things as mean too much to say.
You have to let it drift, to let it float.

The man who did the asking was Manet,
Whose niece's journal treasures the reply.
There are such things as mean too much to say,
But little Julie Manet had a try.

To represent the young, Paul Valéry
Delivered half a speech and then broke down.
He missed his master's deep simplicity.
Then everybody started back to town.

Among those present were Rodin, Bonnard,
Lautrec, Mirbeau, Vallotton, Maeterlinck
And Misia's eternal slave Vuillard.
But Renoir, who had painted her in pink,

Knew ways to tame her when she got annoyed
At how they laughed instead of looking glum.
He thought such moments ought to be enjoyed.
Had not mortality been overcome?

Said Renoir, who had been the poet's friend:
'A Mallarmé does not die every day.'
A sly hint of his own approaching end?
There are such things as mean too much to say.
'I've left that great page blank,' said Mallarmé.

A Gesture towards James Joyce

My gesture towards *Finnegans Wake* is deliberate.
  – Ronald Bush, *T. S. Eliot: A Study in
  Character and Style*

The gesture towards *Finnegans Wake* was deliberate.
It was not accidental.
Years of training went into the gesture,
As W. C. Fields would practise a juggling routine
Until his eczema-prone hands bled in their kid gloves;
As Douglas Fairbanks Sr trimmed the legs of a table
Until, without apparent effort and from a standing start,
He could jump up on to it backwards;
Or as Gene Kelly danced an entire tracking shot over and over
Until the final knee-slide ended exactly in focus,
Loafers tucked pigeon-toed behind him,
Perfect smile exultant,
Hands thrown open saying 'How *about* that?'

The gesture towards *Finnegans Wake* was deliberate.
Something so elaborate could not have been otherwise.
Though an academic gesture, it partook in its final form
Of the balletic arabesque,
With one leg held out extended to the rear
And the equiponderant forefinger pointing demonstratively
Like the statue of Eros in Piccadilly Circus,
Or, more correctly, the Mercury of Giambologna,
Although fully, needless to say, clad.

The gesture towards *Finnegans Wake* was deliberate,
Its aim assisted by the position of the volume,
A 1957 printing in the yellow and orange wrapper
Propped on a sideboard and opened at page 164
So that the gesture might indicate a food-based conceit
About *pudding the carp before doeuvre hors* –
The Joycean amalgam in its ludic essence,
Accessible to students and yet also evincing

9

The virtue of requiring a good deal of commentary
Before what looked simple even if capricious
Emerged as precise even if complex
And ultimately unfathomable.

The gesture towards *Finnegans Wake* was deliberate,
Being preceded by an 'It is no accident, then',
An exuberant 'It is neither accidental nor surprising'
And at least two cases of 'It is not for nothing that',
These to adumbrate the eventual paroxysm
In the same way that a bouncer from Dennis Lillee
Has its overture of giant strides galumphing towards you
With the face both above and below the ridiculous moustache
Announcing by means of unmistakable grimaces
That what comes next is no mere spasm
But a premeditated attempt to knock your block off.

The gesture towards *Finnegans Wake* was deliberate
And so was my gesture with two fingers.
In America it would have been one finger only
But in Italy I might have employed both arms,
The left hand crossing to the tense right bicep
As my clenched fist jerked swiftly upwards –
The most deliberate of all gestures because most futile,
Defiantly conceding the lost battle.

The gesture towards *Finnegans Wake* was deliberate:
So much so that Joyce should have seen it coming.
Even through the eyepatch of his last years.
He wrote a book full of nothing except writing
For people who can't do anything but read,
And now their gestures clog the air around us.
He asked for it, and we got it.

Thoughts on Feeling Carbon-Dated

No moons are left to see the other side of.
Curved surfaces betray once secret centres.
Those plagues were measles the Egyptians died of.
A certain note of disillusion enters.

Were Empson starting now, no doubt exists
That now no doubt exists about space–time's
Impetuosity, his pithy gists
Would still stun, but no more so than his rhymes.

Physics has dished its prefix meta. Science,
First having put black shoes and a blue suit on,
Controls the world's supply of mental giants.
A Goethe now would lack words to loathe Newton.

It's forty years since James Joyce named the quark.
Now nobody's nonplussed to hear light rays
Get sucked down holes so fast they show up dark.
Nor would the converse of that news amaze.

It all gets out of reach as it grows clear.
What we once failed to grasp but still were thrilled with
Left us for someone else, from whom we hear
Assurances about the awe they're filled with.

One night in Cambridge Empson read to us.
He offered us some crisps and seemed delighted
So many young should still want to discuss
Why science once got laymen so excited.

Johnny Weissmuller Dead in Acapulco

Apart possibly from waving hello to the cliff-divers
Would the real Tarzan have ever touched Acapulco?
Not with a one-hundred-foot vine.
Jungle Jim maybe, but the Ape Man never.
They played a tape at his funeral
In the Valley of Light cemetery of how he had sounded
Almost fifty years back giving the pristine ape-call,
Which could only remind all present that in decline
He would wander distractedly in the garden
With his hands to his mouth and the unforgettable cry
Coming out like a croak –
This when he wasn't sitting in his swim-trunks
Beside the pool he couldn't enter without nurses.

Things had not been so bad before Mexico
But they were not great.
He was a greeter in Caesar's Palace like Joe Louis.
Sal, I want you should meet Johnny Weissmuller.
Johnny, Mr Sal Volatile is a friend of ours from Chicago.
With eighteen Tarzan movies behind him
Along with the five Olympic gold medals,
He had nothing in front except that irrepressible paunch
Which brought him down out of the tree house
To earth as Jungle Jim
So a safari suit could cover it up.
As Jungle Jim he wasn't just on salary,
He had a piece of the action,
But coming so late in the day it was not enough
And in Vegas only the smile was still intact.

As once it had all been intact, the Greek classic body
Unleashing the new-style front-up crawl like a baby
Lifting itself for the first time,
Going over the water almost as much as through it,
Curing itself of childhood polio
By making an aquaplane of its deep chest,

Each arm relaxing out of the water and stiffening into it,
The long legs kicking a trench that did not fill up
Until he came back on the next lap,
Invincible, easily breathing
The air in the spit-smooth, headlong, creek-around-a-rock trough
Carved by his features.

He had six wives like Henry VIII but don't laugh,
Because Henry VIII couldn't swim a stroke
And if you ever want to see a true king you should watch
     Weissmuller
In *Tarzan Escapes* cavorting underwater with Boy
In the clear river with networks of light on the shelving sand
Over which they fly weightless to hide from each other behind
     the log
While Jane wonders where they are.
You will wonder where you are too and be shy of the answer
Because it is Paradise.

When the crocodile made its inevitable entry into the clear river
Tarzan could always settle its hash with his bare hands
Or a knife at most,
But Jungle Jim usually had to shoot it
And later on he just never got to meet it face to face –
It was working for the Internal Revenue Service.

There was a chimpanzee at his funeral,
Which must have been someone's idea of a smart promotion,
And you might say dignity had fled,
But when Tarzan dropped from the tall tree and swam out of
     the splash
Like an otter with an outboard to save Boy from the waterfall
It looked like poetry to me,
And at home in the bath I would surface giving the ape-call.

Reflections on a Cardboard Box

Hostathion contains Triazophos,
Controls seed weevil, pea moth, carrot fly.
Of pesticides Hostathion is the boss.
Pests take one sip, kick up their heels and die.

They never find out what Hostathion is.
Triazophos remains the merest word,
Though partly echoed by the acrid fizz
Which suddenly grows too loud to be heard.

Hostathion was once Achilles' friend,
Staunch at his elbow before Ilios,
But now that name brings pea moth a quick end
Assisted by the cruel Triazophos.

Heroic words are too brave for the deeds
They do, yet maybe now they do less evil –
Ferocious but in service to our needs,
Venting our wrath for us on the seed weevil.

Forests of swords on the Homeric plain
Are momentarily invoked. Well, then,
It says much for this age where we complain
Men die like flies, that flies should die like men.

Triazophos sailed with Hostathion
Through centuries as if this were their goal:
Infinite enemies to fall upon,
Killing so common it is called control.

But all the old insanity is gone.
Where are the funeral pyres, the shrieks of loss?
You need to watch only Hostathion.
Hostathion contains Triazophos,

Who once reaped heads by night in no-man's-land
Obeying no man's orders but his own.
Look at him now, Hostathion's right hand –
Cleaning their guns beside the telephone.

The Philosophical Phallus

Female desire aims to subdue, overcome and pacify the unbridled ambition of the phallus.

– Roger Scruton

The unbridled phallus of the philosopher
Was seen last week galloping across the South Downs,
Flame spurting from its flared nostril.

The phallus being a horse in which
Both mane and tail are bunched together at the back end,
This unharnessed piece of horseflesh was of necessity unable
To accompany with a display of shaken neck-hair
The tossing of its head,
But the tossing of its head was tremendous nevertheless,
Like that of Bucephalus, the steed of Alexander.

Where the lush grass curves up to the rim of the chalk cliffs
So that they drop away where you cannot see them
When looking from inland,
Such was the cyclorama against which ran rampant
The unbridled phallus of the philosopher,
Pulling lawn like an emerald treadmill incessantly beneath
The unravelling thunder of its hooves –
Accoutrements which a phallus does not normally possess
But perhaps in this case they were retractable
Like the undercarriage of some large, cigar-shaped aircraft –
The Starlifter, for example, or the C-5A Galaxy.

See where it comes across 'the ontological divide
Separating men and women'!
The unbridled phallus in its frightening hauteur,
Gushing suds with each procreative snort –
Not the small, dog-skulled horse of the Greeks and the Etruscans,
But the horse of the Persians as noted by Herodotus,
Big, built thickly, hefty-headed,
Its two great globular hindquarters throbbing
Like the throats of rutting frogs.

The prancing pudendum curls its lip but says Yes to Life:
It is a yea-neigher.
Not only does it say 'ha-ha!' among the trumpets,
But in the landscaped gardens of fashionable country houses
It trumpets among the ha-has,
And the pulsing vein of its back is not afraid.

Though fleet-footed as an Arab it is stronger than a Clydesdale,
Shouldered like a Shire, bulk-bodied like a Suffolk –
A standing, foam-flanked reproach
To all those of us more appropriately represented
By the Shetland pony,
Or that shrunken, shrivelled toy horse with the mule-tail
Equus przewalskii, Prejvalsky's horse
From the Kobdo district of western Mongolia.

At nightfall the women of storm-swept lonely farms,
Or at casement windows of the grand houses aforesaid,
Or women anywhere who languish 'unfulfilled *qua* women',
Feel their ontological divide transformed to jelly
At the vibrant snuffle in the distance –
Long to subdue it, to overcome it, to pacify it,
Willing it homeward to its chosen stable,
Which will suffer its presence all the more exquisitely
For being neither deep nor wide enough wholly to contain

The unbridled ambition of the philosophical phallus.

Egon Friedell's Heroic Death

Egon Friedell committed suicide
By jumping from his window when he saw
Approaching Brownshirts eager to preside
At rites the recent *Anschluss* had made law.

Vienna's coffee-house habitués
By that time were in Paris, Amsterdam,
London, New York. Friedell just couldn't raise
The energy to take it on the lam.

Leaving aside the question of their looks,
The Jews the Nazis liked to see in Hell
Were good at writing and owned lots of books –
Which all spelled certain curtains for Friedell.

Friedell was cultivated in a way
That now in Europe we don't often see.
For every volume he'd have had to pay
In pain what those thugs thought the fitting fee.

Forestalling them was simply common sense,
An act only a Pharisee would blame,
Yet hard to do when fear is so intense.
Would *you* have had the nerve to do the same?

The normal move would be to just lie still
And tell yourself you somehow might survive,
But this great man of letters had the will
To meet his death while he was still alive.

So out into the air above the street
He sailed with all his learning left behind,
And by one further gesture turned defeat
Into a triumph for the human mind.

The civilized are most so as they die.
He called a warning even as he fell
In case his body hit a passer-by
As innocent as was Egon Friedell.

Homage to Rafinesque

The ichthyologist Constantine Rafinesque-Schmaltz
(Who was pleased to be known as quite simply Rafinesque)
And John James Audubon the famous student of birds
(Whose folios are generally thought too gorgeous for words
Although when opened they envelop your entire desk)
Teamed up in America as if they were dancing a waltz.

It was neither fish nor fowl crabbed their double act.
The flap in their cabin was caused by a humble bat
Which Rafinesque with the nearest thing to hand attacked,
Thus pounding Audubon's beloved violin out flat.

The revenge Audubon took was oblique but sure.
He returned from the Ohio River with drawings, life-size,
Of fish Rafinesque hadn't seen hide nor hair of before,
But belief in Audubon's pencil put scales on his eyes.

He published a book which his enemies loved for its faults.
To pay with his fame for a fiddle was clearly grotesque.
With the object of leading his friend up a similar creek
He might justly have fashioned a phoenix claw or orc beak,
But he showed the forbearance implied by his name, Rafinesque.
Now Audubon's plates are hoarded like gold in the vaults

And only the fish honour Constantine Rafinesque-Schmaltz.

Will Those Responsible Come Forward?

May the Lord have mercy on all those peoples
Who suffer from a perversion of religion –
Or, to put it in a less equivocating way,
Who suffer from an excess of religion –
Or, to come right out with it,
Who suffer from religion.

Let Him tell those catholic Protestants or protestant Catholics
Who in Northern Ireland go to bed on Saturday night
Looking forward to a morning of Holy Worship
That just this once they should make other plans –
Have a heavy cold, a stomach upset or a pulled hamstring
Severe enough to render them immobile,
With something similar for their children –
So that they will not be there to form a congregation
In a church just big enough for a small massacre.
Arrange this reprieve, Lord,
And if you can't manage that much then for Christ's sake
Hand the whole deal over to Allah.

May the Lord with the assistance of Allah
Give heed to the cries of those children in Beirut
Who have the dubious luck to be ten years old and under
While dwelling in the vicinity of a PLO faction
Currently being wiped out by another PLO faction,
And kindly swing it so that the incoming rockets
Do not dismember their small persons irreparably.
Children older than ten years we will give up on,
Not wanting the moon,
And their mothers, needless to say, are for the high jump.
Fix it, Lord. Get Al on to it,
And if it turns out to be more than you can handle
Raise Jehovah on the horn.

May the Lord and Allah with Jehovah's proverbial
In-depth back-up and sales apparatus

Make a concerted effort to cut the crap,
For the following reasons among others:

Lest at least two kinds of Christians during their annual shoot-out
Bisect an old lady who hears the word 'Duck!'
But can't hit the deck because of sciatica
(May her stoop be steep) –

Lest the Druze and the Jews or the Juze and the Drews,
When shelling each other from somewhere each side
Of a ridge or a bridge,
Cascade hot shrapnel on the intervening hospital
Whose patients suffer from mental disorders,
And thus exacerbate in those inherently unstable minds
An already acute sense of insecurity
(May their straitjackets be flak jackets) –

Lest Iraq and Iran or Iran and Iraq go to rack and ruin
Not just in the standard Islamic manner
Of finding each other insufficiently fanatical,
But with an ironic new wrinkle
By which the hitherto unapproachably sordid
Ayatollah or Arsola
Is upstaged by his own appointee,
That even more sadistic fuckwit and fruitcake
The Hayula or Payola,
Who has women tortured in front of their husbands
As a forceful reminder, no doubt supererogatory,
That you can't fight central mosque
(May their screams be deafening) –

Who also, if that doesn't do the trick,
Has the children tortured along with their mothers
(May they all go crazy quickly),
The object being to make the fathers admit
That they plotted the regime's overthrow –
A pretty fantastic charge when you consider
That the regime's overthrow hasn't yet been accomplished
By Allah functioning either on his tod
Or in combination with the Lord, Jehovah,

Buddha, the Great Spirit and each and every other
Recognized form of God –

Always supposing that They are working on it.
Always supposing that They care
About that or anything else.

But this is the sin of despair.

Echo Echo Echo

Changes in temperature entail turmoil.
Petits pois palpitate before they boil.
Ponds on the point of freezing look like oil.
And God knows what goes on below the soil.

God and the naturalists, who penetrate
With camera crews to depths as dark as fate
And shoot scenes hideous to contemplate
Where burrowing Attenboroughs fight and mate.

In outer space the endless turbulence
Seems too far gone to be at our expense.
One likes to think that if a bang's immense
It didn't happen in the present tense.

Still it's unnerving when two galaxies –
One Catherine wheel and one like a Swiss cheese –
Get stuck in with sharp elbows and scraped knees,
Cancelling out their twin eternities.

As for inside the atom here at home,
It makes the cosmos look like *jeu de paume*
Played out around the Houston Astrodome.
We might as well be back in ancient Rome.

Random, unjust and violent universe!
We feel, and those less ignorant feel worse,
Knowing that what's observed must soon disperse
And Phaethon's car turn out to be a hearse.

Hence, or despite that, our concern with form,
Though even here outclassed by nature's norm.
Snowflakes knock spots off Philibert de L'Orme
But something tells us that they are not warm.

Not that *we* are, compared with, say, the worms
Who live on lava, or are those the germs
That breed in butane and eat isotherms?
I'm not much good with scientific terms.

Even for Einstein it remained a dream
To unify the field, which makes it seem
Likely the rest of us won't get a gleam
Of how, or if, the whole works fit a scheme.

One merely hopes that we have made a start.
Our apprehensions might not melt the heart
Or even be heartfelt for the most part,
But from that insufficiency comes art.

We gather ourselves up from the abyss
As lovers after copulation kiss –
Lip-service which, while semaphoring bliss,
Puts in a claim that there was point to this.

Small wonder, therefore, that from time to time,
As dollar millionaires still nickel-and-dime,
The free-form poet knuckles down to rhyme –
Scared into neatness by the wild sublime.

The Anchor of the *Sirius*

Triangular Macquarie Place, up from the Quay,
Is half rainforest, half a sculpture park
Where can be found – hemmed in by palms and ferns,
Trees touching overhead – the Obelisk
From which, one learns, All Public Roads are Measured
Leading to the Interior of the Colony.
Skyscraper cliffs keep this green garden dark.

The Obelisk is sandstone. Thomas Mort
Is also present, bronze on a tall plinth –
His plain Victorian three-piece suit bulks large,
Befitting Sydney's first successful exporter
Of refrigerated foods – while, lower down
This plush declivity, one finds a bubbler
Superfluously shaded by a small
But intricate gun-metal *baldacchino*,
Sure-footed as a Donatello font.

Thus in a sculpture court less up to date
Yet cooler than MOMA's, leafier than the Frick,
One strolls encountering pieces carried out
In traditional materials and is lulled –
Till this free-standing object looms and startles
Like a Calder by Duchamp. It stops you cold,
The anchor of the *Sirius*. It hooks you
More firmly than the fluke which can't be seen
(Because, presumably, buried in the earth)
Could ever have snared the bottom of Sydney Cove.

One is amazed by how it is not old –
Which means the Colony's protracted birth
(The women were outscreamed by the flayed men)
Falls so far short of being long ago
It's hard to grasp. The anchor was brought back
From where the ship ended its history –
I think it tried to sail through Norfolk Island –

To where it began ours. Yes, the First Fleet
Dropped its first anchor just one hundred yards
(Or metres, as they say now) down the street –
And this is it, not much more touched by time
Than now by me, a yokel in the museum.

The crops failed. Phillip was no dynamo,
But Macquarie was, and men like Mort could double
The town's wealth in ten years. The scrub grew long
And lush like Joan Sutherland's throat. Success
Went overseas, took umpteen curtain calls,
Was toasted and had toast named after it,
And now the audience is here. Out on the harbour
Captain Cook II jam-packed with Japanese,
Their Nikons crackling like automatic flak,
Goes swanning past the well-remembered line
Where the submarine nets were when I was young,
Forty years ago – i.e. a full
Fifth of the time Port Jackson's had that name.

And after I'd grown up and gone away
Like the wool-clip to the other end of the world
(Where the wool was turned to suit-cloth and sent back
So Thomas Mort, full of ideas as Dickens,
Might look the part of the philanthropist)
The anchor of the *Sirius* had me pinned –
Spiked, rooted to the spot under these trees
Which filter what light's left by the glass towers
They put up yesterday so that the banks –
Algemene Bank Nederland NV,
Dresdner Bank AG, Banco Nazionale del Lavoro,
Sumitomo International Finance Australia –
Might catch through tinted windows like hot news
Digits conveying all they need to know,
Drawn down from space by ranks of VDUs
And here made manifest as a green glow –
New York and London, Hong Kong, Tokyo,
Sucked in at once to this same lightning rod –
Completing their great journey from afar
As a tired sinner comes at last to God,
As a ship comes in and drops anchor.

The Ferry Token

Not gold but some base alloy, it stays good
For one trip though the currency inflates –
Hard like the ferry's deck of seasoned wood,
The only coin in town that never dates.

Don Juan, as described by Baudelaire,
Before he crossed the Styx to the grim side
Paid Charon *son obole*, his ferry fare.
Was it this very token, worth one ride?

Of course it wasn't. This poor thing will buy
The traveller no myth beyond the dark
Leonine Pinchgut with one beady eye
Fixed on the brilliant, beckoning Luna Park.

At most it takes you back to Billy Blue
Whose ferry linked the Quay to the North Shore
Somewhere about the year of Waterloo –
And probably more after than before.

There's been so little time for grand events.
One ferry sank, but saying those who drowned
Contributed to our historic sense
Would be obscene and logically unsound.

Nevertheless nostalgia impregnates
This weightless disc as sunlight bleaches wood.
Our past is shallow but it scintillates –
Not gold but some base alloy, it stays good.

Funnelweb

The flame reflected in the welder's mask
Burns the board-rider's upstage fingertips
That cut a swathe across the curved sea wall
Inside the Banzai Pipeline's tubular swell.
Sopranos feel the same fire on their lips
Kissing Jochanaan as befits the task.

The crank-winged Chance-Vought F4-U Corsair
When turning tightly spilled white vortices
Behind its wing tips in the cobalt blue.
A mere machine, a Running W
As once brought stuntmen's horses to their knees,
And yet you can't deny it carved the air.

Phenomena like these, it will be said,
Are only incidental at the most
And mostly trivial, to say the least:
Less the confetti at the wedding feast
Than the box it came in, spice without the roast,
Beaches at Tarawa without the dead.

A saturation diver sets his seal
Where even fish can't see reflected flame.
A surfer in the folded tube may form
His signature unnoticed from the foam.
Night fighters' ailerons worked just the same
And Salome might think of her next meal.

True, but not true enough, in my belief.
These things though tenuous aren't set apart.
The casual grace note can't help but imply,
If not the outline of the melody,
Then anyway the impulse at its heart –
And do so all the more for being brief.

Stillness in movement is a waking dream
Movement in stillness has refined from strength.
The river bank must make the drift apparent
Of swans at evening plugged into the current,
But lest they be disorganized at length
Just out of sight they steer to point upstream.

Wristy Makarova's Odette/Odile
(Two lovely people spinning on one toe)
Exemplifies the Body Beautiful
Consumed by its own power to appal.
Watch how the whiplash whirlwind sucks up snow –
A double helix drawn from sex appeal.

Woodcut adoring kings with narrowed eye
Quite clearly find the cradle-capped young Prince
Painful to look at, backed up by his nimbus.
Even His Mother, pierced by the columbus
And haloed in Her own right, seems to wince:
The sun is in the wrong part of the sky.

He could not save Himself, they said with scorn,
But always it has been supposed they erred
And that, armed by His power to distinguish
The star-bursts in His hands from human anguish,
He ultimately went out like a bird
The way that He came in when He was born.

Watching a dear friend go down fast with cancer
Like a raindrop down a window pane, I hold
Her hand of balsa clad with clear doped silk
Pulsating like the skin of simmering milk
Which must boil over soon and leave her cold.
Next time *I'm* coming back a necromancer.

The floorboards in Kyoto's Nijo-jo
Will sing like flocks of birds from their sleeved nails
When someone walks, however light in weight.
Thus Tokugawa shoguns dreamed at night
Equating sudden death with nightingales,
And paper walls seemed real, this being so.

Saito himself committed suicide
The long way round by using the short sword
Before the banzai charge went in at dawn.
Three thousand died before the sun went down.
All night it sounded like a psycho ward.
We sacked out with the corpses open eyed.

What happened the next morning broke your heart.
We saw the whole thing from above the beach.
Mothers threw living babies from the cliff.
The sick lined up to have their heads hacked off.
Those soldiers that the non-coms couldn't reach
Kissed a grenade and blew themselves apart.

Marines you'd swear would never shed a tear
On Saipan wept. And that was all she wrote.
We just got used to it, like swatting flies.
Not even Iwo came as a surprise.
The whole Jap nation would have cut its throat
I swear to God sure as I'm standing here.

For Lichtenberg, wit was a microscope,
Yet in between the lines he seemed to know
His fine analysis did not disperse,
But gave coherence to, the universe.
That strong light touch sums up the rococo:
An epoch blown from clear glass, not from soap.

So do the buildings of Cuvilliés,
The Wittelsbachs' great court-dwarf architect,
Whose play of curlicue and arabesque
Like flame reflected in the welder's mask
Suggests a brilliance beyond intellect,
Fulfilled creation singing its own praise.

His small theatre of the Residenz
In World War II was bombed to smithereens
Yet could be put back as it was, because
Its dazzling inner shell was lath and gauze,
A kit of plaster panels and silk screens
They stashed away until the world saw sense.

At Vegas, the last Grand Prix of the year
Before he died in Belgium, Gilles Villeneuve
Put on his helmet and I saw the sun
Fill up his tinted visor like white wine.
Few poets get the face that they deserve
Or, like Hart Crane, can travel in a tear.

Of course Villeneuve was handsome anyway –
The Rimbaud of the wheel just oozed romance –
But where his class showed was in how that beast
Ferrari drew sweet curves at his behest
Instead of leading him St Vitus' dance.
He charged the earth but gave back art for pay.

If she could *see* herself, the girl on skates –
But she must work by feel in the event,
Assured by how her heavy fingers burn
As in mid-air she makes the triple turn
Explosive effort was correctly spent
And from the whirlpool a way out awaits.

They say that Pipeline surfers deep in white
Whipped water when wiped out may sip the froth
Through pursed lips and thus drown less than they breathe
While buffeted their helpless bodies writhe,
Then once the ruined wave has spent its wrath
Swim resurrected up to the bright light.

Though children in deep shelters could not watch,
Pathfinder flares were sumptuous where they burned
And rustic simpletons found food for thought
In how those coloured chandeliers would float
As if the Son of Man had just returned –
Before the earthquake made them a hotchpotch.

Descending from heaped rubble, 'I composed
Der Rosenkavalier,' Strauss told GIs
Whose billet underneath the *Führerbau*
Reminded them of their hometown hoosegow.
At eighty he was right, if scarcely wise:
From where he stood the episode was closed.

And soon there was another Salome
To propagate his long *legato* phrases,
And, by their shapeliness made feverish,
Lift high the prophet's lopped head in a dish,
And taste the everlasting fire that rages
On those cold lips of *papier mâché*.

She's gone, perhaps to start again elsewhere.
The freezing fens lock up their latent heat.
The rime ice on the river to the touch
Splits in a gash benign neglect will stitch.
Full of potential like briquettes of peat
Atomic bombs enjoy conditioned air.

The Emperor's portrait had survived the blast.
We carried it to safety in the stream
And took turns holding it aloft. The fire
Arched overhead and we succumbed to fear.
The surface of the water turned to steam.
I must say we were very much downcast.

Emerging from a silo of spun spunk
To scan the killing-ground with clustered eyes,
The funnelweb when she appears in person
Reveals a personality pure poison
Should you be tempted to idealize
Her gauze-lined bunker under the tree trunk,

And yet how sweet a tunnel in the mist!
Well might it fascinate as well as frighten.
Looking along such lustrous holes in space
Where indrawn starlight corkscrews down the sluice,
You'll feel your heart first hammer and then lighten
And think God was a gynaecologist.

The Sun so far has only twice touched Earth
With its unmitigated baleful stare.
Flesh turned to pizza under that hot look.
From all the forms of death you took pot luck,
But that by which the occasion was made rare
Showed later on in what was brought to birth.

At KZ Dachau the birthmarked young nun
Beseeching absolution for that place
Won't turn her full face to your chapel pew.
Only her murmurs will admonish you
For thinking to give up pursuit of grace
Simply because such dreadful things were done.

High over Saipan when another plane
Came back above us heading for Japan
As we flew south for home, I never saw
What would have been a chromium gewgaw,
But only what it casually began –
A long straight line of crystal flake cocaine.

Your progeny won't sit still to be told
Nor can you point out through the window how
Air battles of the past left vapour trails
Swirling and drifting like discarded veils,
Scarcely there then and not at all there now,
Except you feel the loss as you grow old.

Black-bottomed whiteware out of nowhere fast
The Shuttle takes fire coming back to us,
A purple storm with silence at the core.
Simmering down, it is the dodgem car
Daedalus should have given Icarus,
Whose wings – a bad mistake – were built to last.

To stay the course you must have stuff to burn.
For life, the ablative is absolute,
And though the fire proceeds against our wishes
Forms are implicit even in the ashes
Where we must walk in an asbestos suit:
A smouldering tip to which all things return.

We may not cavalierly lift the casque
Which separates us from the consequences
Of seeing how the godhead in full bloom
Absolves itself unthinkingly from blame.
It knows us as we know it, through our senses.
We feel for it the warmth in which we bask –
The flame reflected in the welder's mask.

A Valediction for Philip Larkin

You never travelled much but now you have,
Into the land whose brochures you liked least:
That drear Bulgaria beyond the grave
Where wonders have definitively ceased –
Ranked as a dead loss even in the East.

Friends will remember until their turn comes
What they were doing when the news came through.
I landed in Nairobi with eardrums
Cracked by the flight from Kichwa Tembo. You
Had gone, I soon learned, on safari too.

Learned soon but too late, since no telephone
Yet rings in the wild country where we'd been.
No media penetration. On one's own
One wakes up and unzips the morning scene
Outside one's tent and always finds it green.

Green Hills of Africa, wrote Hemingway.
Omitting a preliminary 'the',
He made the phrase more difficult to say –
The hills, however, easier to see,
Their verdure specified initially.

Fifty years on, the place still packs a thrill.
Several reserves of greenery survive,
And now mankind may look but must not kill
Some animals might even stay alive,
Surrounded by attentive four-wheel-drive

Toyotas full of tourists who shoot rolls
Of colour film off in the cheetah's face
While she sleeps in the grass or gravely strolls
With bloody cheeks back from the breathless chase,
Alone except for half the human race.

But we patrolled a less well-beaten trail.
Making a movie, we possessed the clout
To shove off up green hill and down green dale
And put our personal safety in some doubt
By opening the door and getting out.

Thus I descended on the day you died
And had myself filmed failing to get killed.
A large male lion left me petrified
But well alone and foolishly fulfilled,
Feeling weak-kneed but calling it strong-willed.

Silk brushed with honey in the hot noon light,
His inside leg was colonized by flies.
I made a mental note though wet with fright.
As his mouth might have done off me, my eyes
Tore pieces off him to metabolize.

In point of fact I swallowed Kenya whole,
A mill choked by a plenitude of grist.
Like anabolic steroids for the soul,
Every reagent was a catalyst –
So much to take in sent me round the twist.

I saw Kilimanjaro like the wall
Of Heaven going straight up for three miles.
The Mara river was a music hall
With tickled hippos rolling in the aisles.
I threw some fast food to the crocodiles.

I chased giraffes who floated out of reach
Like anglepoise lamps loose in zero g.
I chased a *mdudu* with a can of bleach
Around my tent until I couldn't see.
Only a small rhinoceros chased me.

The spectral sun-bird drew the mountain near,
And if the rain-bird singing *soon soon soon*
Turned white clouds purple, still the air was clear –
The radiant behind of a baboon
Was not more opulent than the full moon.

So one more tourist should have been agog
At treasure picked up cheaply while away –
Ecstatic as some latter-day sea dog,
His trolley piled high like a wain of hay
With duty-free goods looted from Calais.

For had I not enlarged my visual scope,
Perhaps my whole imaginative range,
By seeing how that deadpan antelope,
The topi, stands on small hills looking strange
While waiting for the traffic lights to change?

And had I not observed the elephant
Deposit heaps of steaming excrement
While looking wiser than Immanuel Kant,
More stately than the present Duke of Kent?
You start to see why I was glad I went.

Such sights were trophies, ivory and horn
Destined for carving into *objets d'art*.
Ideas already jumping like popcorn,
I climbed down but had not gone very far
Between that old Dakota and the car

When what they told me stretched the uncrossed space
Into a universe. No tears were shed.
Forgive me, but I hardly felt a trace
Of grief. Just sudden fear your being dead
So soon had left us disinherited.

You were the one who gave us the green light
To get out there and seek experience,
Since who could equal you at sitting tight
Until the house around you grew immense?
Your bleak bifocal gaze was so intense,

Hull stood for England, England for the world –
The whole caboodle crammed into one room.
Above your desk all of creation swirled
For you to look through with increasing gloom,
Or so your poems led us to assume.

Yet even with your last great work 'Aubade'
(To see death clearly, did you pull it close?)
The commentator must be on his guard
Lest he should overlook the virtuose
Technique which makes majestic the morose.

The truth is that you revelled in your craft.
Profound glee charged your sentences with wit.
You beat them into stanza form and laughed:
They didn't sound like poetry one bit,
Except for being absolutely it.

Described in English written at its best
The worst of life remains a bitch to face
But is more shared, which leaves us less depressed –
Pleased the condition of the human race,
However desperate, is touched with grace.

The seeming paradox is a plain fact –
You brought us all together on your own.
Your saddest lyric is a social act.
A bedside manner in your graveyard tone
Suggests that at the last we aren't alone.

You wouldn't have agreed, of course. You said
Without equivocation that life ends
With him who lived it definitely dead
And buried, after which event he tends
To spend a good deal less time with his friends.

But you aren't here to argue. Where you are
By now is anybody's guess but yours.
I'm five miles over Crete in a Tristar
Surrounded by the orchestrated snores
Induced by some old film of Roger Moore's.

Things will be tougher now you've proved your point,
By leaving early, that the man upstairs
Neither controls what happens in the joint
We call the world, nor noticeably cares.
While being careful not to put on airs,

It is perhaps the right time to concede
That life is all downhill from here on in.
For doing justice to it, one will need,
If not in the strict sense a sense of sin,
More *gravitas* than fits into a grin.

But simply staying put makes no one you.
Those who can't see the world in just one street
Must see the world. What else is there to do
Except face inescapable defeat
Flat out in a first-class reclining seat?

You heard the reaper in the Brynmor Jones
Library cough behind your swivel chair.
I had to hear those crocodiles crunch bones,
Like cars compressed for scrap, before the hair
Left on my head stood straight up in the air.

You saw it all in little. You dug deep.
A lesser man needs coarser stimuli,
Needs coruscating surfaces . . . needs sleep.
I'm very rarely conscious when I fly.
Not an event in life. To sleep. To die.

I wrote that much, then conked out over Rome,
Dreamed I'd been sat on by a buffalo,
Woke choking as we tilted down for home,
And now see, for once cloudless, the pale glow
Of evening on the England you loved so

And spoke for in a way she won't forget.
The quiet voice whose resonance seemed vast
Even while you lived, and which has now been set
Free by the mouth that shaped it shutting fast,
Stays with us as you turn back to the past –

Your immortality complete at last.

Jet Lag in Tokyo

Flat feet kept Einstein out of the army.
The Emperor's horse considers its position.
In Akasaka men sit down and weep
Because the night must end.

At Chez Oz I discussed my old friend's sex change
With a lovely woman who, I later learned,
Had also had one. The second movement
Of the Mahler Seventh on my Boodo Kahn
Above the North Pole spoke to me like you.

Neutrinos from 1987A
Arrived in the Kamikande bubble chamber
Three hours before the light. Shinjuku neon
Is dusted with submicroscopic diamonds.

Our belled cat keeps blackbirds up to scratch
With the fierce face of a tiger from the wall
Of the Ko-hojo in the Nanzen-ji, Kyoto.
You would not have been looking for me,
God told Pascal,
If you had not found me.

What will we do with those Satsuma pots
When the sun dies? Our Meissen *vieux Saxe* girl
Was fired three times. The car will be OK:
A Volkswagen can take anything.

An age now since I wrote about your beauty,
How rare it is. Tonight I am reminded.
Sue-Ellen Ewing says *Gomen nasai*.
Perhaps the Emperor's horse is awake also.
I think this time I've gone too far too fast.

The Light Well

Nacimos en un país libre que nos legaron nuestros padres, y
primero se hundirá la Isla en el mar antes que consintamos
en ser esclavos de nadie.

 —Fidel Castro, *La historia me absolverá*

From Playa de Giron the two-lane blacktop
Sticks to the shoreline of the Bay of Pigs –
The swamp's fringe on your left showing the sea
Through twisted trees, the main swamp on your right –
Until the rocks and tangled roots give way
To the soft white sand of Playa Larga,
The other beach of the invasion. Here
Their armour got stopped early. At Giron
They pushed their bridgehead inland a few miles
And held out for two days. From the air
Their old B-26s fell in flames.
High-profile Shermans doddered, sat like ducks
And were duly dealt with. Fidel's tanks,
Fresh in from Russia and as fast as cars,
Dismembered everything the Contras had,
Even the ships that might have got them out.
Also the People, who were meant to rise –
Chuffed at the thought of being once again
Free to cut cane all day for one peso
On land owned by the United Fruit Company –
Unaccountably stayed where they were. The swamp
Didn't notice a thing. The crocodiles
Haven't given it a thought in years,
Though wayward bombs from 4.2" mortars
Must, at the time, have made some awfully big
Holes in the mud. Apart from the vexed question
Of which genius ever picked it as the venue
For a military initiative whose chance
Paled beside that of a snowball in Hell,
The area holds no mysteries. Except one.
Somewhere about a mile along the road,

Look to the right and you can see a hint
Of what might be a flat spot in the swamp.
It is. A sketchy dirt track through the trees
Leads to a pool just forty feet across
Connected to the sea at such a depth
That though as clear as air and always calm
It shades down into darkness. Sufferers
From vertigo can't swim there. Parrot fish
Like clockwork paperweights on crystal shelves,
Their colour schemes preposterous, exchange
Positions endlessly. Shadows below
Look no more dense than purity compressed
Or light packed tight. Things were clear-cut
At that great moment of assault repulsed,
The victors proud yet chivalrous to a fault.
White flags, no matter how unsavoury
The hands that held them, were respected. Two
Of Batista's most notorious torturers,
Still wearing their original dark glasses
(Through which they'd both looked forward to a prompt
Resumption of a glittering career),
Were singled out and shot, but otherwise
Nobody missed a change of socks. They all
Got shipped back undamaged to Miami –
A better deal than they'd have handed out.
That day the Cuban revolution showed
A cleanliness which in the memory
Dazzles the more for how it has been spoiled:
What had to happen sullied by what might
Have been avoided, had those flagrant beards
Belonged to wiser heads – or so we think,
We who were young and thrilled and now are neither.
Credit where credit's due, though. Let's be fair.
Children cut cane here still, but go to school,
And don't get sick; or, if they do, don't die.
La cienega is a charnel house no longer,
And in this pool, which they call El Senote,
Young workers float at lunchtime like tree frogs
Poised on an air column. Things have improved
In some ways, so when they get worse in others

It's easier to blame Reagan than accept
The plain fact that the concentrated power
Which makes sick babies well must break grown men –
The logic so obvious it's blinding.
From armchairs far away we watch the brilliant
Picture grow dim with pain. On the Isle of Pines
The men who wear dark glasses late at night
Are back in business. Anyone smart enough
To build a raft from inner tubes and rope
Would rather run the gauntlet of the sharks
On the off-chance of encountering Florida
Than take the risk of listening to one more
Speech by Fidel – who, in his unrelenting
Urge to find friends among the non-aligned
Countries, now heaps praise on the regime
Of the Ayatollah Khomeini. Russian oil
Pollutes Havana. How opaque, we feel,
Those erstwhile glories have become, how sad –
Preferring, on the whole, to leave it there
Than enter beyond one long, ravished glance
That cistern filled with nothing but the truth,
Which we partake of but may not possess
Unless we go too deep and become lost,
By pressure of transparency confounded –
Trusting our eyes instead of turning back,
Drawn down by clarity into the dark,
Crushed by the prospect of enlightenment,
Our lungs bursting like a revelation.

The Artificial Horizon

Deus gubernat navem

The artificial horizon is no false dawn
But a tool to locate you in the sky.
A line has been drawn.
If it tilts, it is you that are awry.
Trust it and not your eye.

Or trust your eye, but no further than it goes
To the artificial horizon.
Only if that froze
Would you look out for something on the level
And pray you didn't spot it too late.
To stay straight
You can't just follow your nose –

Except when the true horizon's there.
But how often is that?
The sea at sunset shades into the air.
A white cloud, a night black as your hat –
What ground you glimpse might be at an angle,
While looking flat.

So the artificial horizon is a court
Of appeal, your first line of defence
And last resort:
A token world whose import is immense.

Though it seem unreal,
If it moves it can't be broken.
Believe that it makes sense
Or else be brought up short.

The artificial horizon
Is your Dr Johnson:
It's got its own slant.

It says clear your mind of cant.

What Happened to Auden

His stunning first lines burst out of the page
Like a man thrown through a windscreen. His flat drawl
Was acrid with the spirit of the age –
The spy's last cigarette, the hungry sprawl
Of Hornby clockwork train sets in 'O' gauge,
Huge whitewashed slogans on a factory wall –
It was as if a spotlight when he spoke
Brilliantly pierced the histrionic smoke.

Unsentimental as the secret police,
Contemporary as a Dinky Toy,
On holiday in Iceland with MacNeice,
A flop-haired Cecil Beaton golden boy,
Auden pronounced like Pericles to Greece
The short time Europe had left to enjoy,
Yet made it sound as if impending doom
Could only ventilate the drawing room.

Splendidly poised above the ashtray's rim,
The silver record-breaking aeroplane
For streamlined utterance could not match him.
Oblique but no more often than the rain,
Impenetrable only to the dim,
Neurotic merely not to be insane,
He seemed to make so much sense all at once
Anyone puzzled called himself a dunce.

Cricket pavilion lust looked a touch twee
Even to devotees, but on the whole,
Apart from harsh reviews in *Scrutiny*,
All hailed his triumph in Cassandra's role,
Liking the *chic* he gave her, as if she
Wore ankle-strap high heels and a mink stole –
His ambiguity just further proof
Here was a man too proud to stand aloof.

By now, of course, we know he was in fact
As queer as a square grape, a roaring queen
Himself believing the forbidden act
Of love he made a meal of was obscene.
He could be crass and generally lacked tact.
He had no truck with personal hygiene.
The roughest trade would seldom stay to sleep.
In soiled sheets he was left alone to weep.

From the Kurfürstendamm to far Shanghai
He cruised in every sense with Isherwood.
Sadly he gave the talent the glad eye
And got out while the going was still good.
New York is where his genius went to die
Say those who disapproved, but though they could
Be right that he lost much of his allure,
Whether this meant decline is not so sure.

Compatriots who stuck it out have said
Guilt for his getaway left him unmanned,
Whereat his taproot shrivelled and went dead,
Having lost contact with its native land.
Some say it was the sharing of his bed
With the one man nobody else could stand
That did him in, since poets can't afford
The deadly risk of conjugal concord.

But Chester made bliss hard enough to take,
And Wystan, far from pining for his roots,
Gaily tucked into the unrationed steak.
An international figure put out shoots.
Stravinsky helped the progress of the rake:
Two cultural nabobs were in cahoots.
No, Auden ageing was as much at home
On the world stage as Virgil was in Rome,

If less than *salonfähig* still. Regret
By all accounts he sparingly displayed
When kind acquaintances appeared upset,
Their guest rooms wrecked as if by an air raid.

He would forgive himself and soon forget.
Pig-like he revelled in the mess he made,
Indecorous the more his work lost force,
Devoid of shame. Devoured, though, by remorse,

For had he not gazed into the abyss
And found, as Nietzsche warned, that it gazed back?
His wizardry was puerile next to this.
No spark of glamour touched the railway track
That took whole populations to the hiss
Of cyanide and stoked the chimney stack
Scattering ash above a vast expanse
Of industry bereft of all romance.

The pit cooled down but still he stood aghast
At how far he had failed to state the case
With all those tricks that now seemed so half-arsed.
The inconceivable had taken place.
Waking to find his wildest dreams outclassed
He felt his tongue must share in the disgrace,
And henceforth be confined, in recompense,
To no fine phrase devoid of plain prose sense.

The bard unstrung his lyre to change his tune,
Constrained his inspiration to repent.
Dry as the wind abrading a sand dune,
A tightly drafted letter of intent,
Each rubric grew incisive like a rune,
Merest suggestions became fully meant.
The ring of truth was in the level tone
He forged to fit hard facts and praise limestone.

His later manner leaves your neck-hair flat,
Not standing up as Housman said it should
When poetry has been achieved. For that,
In old age Auden simply grew too good.
A mortal fear of talking through his hat,
A moral mission to be understood
Precisely, made him extirpate the thrill
Which, being in his gift, was his to kill.

He wound up as a poor old fag at bay,
Beleaguered in the end as at the start
By dons appalled that he could talk all day
And not draw breath although pissed as a fart,
But deep down he had grown great, in a way
Seen seldom in the history of his art –
Whose earthly limits Auden helped define
By realizing he was not divine.

Last Night the Sea Dreamed It Was Greta Scacchi

Last night the sea dreamed it was Greta Scacchi.
It wakes unruffled, lustrous, feeling sweet –
Not one breath of scandal has ever touched it.

At a higher level, the rain has too much power.
Grim clouds conspire to bring about its downfall.
The squeeze is on, there is bound to be a shake-out.

The smug sea and the sky that will soon go bust
Look like antagonists, but don't be fooled:
They understand each other very well.

We are caught between the hammer and the anvil.
Our bodies, being umpteen per cent water,
Are in this thing up to the neck at least.

If you want to feel detached from a panorama,
Try the Sahara. Forget about Ayers Rock –
The sea was once all over it like a rash.

The water in the opal makes it lovely,
Also unlucky. If not born in October
You might be wearing a cloudburst for a pendant.

The ban on flash photography is lifted.
The reception area expectantly lights up.
No contest. It's just life. Don't try to fight it –

You'll only get wet through, and we are that
Already. Every dimple in the swell
Is a drop in the ocean, but then who isn't?

No, nothing about women is more sensual
Than their sea smell. Look at her lying there,
Taking what comes and spreading it on her skin –

The cat, she's using her cream as moisturizer.
Milt Jackson's mallets bounce on silver leaves.
Strafed by cool riffs she melts in silent music:

Once we walked out on her, but we'll be back.

Drama in the Soviet Union

When Kaganovich, brother-in-law of Stalin,
Left the performance barely halfway through,
Meyerhold must have known that he was doomed,
Yet ran behind the car until he fell.
In *Pravda* he'd been several times condemned
For Stubborn Formalism. The ill will
Of the All Highest himself was common knowledge,
Proved by a mud slide of denunciations
And rubbed in by the fact that the Great Teacher
Had never personally entered the theatre
Which this enemy of the people had polluted
With attitudes hostile to the State.

Thus Meyerhold was a dead man of long standing:
Behind the big black car it was a corpse
That ran, a skull that gasped for air,
Bare bone that flailed and then collapsed.
His dear friend Shostakovich later said
How glad he was that he had never seen
Poor Meyerhold like that. Which was perhaps
Precisely why this giant of his art
Did such a thing: to dramatize the fear
Which had already eaten him alive
And make it live.

            Stalin, meanwhile,
Who didn't need to see how it was done
To know that the director's trick of staging
A scene so it could never be forgotten
Had to be stamped on, was the acknowledged master
Of the one theatrical effect that mattered –
He knew how to make people disappear.

So Meyerhold, having limped home, plummeted
Straight through the trapdoor to oblivion.
Nobody even registered surprise.

Specific memories were not permitted.
People looked vague, as if they didn't have them.
In due course his widow, too, was murdered –
Stabbed in the eyes, allegedly by thieves.

Budge up

Flowering cherry pales to brush-stroke pink at blossom fall
Like watermelon bitten almost to the rind.
It is in his mind because the skin is just that colour
Hot on her tight behind
As she lies in the bath, a Bonnard flipped like a flapjack.

His big black towel turns a naiad to a dryad,
No pun intended. Then,
An unwrapped praline,
She anoints herself with liberal Oil of Ulay.
It looks like fun.
Her curved fingers leave a few streaks not rubbed in.
He says: here, let me help.

The night is young but not as young as she is
And he is older than the hills.
Sweet sin
Swallows him at a gulp.

While cherry blossom suds dry on the lawn
Like raspberry soda
He attends the opening of the blue tulip
Mobbed at the stage door by forget-me-nots.

For a short season
He basks in her reflected glory.

Pathetic fallacy,
Dispelled by the clattering plastic rake.

Bring Me the Sweat of Gabriela Sabatini

Bring me the sweat of Gabriela Sabatini
For I know it tastes as pure as Malvern water,
Though laced with bright bubbles like the *aqua minerale*
That melted the kidney stones of Michelangelo
As sunlight the snow in spring.

Bring me the sweat of Gabriela Sabatini
In a green Lycergus cup with a sprig of mint,
But add no sugar –
The bitterness is what I want.
If I craved sweetness I would be asking you to bring me
The tears of Annabel Croft.

I never asked for the wristbands of Maria Bueno,
Though their periodic transit of her glowing forehead
Was like watching a bear's tongue lap nectar.
I never asked for the blouse of Françoise Durr,
Who refused point-blank to improve her soufflé serve
For fear of overdeveloping her upper arm –
Which indeed remained delicate as a fawn's femur,
As a fern's frond under which cool shadows gather
So that the dew lingers.

Bring me the sweat of Gabriela Sabatini
And give me credit for having never before now
Cried out with longing.
Though for all the years since TV acquired colour
To watch Wimbledon for even a single day
Has left me shaking with grief like an ex-smoker
Locked overnight in a cigar factory,
Not once have I let loose as now I do
The parched howl of deprivation,
The croak of need.

Did I ever demand, as I might well have done,
The socks of Tracy Austin?

Did you ever hear me call for the cast-off Pumas
Of Hana Mandlikova?
Think what might have been distilled from these things,
And what a small request it would have seemed –
It would not, after all, have been like asking
For something so intimate as to arouse suspicion
Of mental derangement.
I would not have been calling for Carling Bassett's knickers
Or the tingling, Teddy Tinling B-cup brassière
Of Andrea Temesvari.

Yet I denied myself.
I have denied myself too long.
If I had been Pat Cash at that great moment
Of triumph, I would have handed back the trophy
Saying take that thing away
And don't let me see it again until
It spills what makes this lawn burst into flower:
Bring me the sweat of Gabriela Sabatini.

In the beginning there was Gorgeous Gussie Moran
And even when there was just her it was tough enough,
But by now the top hundred boasts at least a dozen knockouts
Who make it difficult to keep one's tongue
From lolling like a broken roller blind.
Out of deference to Billie-Jean I did my best
To control my male chauvinist urges –
An objectivity made easier to achieve
When Betty Stove came clumping out to play
On a pair of what appeared to be bionic legs
Borrowed from Six Million Dollar Man.

I won't go so far as to say I harbour
Similar reservations about Steffi Graf –
I merely note that her thigh muscles when tense
Look interchangeable with those of Boris Becker –
Yet all are agreed that there can be no doubt
About Martina Navratilova:
Since she lent her body to Charles Atlas
The definition of the veins on her right forearm

Looks like the Mississippi river system
Photographed from a satellite,
And though she may unleash a charming smile
When crouching to dance at the ball with Ivan Lendl,
I have always found to admire her yet remain detached
Has been no problem.

But when the rain stops long enough for the true beauties
To come out swinging under the outshone sun,
The spectacle is hard for a man to take,
And in the case of this supernally graceful dish –
Likened to a panther by slavering sports reporters
Who pitiably fail to realize that any panther
With a topspin forehand line drive like hers
Would be managed personally by Mark McCormack –
I'm obliged to admit defeat.

So let me drink deep from the bitter cup.
Take it to her between any two points of a tie-break
That she may shake above it her thick black hair,
A nocturne from which the droplets as they fall
Flash like shooting stars –
And as their lustre becomes liqueur
Let the full calyx be repeatedly carried to me.
Until I tell you to stop,
Bring me the sweat of Gabriela Sabatini.

Fridge Magnet Sonnets

Except for the punctuation and capitalization, these sonnets were assembled on a refrigerator door entirely within the restrictions imposed by the Basic Magnetic Poetry Kit and the Cerebra Supplemental Kit. Whether the resulting, apparently unavoidable, pastiche of Wallace Stevens was dictated by a propensity in the mind of the author or by the nature of magnetic poetry would be nice to know. If the latter, there must now be refrigerators all over the world that look like the galley proofs of *Harmonium*.

I

I ribald sophist, you deft paragon,
Whet in our cloister languid dreams of sweet
Tongue-worship for the storm we cudgel on
With profligate palaver of bare feet.
But fiddle as we may, the shadows fall
Blue, tawdry, obdurate and lachrymose –
A torpid, adolescent caterwaul
Like tumid skin of a morose morass.
'So what?' you cry, and quashed I must eschew
Arid alacrity of epithet,
Be cool, austere, brusque, trenchant, true like you,
Not vapid and verbose as I am yet:
From here on in spurn brazen lusciousness,
Fetter my fecund zeal and chant fluff less.

II

Unctuous misanthrope, abscond to life!
Pant in a lather for a peachy breast.
Ascetic gynophobes usurp their lust,
Rip with the tacit rusty temporal knife
Of stultifying pallid acumen
The gorgeous mist of frantic puppy love

And enervate it to the putative.
No affable abeyance can supplant
Hot need, stalwart pariah and miscreant.
Let unrequited priapism, then,
Capriciously lambaste banal repose,
Ache, pound, boil, heave, drool juice and fulminate.
Delirious love is never delicate:
A florid blood-red spring rain shakes the rose.

Go Back to the Opal Sunset

Go back to the opal sunset, where the wine
Costs peanuts, and the avocado mousse
Is thick and strong as cream from a jade cow.
Before the passion fruit shrinks on the vine
Go back to where the heat turns your limbs loose.
You've worked your heart out and need no excuse.
Knock out your too-tall tent pegs and go now.

It's England, April, and it's pissing down,
So realize your assets and go back
To the opal sunset. Even autumn there
Will swathe you in a raw-silk dressing gown,
And through the midnight harbour lacquered black
The city lights strike like a heart attack
While eucalyptus soothes the injured air.

Now London's notion of a petty crime
Is simple murder or straightforward rape
And Oxford Street's a bombing range, to go
Back to the opal sunset while there's time
Seems only common sense. Make your escape
To where the prawns assume a size and shape
Less like a newborn baby's little toe.

Your tender nose anointed with zinc cream,
A sight for sore eyes will be brought to you.
Bottoms bisected by a piece of string
Will wobble through the heat-haze like a dream
That summer afternoon you go back to
The opal sunset, and it's all as true
As sandfly bite or jelly-blubber sting.

What keeps you here? Is it too late to tell?
It might be something you can't now define,
Your nature altered as if by the moon.

Yet out there at this moment, through the swell,
The hydrofoil draws its triumphant line.
Such powers of decision should be mine.
Go back to the opal sunset. Do it soon.

Lament for French Deal

feror ingenti circumdata nocte

God bless the nurses of the Sacred Heart
Who bring His great gift, morphine, to annul
The agony which tears French Deal apart.
Heaven be praised
That Science makes her once keen senses dull.

We thought of wattle sprays and willow wands
When we first saw French Deal in those young years –
Of frangipani petals and palm fronds.
Lord, she was sweet:
Gamblers and poets were both moved to tears.

To tears of lust as well, for though her face
Beat any angel's hollow, her loose limbs
And languorous figure had a pagan grace
To make a priest
Compose risqué new words for well-known hymns.

A gambler gave French Deal her name. Today,
Though sick himself, he sits beside her bed.
I know he will, while I am far away,
Kiss her goodbye
On my behalf as I would in his stead.

He named her for a racehorse that came in.
Fresh from the country, Janet was impressed
And as French Deal embraced a Life of Sin –
Since in those days
Free love was damned no sooner than confessed.

But not so at the Royal George Hotel,
Headquarters of the Downtown Push, for there
Bohemians defied the threat of Hell.
Lapsed Catholics
Sang blasphemously to the evening air.

Hot nights, cold beer and filtered cigarettes
Plucked proudly from the new-style flip-top box!
Philosophers pronounced, gamblers made bets –
It was a home
Away from home, that thieves' den by the docks.

Push women were the equals of their men,
Or so the theory went the men advanced
With all their other theories while, as then
Was still the rule,
The women were required to sit entranced.

Oasis faces in a boundless waste
Of words, and one face fairer than the rest:
Across the room, still smarting at the taste
Of my first beer,
I winced but gazed unblinking and felt blessed.

She was the gambler's girl and not to be
Approached by one so clearly short of clues,
But when I sailed away her memory
Smoked in my mind,
A brand evoking all I stood to lose.

The white light, the sweet heat, the open air,
The opal sunset and the sudden dawn,
You saw them all when she swept back her hair –
Her upraised arms
Outlined the paradise where we were born.

London was cold and girls in pubs would show
No skin below the neck except their hands.
Only blood shining out made their skins glow:
No sun shone in.
A man's eyes risked death in such frozen lands.

But come the second winter my despair
Cracked and dissolved. Out of the fog there stepped
French Deal and gathered me into her care.
Until the spring
It was together that we woke and slept.

She made it clear that she had come away
Only to show the gambler she was free.
For her this was a working holiday
From too much love,
A break from him. A bigger break for me,

My longed-for first great love affair unloosed
Not just desire but the desire to please.
Just as Narcissus was himself seduced
As he gazed down
To see the loved one's face in ecstasies,

I made her gasp and took it for applause:
It was my wretched ego I caressed.
No doubt I had confused effect and cause,
But equally
There could be no doubt I had Passed a Test.

Bursting with butch conceit I said goodbye.
She sailed home to be married. I stayed on,
And fifteen years unravelled before I
Saw her again.
Sydney had changed a lot while I was gone.

The Opera House was finished, there were tall
Buildings ablaze at night behind the Quay.
The Royal George was lost beyond recall
In concrete roads
Whose coils had squeezed it dry of mystery.

But one thing had remained the same: French Deal.
Tea on the lawn in my case proved unwise.
Unused to it, I judged the sun unreal.
Spread at our feet
Careening Cove was too bright for my eyes.

Dazzled I listened while she told me how
Marriage had come and gone. She had been ill
With meningitis but was better now.
She dropped a hint:
She and the gambler were true lovers still.

Long before sunset she took me inside
To lavish lotion on my burning skull.
I heard the ripple of the ebbing tide
Rocking a boat:
The chink of wind chimes and the slapping hull.

From that night on for fifteen years again
Whenever I flew home I came to tea,
And so in her life's prime the same two men
She started with
Shared her affection and her courtesy.

The gambler got the lion's share, of course:
To throw his life away yet keep her near
Was his reward for backing the right horse.
Each evening there
He warmed to her while it was morning here.

Conversely in my night she took the train
To Burwood where her girls thought her the best
Teacher in history and offset the pain
Of childlessness –
While he made sure he got a lot of rest.

Yes, all the time I toiled with diligence,
Apart from placing bets his only fame
He got from demonstrating in defence
Of a few trees –
His colleagues in the vegetation game.

Two men who scarcely added up to one,
One work-shy and the other a machine:
Both, when they sat beside her in the sun,
Were at their best.
Each was the better man he might have been.

Born of the fragile truce between us two,
Who never met except in her regard,
Her love life lasted yet was always new –
An ebb and flow
Like the tide at the foot of her front yard.

By rights we should all three have gone to hell
Together, but blind chance chose her to face
The silent forecast of her own death knell –
A cruel shadow
Which will soon, says the Sister's voice through space,

At last have done. The roses that I left
Fade in their vase. Bending to kiss her eyes
He can precisely see himself bereft
Where I must guess –
Yet I can paint the picture when she dies.

On High Street wharf at midnight she alone
Waits for the small white ferry with no crew
To grumble close. Its soft ropes on their own
Throw quiet loops.
Weightless she steps aboard as we will do

When our turn comes, gambler: but not tonight.
Tonight we are those two gulls overhead
Gliding against the wind to match our flight
With the ghost ship
That will not cross the harbour, but instead

Slips on the tide towards the open sea
Whose darkness, which already reaches deep
Into the brilliant city, soon will be
All that there is,
As she sails out across the curve of sleep –

Too far to follow, even for you and me.

The Eternity Man

Never filmed, he was photographed only once,
Looking up startled into the death-trap flash
Like a threatened life form.
Still underlining his copybook one-word message
With the flourish that doubled back under the initial 'E',
He was caught red-eyed with the stark white chalk in his hand
Writing Eternity.

Before he died in 1967
At the age of eighty-eight
He had managed to write it five hundred thousand times,
And always in copperplate script.
Few streets or public places in the city of Sydney
Remained unmarked by the man with a single obsession –
Writing Eternity.

Wherever you lived, sooner or later he'd reach you.
Hauling their billycarts up for the day's first run
Small boys swarmed when they came to the word
Arrestingly etched in the footpath.
It was self-protected by its perfect calligraphy –
The scrupulous sweep of a hand that had spent its lifetime
Writing Eternity.

He was born in a Balmain slum and raised underneath it,
Sleeping on hessian bags with his brothers and sisters
To keep beyond fist's reach of his dipso parents.
His name was Arthur Stace.
He had no one to use it apart from his family.
His fate was to die as a man and return as a portent,
Writing Eternity.

His sisters grew up to be prostitutes. He was a pimp,
But in 1930, in his early forties, on meths,
He heard the Reverend John Ridley at Burton Street
Baptist Church, Darlinghurst,

And scrapped his planned night in the down-and-out sanctuary.
The piss artist had his vocation revealed unto him –
Writing Eternity.

'I wish I could shout one word through the streets of Sydney!'
The Reverend Ridley shouted. 'Eternity! You
Have got to meet it! You! Where will you spend
Eternity?' Alone in his pew,
Avoided by all for his smell strong enough to see,
A man reborn saw the path stretch ahead he would stoop to,
Writing Eternity.

In New South Wales for more than a hundred years
We all had to learn that script in school,
But what school did he ever go to, and where
Did his chalk come from? How did he eat?
These nagging conundrums were mulled over endlessly
As he roamed unseen through the city without rhyme or reason
Writing Eternity.

In a blaze of glory the Thousand Year Reich was announced.
Old Bolsheviks shyly confessed with downcast eyes
And the first reffos arrived at Woolloomooloo.
Our troops sailed off to prop up the Middle East
Until Singapore fell and the Yanks overtipped for a taxi –
Yet still through the blacked-out streets he kept his own schedule
Writing Eternity.

But a mere word was ceasing to hold any terrors.
Belief in the afterlife faded. Where was God
When the Christmas snow came fluttering into the death camps?
Those kindling children, their piles of little shoes,
Condemned Divine Justice past hope of apology:
To rage at the storm and expect it to stop made more sense than
Writing Eternity.

He wrote it on the same night Hitler burned.
He wrote it as the Japanese cities melted
And the tanks rolled into Budapest.
While Sputnik skimmed through the stars he bent to his task

As if we believed there was still any Hell except history,
And Heaven could be rebuilt by one scuttling ratbag
Writing Eternity.

The rain didn't always wash his word away.
He sometimes used more than chalk. Near my place once
I found it fingertip deep in the new white concrete.
It was lined with crimson enamel, a rune punched in
By a branding-iron from space. Down on one knee
I chipped out the paint with my penknife as if I could stop him
Writing Eternity.

He wouldn't have known. He didn't have time to go back,
Not even to visit his real bravura efforts
Which culminated in his famous Australia Square
Incised masterpiece filled with stainless steel.
Some snot-nosed kid with a grudge there would always be,
But he put all that behind him and kept on going,
Writing Eternity.

By the time he died I was half the world away
And when I came back I never gave him a thought.
It was almost fifty years after I unpicked it
That I pondered his word again,
On the dawn of the day when the laughing stock was yours truly
Who would have to go on alone and be caught in the spotlight
Writing Eternity.

From the thirty-third floor of the Regent I looked down naked.
The Opera House was sold out. I was afraid,
But the Harbour was flat calm all the way to the sea,
Its shaped, linked loops flush with silver,
And I suddenly saw what that showpiece of geology
Had really been up to ever since the magma cooled –
Writing Eternity.

That word again, and this time I could read it.
It said your life is on loan from those before you
Who had no chance, and before it is even over
Others will come to judge you, if only by

Forgetting your name; so better than glittering vainly
Would be to bend down in the dark half a million times
Writing Eternity.

Where will we spend it? Nowhere except here.
Life everlasting ends where it begins,
On Earth, but it is present at every moment.
We must seek grace now and not for ourselves alone
Was what that crazed saint meant in his ecstasy –
Since time is always, with chalk made from children's ashes,
Writing Eternity.

Reflections in an Extended Kitchen

Late summer charms the birds out of the trees
On to our lawn, where the cat gets them.
Aware of this but not unmanned, Matisse
Makes the whole room as sexy as the girl.

'Distributed voluptuousness,' he said,
Matching the decor to her lazy gaze.
Just book me on the first flight to Morocco.
You see what I see? Feathers on the grass.

Nothing so sordid in Henri's back yard
Where coloured shapes may touch, but not to crush.
Look at that death trap out there, lined with roses!
We grew a free-fire zone with fertilizer.

Caught on the ground like the Egyptian Air Force
A wrecked bird on its back appears outraged:
It could have been a contender. What a world
Of slam-bang stuff to float one fantasy

Amongst her figured curtains, blobs for flowers,
Lolling unlocked in filmy harem pants!
Where did we see her first? That place they called
Leningrad. She looked like History's cure,

And even he could use that. When he turned
An artful blank back on his wife and child
They were arrested, leaving him to paint
In peace a world with no Gestapo in it –

A dream that came true. Agonies recede,
And if his vision hid harsh facts from him
It sharpens them for us. Best to believe
He served an indispensable ideal:

Douceur de vivre on a heroic scale –
Heaven on Earth, the Land of Oobladee,
Cloud Nine and Shangri-la hooked to the wall
As bolt holes for the brain, square wishing wells.

Suppose that like his brush my pen could speak
Volumes, our cat might stay in shape to pounce,
But only on the arm of that soft chair
You sit in now and where you would lie lulled,

An ageless, in-house *odalisque couchée*
Never to be less languorous than this,
Always dissolving in the air around you
Reality's cruel purr with your sweet whisper –

And nothing would be terrible again,
Nor ever was. The fear that we once felt
For daughters fallen ill or just an hour
Late home: it never happened. That dumb bird
Stayed in its tree and I was true to you.

In Praise of Marjorie Jackson

In 1999, the year before the Sydney Olympics,
Her face all laugh lines, regal in her scarlet coat,
The gold in her teeth aglow like her set of gold medals,
At the brand-new stadium she said exactly the right thing:
'What a heritage for our kids! It's lovely.'
As usual her words rang bells all over Australia.
She could always do that, tap into the national pride.

Fifty years back, she was the fastest kid in Lithgow.
She could run the boys into the earth,
And when she ran the legs off Fanny Blankers-Koen
(Who, visiting Sydney, expected to win in a walk)
The good citizens of Lithgow were not surprised –
Unlike the rest of Australia, whose collected sporting scribes,
When their mouths had returned to the normal, merely open,
     position,
Gave her an express train's name to match the way she ran –
She was the Lithgow Flash.
Young Marjorie, who could always do the right thing,
Went back to Lithgow with a modest, pre-cosmetic smile,
Quietly amused at the ratbag outside world.

Lithgow, hemmed in by its hills and one storey high
At its highest, didn't even have a running track.
They cleared her a stretch of ground to prepare for the Olympics.
Tired after work, she would train there in the dark:
Lit up by car headlights that turned the loitering fog
Into the nimbus of a legend about to happen
As she sailed like an angel through the clouds of her first glory,
The most brilliant thing Lithgow had ever seen –
The right thing, the thing she could always do
With a whole heart, putting one foot in front of the other
Like the fists of Jimmy Carruthers tapping a punchball.

At Helsinki she ran in metres instead of yards
So the stretch for the sprints was just that little bit longer

Each time, two ghosts of a chance for the others to catch her
After her start that uncoiled like Hector Hogan's –
But they never got near her.
In both events, she won scooting away like a wallaby
With its tail on fire, and collared those twin gold medals
With a smile for the camera that signalled her gratitude
To God and the world, to Finland, Australia and Lithgow –
The right smile, again the right thing exactly.

She came home in triumph, with ninety-six miles of people
From Sydney to Lithgow shouting congratulations –
The kind of acclaim that used to make Roman generals
Decide it might just be their turn to go for the title.
It would go to anyone's head, but it didn't to hers
Because it wouldn't have been the right thing:
She married her cyclist Peter and the people of Lithgow
Collected a total of seventy-seven pounds for the wedding –
The nearest she ever got to the big money
And the nearest she wanted.

When the last of Peter's health melted, what could she do
Except the right thing? She lent her undying lustre
To fundraising for leukaemia research.
She groomed herself as a speaker, walked with the poise
That only those who have danced on air can possess
(Or walked on water, like the Rivercat named for her
You can catch tomorrow from the Quay to Paramatta,
Watching the way its keels, like the spikes of a sprinter,
In their lightweight trajectory barely impinge on the world)
And still, with her seventieth year coming close to her heels,

She looked fit to make that spanking new surface at Homebush
Unroll from the balls of her feet like a belt going backwards
Into the past, into the headlight-lit mist
Where she was the quickest of all my fantastic girls –
Than Shirley Strickland, than even Betty Cuthbert she was
     quicker –
The very first of the fleet-foot females Movietone flung
Flying towards me but forever out of reach
Up there on the screen, their green and gold strip black and white

To the lens, but to my pre-teen eyes spilling fire
From the warmth of their bodies, the strength of their softness,
     the sweet
Line of their slimness propelled by the will to excel
And cold lamb cutlets for breakfast.

Yes, still in short pants I was out of my mind for them all,
But somehow I knew – I don't know, it was something about her –
That she – the unglamorous one but in motion a goddess –
That she was the one who, had I been able to catch her
And run at her side for a while as I gasped out my feelings,
Would have done the right thing,
And smiled without laughing before she raced on and away –

Or even said, even though it wasn't true,
That if I'd had the luck to have been born and brought up in
     Lithgow
Where the nights were cool, the stars were close and the people
     real,
I could have been a sprinter too,
And run for my country at the same amazing time
As the Lithgow Flash shot through like the Bondi Special
Into the language, and Australia rose to its feet –
Cheering the champion, which, even when all are equal,
And sometimes especially then, is the right thing to do.

Simple Stanzas about Modern Masters

If T. S. Eliot and Ezra Pound
Came back to life, again it would be found
One had the gab, the other had the gift
And each looked to the other for a lift.

The Waste Land, had not Pound applied his blue
Pencil, might well have seemed less spanking new.
Pound was a crackpot but that made his critical
Prowess particularly analytical.

Embarrassing, however, there's no doubt:
Increasingly too crass to have about.
While Eliot held discreetly right-wing views
Pound yelled obscenities about the Jews.

For Eliot, the time to cause a stir
Was past, and dignity was *de rigueur*,
But Pound preferred to hang out with the boys
In boots and black shirts who made lots of noise.

For Eliot the war brought veneration:
He seemed to speak for his adopted nation.
When Pound spoke it reminded Mussolini
What it had cost them to lose Toscanini.

Pound wound up in a cage and might have swung
Or died strapped down if he had not been sprung;
A big prize for the *Cantos* saved his neck
Though even he half-guessed they were a wreck.

The rackety campaign in Pound's support
Worked only because Eliot took thought
On how *il miglior fabbro* might best be
Saved for a dignified senility.

His tactic was to let it be inferred
That though he nowadays thought Pound absurd,
The established master and his erstwhile mentor
Were still somehow one creature, like a centaur.

One was the head, the other the hindquarters
(A point made by the more astute reporters)
But few dared to protest at a free pass
For such a well-connected horse's arse.

Pound in his dotage made no spark of sense
But Eliot, still staunch in his defence,
Remembered how it took a cocksure friend
To help unscramble radium from pitchblende.

Pound falling silent, Eliot sat in state.
Though some said what he did was etiolate,
Most regally he'd kept the palace rule –
Never lose sight of what you owe your fool.

Son of a Soldier

My tears came late. I was fifty-five years old
Before I began to cry authentically:
First for the hurt I had done to those I loved,
Then for myself, for what had been done to me
In the beginning, to make my heart so cold.

When the floodgates opened, the flood was not like rain.
With the undammed water came the sad refuse:
The slime, the drowned rats and the bloated corpse
Of the man whose absence had plugged up the sluice
That now gushed junk into my neat domain.

Not older by all that much than my dear daughters
He lay disfiguring a flower bed,
As if by bubbling gas a shallow grave
Of massacre had thrust up one of its dead,
Not to be washed clean by the clearest waters.

I took leave of my wife and knelt beside him
Who could have been my son, though I was his,
And everything he had not come back to tell me
About how everlasting true love is
Was a mouth of mud, so thick did woe betide him.

'Had you come home, I would not be what I am,'
I cried. 'I could have loved my mother less
And not searched for more like her among others,
Parched for a passion undimmed by distress
While you lay deep behind that looming dam.'

The wet earth swallowed him. This time his grave
Was marked: at least I knew now where he was.
I turned to meet her eyes. 'Let me explain,'
I said to her. 'My tears were trapped because
He left me to be tender, strong and brave

Who was none of those things. Inflamed by fright,
The love that he did not return to make
To the first woman I knew and could not help,
Became in me a thirst I could never slake
For one more face transfigured by delight,

Yet needing nothing else. It was a doomed quest
Right from the start, and now it is at an end.
I am too old, too raddled, too ashamed.
Can I stay in your house? I need a friend.'
'So did I,' she said truly. 'But be my guest:

God knows I too have waited wasted years
To have my husband home. Our parents wept
For history. Great events prised them apart,
Not greed, guilt, lies and promises unkept.
Pray they come not too late, these healing tears.'

The house we live in and that man-sized mound
Are a long walk between, yet both are real.
Like family life, his flowers have their weeds
To save them from a sanitized ideal.
I hope this balance holds until the ground

Takes me down, too. But I fear they will go on thronging,
Those pipe-dream sprites who promise a fresh start –
Free, easy furies haunting a cot case
That never lived, or loved, with a whole heart –
Until for one last time I die of longing.

What will I tell her then, in that tattoo
Of the last breath, the last gasp, the death rattle?
The truth: that in my life stolen from him
Whose only legacy was a lost battle,
The one thing that belonged to me was you.

Where the Sea Meets the Desert

Antony and Cleopatra swam at Mersa Matruh
In the clear blue shallows.
Imagine the clean sand, the absence of litter –
No plastic bottles or scraps of styrofoam packing,
No jetsam at all except the occasional corpse
Of a used slave tossed off a galley –
And the shrieks of the dancing Queen as the hero splashed her
While her cheer-squad of ladies-in-waiting giggled on cue,
The eunuchs holding the towels.
With salt in her eyes did she wrinkle the perfect nose
Of which Pascal would later venture the opinion
That had it been shorter (he didn't say by how much)
History would have been different?
They were probably both naked. What a servant saw
Did not count. They might even have boffed each other
Right there at the water's edge like a pair of dolphins
Washed up in the middle of a mad affair,
With her unable to believe the big lunk would ever
Walk away from this, and him in his soul
Fighting to forget that this was R&R
And there was still the war.

There is always the war. The Aussies in Tobruk
Could hear the German bombers at El Adem
Warming up on the airfield
For the five-minute flight that is really the only distance
Between bliss and blitz.
Ears still ringing from kookaburras and whipbirds
Were heckled by Heinkels.
When Antony eyeballed her Coppertone tits and bum
He was looking at Actium.

Shake it, lady.
Shake it for the Afrika Korps.
Where the sea meets the desert there is always,
There is always the war.

The Lions at Taronga

The leaves of Tower Bridge are rigged to open
For any taxi I might chance to catch.
They say that when the ravens leave the Tower

It means they'll use my rain-stained study skylight
As a toilet. I can see Canary Wharf,
A Russian rocket packed around with boosters

Lit up to launch at dawn from Baikonur.
The Blade of Light is cleared for butterflies
To crash-land. When that lens-shaped office block

Is finished it will bend a ray from space
To burn the *Belfast* like a sitting duck.
I've known the NatWest Tower since it was knee-high

To the Barbican, another high-tech know-how
HQ that used to look like the last word.
From my place I can see last words in vistas

As far downriver as the spreading spikes
Of the Dome, some sad bitch of a sea urchin
Losing its battle with a stray Dutch cap

While hothouse pleasure boats leak foreign voices
Like tourist minibuses nose to tail
In the corridors of Buckingham Palace.

Been there, done that. The Queen, she hung one on me.
I've got it in a box. The box to frame
My body will be built here, like as not,

And probably quite soon. I've lived in London
For longer than some people live all told.
Except for the way out, I know it backwards.

So at night when the lions at Taronga
Roar in my memory across the water
I feel the way they must have felt, poor bastards –

Gone in the teeth. The food dead. On display
All day and every day. Sleep in a fortress.
Every familiar walkway leads to strangers.

Dream Me Some Happiness

John Donne, uneasiest of apostates,
Renouncing Rome that he might get ahead
In life, or anyway not wind up dead,
Minus his guts or pressed beneath great weights,

Ascribed his bad faith to his latest flame
As if the fact she could be bent to do
His bidding proved that she would not stay true:
Each kiss a Judas kiss, a double game.

Compared with him, the mental muscle-man,
Successors who declared his numbers rough
Revealed by theirs they found the pace too tough:
The knotty strength that made him hard to scan

Left him renowned for his conceits alone,
Figments unfading as the forms of death
Prescribed for Catholics by Elizabeth –
Tangles of gristle, relics of hair and bone.

Brought back to favour in an anxious time
Attuned to his tormented intellect,
By now he charms us, save in one respect:
Framing his women still looks like a crime.

We foist our fault on her we claim to love
A different way. Pleased to the point of tears,
She tells us that the real world disappears.
Not quite the Donne thing, when push comes to shove:

He wrote betrayal into her delight.
We have a better reason to deceive
Ourselves as we help her help us believe
Life isn't like that: at least, not tonight.

Deckard Was a Replicant

The forms of nature cufflinked through your life
Bring a sense of what Americans call closure.
The full-blown iris swims in English air
Like the wreckage of an airbag jellyfish
Rinsed by a wave's thin edge at Tamarama:
The same frail blue, the same exhausted sprawl,
The same splendour. Nothing but the poison
Is taken out. In the gallery, that girl
Has the beauty that once gave itself to you
To be turned into marriage, children, houses.
She will give these things to someone else this time.

If this time seems the same time, it's because
It is. The reason she is not for you
Is she already was. Try to remember
What power they have, knowing what sex is for:
Replacing us. The Gainsborough chatelaine
She studies wears a shawl dipped in the hint
Of jacaranda blossoms, yet it might
Remind her of sucked sweets, or the pale veins
Of her own breasts. Setting the Thames on fire,
The tall white-painted training ship from Denmark
Flaunts the brass fittings of the little ferry
That took you as a child to Kirribilli
On its way to Wapping, then the Acheron
And Hades. Those gulls that graze the mud
Took sixty years to get here from Bundeena.

At an average speed of forty yards an hour
They barely moved. It seems you didn't either.
You stood still with your head wrapped in the armour
Of perception's hard-wired interlocking habits.
Ned Kelly was the ghost of Hamlet's father.
Dazzled by lipstick pulped from waratahs,
The smoker coughs, having been born again.

Lucretius the Diver

Things worn out by the lapse of ages tend
Toward the reef, that motley wrecking crew
Of living polyps who, to get ahead,
Climb ruthlessly all over their own dead,
But facts like those Lucretius never knew:
He merely meant we can't long buck the trend
That winds up hard against a watershed.

Horace had godly names for every breeze.
Ovid himself was stiff with sacred stuff.
Virgil talked turkey just once, about bees.
Of ancient wits Lucretius alone,
Without recourse to supernatural guff,
Uncannily forecast the modern tone –
Viewing the world as miracle enough.

Imagine him in scuba gear, instead
Of whatever kit a Roman poet wore –
To find his fruitful symbol for the grave
Not just inevitable but alive
Would surely suit him down to the sea floor.
Suspended before such a flower bed
He'd bubble with delight beneath the wave.

The reef, a daughter, and the sea, its mother,
In a long, white-lipped rage with one another
Would shout above him as he hung in space
And saw his intuition had been right:
Under a windswept canopy of lace,
Even down there in that froth-filtered light,
The World of Things is clearly the one place –

Death lives, life dies, and no gods intervene.
It's all so obvious, would be his thought:
But then, it always was, at least to him,
And why the rest of them were quite so dim

On that point is perhaps a theme we ought
To tackle, realizing it could mean
Our chances going in are pretty slim

Of drawing comfort from a Golden Age
So lethally haphazard no one sane
Could contemplate the play of chance was all
There was to life. That took the featherbrain
Lucretius seemed to them, and not the sage
He seems to us, who flinch from his disdain
As he stares seaward at the restless wall

Of ruined waves, the spray that falls like rain.

One Man to Another

Salute me! I have tamed my daughter's face
With hot oil, and my honour has been saved.
It's not to be defied that I have slaved.
She talks a lot less now she knows her place.

Most of her mouth can still move, and one eye
Could stare in hatred if she wanted to.
I'm proud to say her protests have been few
Apart from that absurd initial cry.

That was the evil spirit leaving her.
She really should have dealt with it herself.
She said she'd rather end up on the shelf
Than marry our best choice. What thoughts occur

To girls nowadays! Next they will want a say
In what to wear and when to buy a book.
Here, take your mother's mirror. Take a look.
What have you got in store for me today?

You thought to shake my faith? Well, you have found
My faith shakes you, and will again, I swear,
If you continue with that hangdog air:
If you continue with that whining sound.

Can't you be grateful we still keep you here?
We could have sent you out there to the dust
Where people fight for every cowpat crust.
We don't ask for a grin from ear to ear,

But now no man would want you, we still do,
So cut the sulky pout. To many another
Far worse than this has happened. Ask your mother.
I don't know what the world is coming to.

See how she slinks inside. If not with grace
She seems to have accepted, more or less,
Some limit to a woman's wilfulness.
The lesson hurt us both, but met the case.

Salute me! I have tamed my daughter's face.

Stolen Children

From where I sit for cool drinks in the heat
The Covent Garden Jumpzone seems to fling
Kids over rooftops in a bungee dive
The wrong way, and the thrill it is to swing
Straight up and down you see when they arrive,
In Heaven as on Earth, with kicking feet,

And so depart. One flier takes the pip
By somersaulting in her harness when,
High overhead, there is a moment's pause
For rubber to recuperate. Not then,
But later, as she signals for applause
With a slow stride instead of a last flip,

The penny drops. I've seen this girl before.
Above the birthplace of the Son of God
It had pleased Botticelli to impose
The perfect circle of a trained cheer-squad
Dancing barefoot with light fantastic toes
As angels do, the cloudless blue their floor.

The second from the left was my dream girl.
Outside, Trafalgar Square filled up with snow.
Winter in England was a culture shock
More ways than one. The gallery's warm glow
Seemed concentrated in a flowing frock,
A flash of ankle gleaming like a pearl.

Back down with us, she saunters past my chair.
About thirteen, with more than blips for breasts,
She wasn't born before I saw her first
On a glass board surfing the troughs and crests
Of the air waves. Nor was her mother. Worst
Of all is how the longing lingers there

Yet leaves us nothing else to bless at last
Except our luck that we were not insane.

The *Standard* says the missing girls are still
Not found. A man is held. The writers strain
The law's pale letter, closing for the kill
As once the mob did, not far in the past.

Suppose he did it, don't I know that face?
I shave it every morning. The same eyes
Plead innocent. In his case, one loose screw
Switched the desire a priest can't neutralize
To children, and permitted him to do
What we don't dream of even when God's grace

Stuns us with glory walking in the sky.
Grace, but not justice. If an impulse makes
Mere fools of most but monsters of the rest,
A balance sheet of what it gives and takes
Implies a mediator who knows best
If you can just surrender. Nor can I.

Think of the fathers, praying. They must know
No one exists to listen who did not
Choose them for this, but where else can they ask
The same exemption all the others got
By chance? They beg for mercy from a mask.
Had it a mind, they'd not be weeping so.

Time to go home. The things I tried to tell
My own two daughters churn in my hot head.
The stranger won't come on like Captain Hook.
He'll laugh like me, crack jokes, yet want you dead.
Good story, Dad. I turn for one last look
At Paradise, and how we rose and fell.

Young Lady in Black

The Russian poets dreamed, but dreamed too soon,
Of a red-lipped, chalk-white face framed in black fur:
Symbol of what their future would be like –
Free, lyrical and elegant, like her.
In the love songs of their climacteric
I met you before I met you, and you were
The way you are now in these photographs

Your father took outside the Hermitage.
You stand on snow, and more snow in the air
Arrives in powdered form like rice through space.
It hurts to know the colour of your hair
Is blacker than your hat. Such is the price
Figments exact by turning real: we care
Too much. I too was tricked by history,

But at least I saw you, close enough to touch,
Even as time made touch impossible.
The poets never met their richly dressed
Princess of liberty. The actual girl
Was lost to them as all the rest was lost:
Only their ghosts attended the snowfall
The camera stopped when you stood in the square,

Fiction made fact at long last and too late.
My grief would look like nothing in their eyes.
I hear them in the photographs. The breath
Of sorrow stirs the cold dust while hope dies
The worst way, in the vision of rebirth,
As by whole generations they arise
From pitted shallows in the permafrost

And storm the Winter Palace from the sky.
Each spirit shivering in a bead of light,
They fall again for what they once foretold –

For you, dawn burning through its cloak of night.
They miss what I miss, and a millionfold.
It all came true, it's there in black and white:
But your mouth is the colour of their blood.

In Town for the March

Today in Castlereigh Street I
Felt short of breath, and here is why.
From the direction of the Quay
Towards where Mark Foys used to be,
A glass and metal river ran
Made in Germany and Japan.
Past the facade of David Jones
Men walked their mobile telephones,
Making the footpath hideous
With what they needed to discuss.
But why so long, and why so loud?
I can recall a bigger crowd
In which nobody fought for space
Except to call a name. The face
To fit it smiled as it went by
Among the ranks. Women would cry
Who knew that should they call all day
One face would never look their way.
All this was sixty years ago,
Since when I have grown old and slow,
But still I see the marching men,
So many of them still young then,
Even the men from the first war
Straight as a piece of two-by-four.
Men of the Anzac Day parade,
I grew up in the world you made.
To mock it would be my mistake.
I try to love it for your sake.
Through cars and buses, on they come,
Their pace set by a spectral drum.
Their regimental banners, thin
As watercolours fading in
The sun, hint at a panoply
Dissolving into history.

As the rearguard outflanks Hyde Park,
Wheels right, and melts into the dark,
It leaves me, barely fit to stand,
Reaching up for my mother's hand.

Six Degrees of Separation from Shelley

In the last year of her life I dined with Diana Cooper
Who told me she thought the best thing to do with the poor
Was to kill them. I think her tongue was in her cheek
But with that much plastic surgery it was hard to tell.

As a child she had sat on the knee of George Meredith,
More than forty years after he published *Modern Love.*
Though she must have been as pretty as any poppet
Who challenged the trousers of Dowson or Lewis Carroll,

We can bet Meredith wasn't as modern as that.
By then the old boy wouldn't have felt a twinge
Even had he foreseen she would one day arrive
In Paris with an escort of two dozen Spitfires.

The book lamented his marriage to one of the daughters
Of Peacock. Peacock when young rescued Shelley
From a coma brought on through an excess of vegetarianism
By waving a steak under his sensitive nose.

Shelley never quite said that the best thing to do with the rich
Was to kill them, but he probably thought so.
Whether the steak was cooked or raw I can't remember.
I should, of course. I was practically there:

The blaze of his funeral pyre on the beach at night
Was still in her eyes. At her age I hope to recall
The phial of poison she carried but never used
Against the day there was nothing left to live for.

Occupation: Housewife

Advertisements asked 'Which twin has the Toni?'
Our mothers were supposed to be non-plussed.
Dense paragraphs of technical baloney
Explained the close resemblance of the phoney
To the Expensive Perm. It worked on trust.

The barber tried to tell me the same sheila
With the same Expensive Perm was pictured twice.
He said the Toni treatment was paint-sealer
Re-bottled by a second-hand car dealer
And did to hair what strychnine did to mice.

Our mothers all survived, but not the perms.
Two hours at most the Toni bobbed and dazzled
Before the waves were back on level terms,
Limp as the spear-points of the household germs
An avalanche of Vim left looking frazzled.

Another false economy, home brew
Seethed after nightfall in the laundry copper.
Bought on the sly, the hops were left to stew
Into a mulch that grunted as it grew.
You had to sample it with an eye-dropper,

Not stir it with a stick as one mum did.
She piled housebricks on top, thinking the gas
Would have nowhere to go. Lucky she hid
Inside the house. The copper blew its lid
Like Krakatoa to emit a mass

Of foam. The laundry window bulged and broke.
The prodigy invaded the back yard.
Spreading across the lawn like evil smoke
It murdered her hydrangeas at a stroke
And long before the dawn it had set hard.

On a world scale, one hardly needs to note,
Those Aussie battlers barely had a taste
Of deprivation. Reeling from the boat
Came reffo women who had eaten goat
Only on feast days. Still, it is the waste

I think of, the long years without our men,
And only the Yanks to offer luxuries
At a price no decent woman thought of then
As one she could afford, waiting for when
The Man Himself came back from Overseas.

And then I think of those whose men did not:
My mother one of them. She who had kept
Herself for him for so long, and for what?
To creep, when I had splinters, to my cot
With tweezers and a needle while I slept?

Now comes the time I fly to sit with her
Where she lies waiting, to what end we know.
We trade our stories of the way things were,
The home brew and the perm like rabbit fur.
How sad, she says, the heart is last to go.

The heart, the heart. I still can hear it break.
She asked for nothing except his return.
To pay so great a debt, what does it take?
My books, degrees, the money that I make?
Proud of a son who never seems to learn,

She can't forget I lost my good penknife.
Those memories of waste do not grow dim
When you, for Occupation, write: Housewife.
Out of this world, God grant them both the life
She gave me and I had instead of him.

Jesus in Nigeria

Let him so keen for casting the first stone
Direct a fast ball right between her eyes,
So it might be from one quick burst of bone,
Not from a mass of bruises, that she dies.

I'm pleased to see, of all you without sin,
The cocky dimwit is so young and strong
Who won the draw to let the games begin.
He looks the type, unless I'm very wrong,

Who'll hog the glory with his opening shot.
With any luck at least he'll knock her out.
His rivals in this miserable lot
Are hard pressed to jump up and down and shout.

That old one there has just put out his back
Lifting a boulder he could barely throw
For half a yard without a heart attack,
But you can bet, just to be in the show,

He'd shuffle up and drop it on her head.
I hate to take my father's name in vain
But God almighty, how they want her dead:
How sure they are that she should die in pain.

The woman taken in adultery:
It's one of the best stories in my book.
Some scholars call it the essential me.
If my writ ran here, you could take a look.

Alas, it doesn't. I wield little power
Even with my bunch, let alone with yours.
Long, long ago I had my public hour.
My mission failed. The maniacs and bores

Took over. I still weep, but weep in fear
Over a world become so pitiless
I miss that blessed soldier with the spear
Who put an early end to my distress.

Merely a thug and not a mental case,
He showed the only mercy I recall.
A dumb but reasonably decent face:
The best that we can hope for, all in all.

Step up, young man. Take aim and don't think twice.
No matter what you both believe is true,
Tonight she will be with me in Paradise.
I'm sorry I can't say the same for you.

The Place of Reeds

Kogarah (suppress the first 'a' and it scans)
Named by the locals for the creek's tall reeds
That look like an exotic dancer's fans
When dead, was where I lived. Born to great deeds

I stripped the fronds and was a warrior
Whose arrows were the long thin brittle stem
With a stiff piece of copper wire or
A headless nail to make a point for them.

The point went in where once the pith had been
Before it crumbled. The capillary
Was open at the other end. Some keen
Constructors mastered the technology

For fitting in a feathery tailpiece,
But they made model aeroplanes that flew.
Mine didn't, and my shafts, upon release
Wobbled and drifted as all missiles do

With nothing at the back to guide their flight.
Still, I was dangerous. My willow bow
Armed an Odysseus equipped to smite
Penelope and let her suitors go.

The creek led through a swamp where each weekend
Among the tangled trees we waged mock war.
At short range I could sometimes miss a friend
And hit the foe. Imagine Agincourt

Plus spiders, snakes and hydroponic plants.
I can't forget one boy, caught up a tree
By twenty others, peeing his short pants
As the arrows came up sizzling. It was me.

Just so the tribesmen, when our ship came in
Bringing the puffs of smoke that threw a spear
Too quick to see, realized they couldn't win.
It was our weaponry and not their fear

Defeated them. As we who couldn't lose
Fought with our toys, their young men dived for coins
From the wharf across the bay at La Perouse,
Far from us. Now, in age, my memory joins

Easy supremacy to black despair
In those enchanted gardens that they left
Because they knew they didn't have a prayer:
Lately I too begin to feel bereft.

Led by the head, my arrow proves to be
My life. I took my life into my hands.
I loosed it to its wandering apogee,
And now it falls. I wonder where it lands.

Hard-Core Orthography

In porno-speak, reversion to the Latin
Consoles us. 'Cum.' *Cum laude* we construe
As an audible orgasm. By that pattern,
Cum grano salis overturns the salt
With a thrashing climax when her urge to screw
Right there at dinner must be satisfied.
Cum vulpibus vulpinandum. While with foxes –
Caught *in flagrante*, high-heeled shoes flung wide
In satin sheets – do as the foxes do.
With aching wrist and pouting like a dolt,
Linguistically we still tick the right boxes:
You made *mecum*, she moans as she comes to.
Thus moved, her airbag lips look cumbersome
In the best sense. Maybe she's not so dumb.
Dum spiro, spero. How was it for you?

Ramifications of Pure Beauty

Passing the line-up of the narrowboats
The swans proceed down river. As they go
They sometimes dip and lift an inch or so.
A swan is not a stick that merely floats
With the current. Currents might prove too slow
Or contrary. Therefore the feet deploy:
Trailed in the glide, they dig deep for the thrust
That makes the body bob. Though we don't see
The leg swing forward and extend, it must
Do so. Such a deduction can't destroy
Our sense-impression of serenity,
But does taint what we feel with what we know.

Bounced from up-sun by Focke-Wulf 'Long Nose'
Ta-152s, Pierre Clostermann
Noted their bodies 'fined down by the speed':
And so they were, to his eyes. Clipped wingspan,
Long legs and close-cowled engine made the pose
Of that plane poised when stock-still. In the air,
High up and flat out, it looked fleet indeed.
What pulled it through the sky was left implied:
You had to know the turning blades were there,
Like the guns, the ammo and the man inside
Who might have thought your Tempest pretty too –
But not enough to stop him killing you.

The crowds for Titian cope with the appeal
Of flayed Actaeon. Horror made sublime:
We see that. Having seen it, we relax
With supine ladies. Pin-ups of their time,
Surely they have no hinterland of crime?
Corruption would show up like needle-tracks.
No, they are clean, as he was. All he knew
Of sin was painting them with not much on.
Even to fill a Spanish contract, he

Brought on the girls and called it poetry.
Philip II felt the same. Why think
At this late date about the mortal stink
Of the war galley, graceful as a swan?

Flashback on Fast Forward

The way his broken spirit almost healed
When he first saw how lovely she could look,
Her face illuminated by a book,
Was such a holy moment that he kneeled
Beside her; and the way his shoulders shook
Moved her caressing hand. Their love was sealed.

They met again. A different, older place
Had drawn her to its books, but still the glow
Of white between the words lit up her face
As if she gazed on freshly fallen snow.
He knew his troubled heart could not forego,
Not even for her sake, this touch of grace.

He asked her hand in marriage. She said yes.
Later he often said she must have known
To be with him was to be left alone
With the sworn enemy of happiness,
Her house a demilitarized zone
At best, and peace a pause in the distress.

When finally it broke her, he helped bring
Her back to life. Give him that much at least:
His cruelty was but a casual thing,
Not a career. Alas, that thought increased
His guilt he'd talked her into sheltering
Him safe home from the storm that never ceased,

Nor ever would. And so the years went by,
And, longer wed than almost all their friends,
Always in silence they would wonder why,
And sometimes say so. When a marriage ends,
They noticed, it's from good will running dry,
Not just from lack of means to make amends.

He could not save himself: that much she knew.
Perhaps she'd felt it forty years before
When he quaked where he knelt, and what was more
She was aware that saying 'I love you'
To one who hates himself can only store
Up trouble earthly powers can't undo.

But revelation can. There at the start,
It came again to mark their closing years.
Once more, and this time through and through, his heart
Was touched. The ice he half prized turned to tears
As the last hailstone melts and disappears
In rain. By just a glass door set apart,

She in her study, he in the garden, they
Looked separate still, but he saw, in her eyes,
The light of the white paper. How time flies
Revealed its secret path from their first day.
He did a dance to make her look his way.
She smiled at him, her devil in disguise,

Almost as if at last he had grown wise.

PARODIES, IMITATIONS
AND LAMPOONS

From Robert Lowell's Notebook

Notes for a Sonnet

Stalled before my metal shaving mirror
With a locked razor in my hand I think of Tantalus
Whose lake retreats below the fractured lower lip
Of my will. Splinter the groined eyeballs of our sin,
Ford Madox Ford: you on the Quaker golf course
In Nantucket double-dealt your practised lies
Flattering the others and me we'd be great poets.
How wrong you were in their case. And now Nixon,
Nixon rolls in the harpoon ropes and smashes with his flukes
The frail gunwales of our beleaguered art. What
Else remains now but your England, Ford? There's not
Much Lowell-praise left in Mailer but could be Alvarez
Might still write that book. In the skunk-hour
My mind's not right. But there will be
Fifty-six new sonnets by tomorrow night.

Revised Notes for a Sonnet

On the steps of the Pentagon I tucked my skull
Well down between my knees, thinking of Cordell Hull
Cabot Lodge Van du Plessis Stuyvesant, our gardener,
Who'd stop me playing speedway in the red-and-rust
Model A Ford that got clapped out on Cape Cod
And wound up as a seed shed. Oh my God, my God,
How this administration bleeds but will not die,
Hacking at the ribcage of our art. You were wrong, R. P.
Blackmur. Some of the others had our insight, too:
Though I suppose I had endurance, toughness, faith,
Sensitivity, intelligence and talent. My mind's not right.
With groined, sinning eyeballs I write sonnets until dawn
Is published over London like a row of books by Faber –
Then shave myself with Uncle's full-dress sabre.

Notes for a Revised Sonnet

Slicing my head off shaving I think of Charles I
Bowing to the groined eyeball of Cromwell's sinning will.
Think too of Orpheus, whose disembodied head
Dumped by the Bacchants floated singing in the river,
His love for Eurydice surviving her dumb move
By many sonnets. Decapitation wouldn't slow me down
By more than a hundred lines a day. R. P. and F. M. F.
Play eighteen holes together in my troubled mind,
Ford faking his card, Blackmur explicating his,
And what is love? John Berryman, if you'd had what it took
We could have both blown England open. Now, alone,
With a plush new set-up to move into and shake down,
I snow-job Stephen Spender while the liquor flows like lava
In the parlour of the Marchioness of Dufferin and Ava.

Once Smitten, Twice Smitten

Peter Porter as Enobarbus

There goes her barge without me. Did she spot
Me lurking in the reeds as she swept by?
Ra only knows. What gets her I've not got.
No ranks below Triumvir need apply.

I'm just a scribe in plastic sandals. She
Squats on a golden throne, I on this log.
How does it feel to screw a dynasty?
Caesar found out, but he was not a wog.

And now it's Antony that fuels her fires.
The lucky bastard lies in wait down-Nile.
Some Keystone Copts are shouting. It transpires
I'm sitting on a sacred crocodile.

Adrian Henri Wants to Write Poems

Remembering the day I walked five miles in my short trousers
To draw a picture of a plover's nest
And found out when I got there
That my pencil was broken and I had nothing to sharpen it with
A Heinkel one-eleven flew overhead looking for Liverpool
Or was it a Zeppelin, it's hard to remember how old
you are when you've been working on a youth image this long
cranes in the dockyards foghorns on the water clouds in the sky
lying on my back in grandad's allotment discovering Mallarmé
seeing the world for the first time flowers earth grass weeds
a sad young poet needing something to bring the brilliance of his
     perceptions
into focus

EUNICE tall dark schoolgirl breasts like fairy cakes you show me
yours running up the sand hills sudden flash of knickers
     illuminating
a young poet's mind and showing him his future
SHARON small fair schoolgirl transforming herself at night into a
     ponytail teenager pressed up against me dancing to Guy
     Mitchell
breast knickers breast knickers knickers
SHARON'S MOTHER love-starved scolding horror screaming at
     the sad young poet saying what have you done to my Sharon
     playing
hospitals realizing with a shock that Sharon's mother wears
knickers
too

on a bus to London
reading Leopardi in the Heath-Stubbs translation
getting off at Victoria with an air-force holdall
full of spare cuddle-pie pea jackets, horn-rimmed glasses
and four thousand seven hundred pages of single-spaced manuscript
Pete Brown running towards me inspired liberated cute
yelling hey Adrian the whole poetry-reading circuit is opening up
     the way Eunice used to and me yelling back

watch out for that bus
too late
in the Royal Free hospital Pete with all four limbs in traction
a splint up his nose and his mouth wired together
and the sad young poet sitting beside his bed
reads the whole manuscript Pete signalling gratitude
     with his left eyebrow

Edinburgh Festival lights fame repression
streets full of scotsmen Royal Mile chips haggis
Traverse theatre lunchtimes reading with Roger McGough
girls packed along the walls drinking in every word
knickers knickers knickers knickers

then you happened
middle-aged woman with body of a schoolgirl
lying all night on top of you like Moby Dick in dry dock
reciting Mallarmé to the rhythm of your loving
saying are you really twenty years old and hearing you sob
no thirty-four

then she happened
girl beautiful as cupcakes frilly-edged knickers
lying all night on top of her reciting Leopardi
saying are you really twenty years old and hearing her sob
no eleven

In Wormwood scrubs the sad young poet reads Rimbaud in the
     library
working on the autobiography Cape yelling for more instalments
dreaming of schoolgirls in cell at night
warm young bodies under blue gym slips open mouths questing
     hands
rain slanting down past the barred window
Brown making a million writing lyrics for Cream
got to get out of here, back in amongst it
fame knickers wealth adulation wealth knickers fame knickers
knickers
sad young poet writing on into the night

R. S. Thomas at Altitude

The reason I am leaning over
At this pronounced angle is simply
That I am accustomed to standing
On Welsh hillsides
Staring out over escarpments stripped
And pitiless as my vision,
Where God says: Come
Back to the trodden manure
Of the chapel's warm temptation.
But I see the canker that awaits
The child, and say no.
I see the death that ends
Life, and say no.
Missing nothing, I say
No, no.
And God says: you can't
Say no to me, cully,
I'm omnipotent.
But I indicate the
Flying birds and the
Swimming fish and the trudging
Horse with my pointing
Finger and with customary
Economy of language, say
Nothing.
There is a stone in my mouth,
There is a storm in my
Flesh, there is a wind in
My bone.
Artificer of the knuckled, globed years
Is this your answer?
I've been up on this hill
Too long.

Edward Estlin Cummings Dead

what time el Rouble & la Dollar spin
'their' armies into ever smaller change,
patrolling Kopeks for a Quarter search
& Deutschfranc, after decimating Yen
inflates with sterling Rupee in a ditch

(what time, i.e., as moneys in their 'death'
throes leave room for unbought souls to breathe)

that time, perhaps,
                        I'm him believing (i.
e., cummings
    hold it
    CUMMINGS) dead (

p   e   g   g   e   d   o   u   t
) & I will leave him lie

John Wain's Letters to Five More Artists

I

Now that I am Oxford Professor of Poetry, Django Reinhardt,
I salute your memory with more humility than ever.
You with crippled hands
Plucked everlasting beauty on that Dicky Wells
Paris Concert LP that I wore out.
You thought that different moons shone over France and England
But you played something superlative every time. No intellectual,
You were all artist. I wish, increasingly, that I were less
Intellectual. I would like to be a gipsy guitarist
With his fingers burned off playing with Dicky Wells,
Matching glittering silver guitar-runs to the black ripeness
Of his golden horn. I find, myself,
That to be prolific comes easily
But to be memorable takes effort. I wish
I could do what you did on *La Mer*. Wish also, Django, *mon cher*,
That I could be more humble.

II

Now that I am Oxford Professor of Poetry, Michelangelo Buonarotti,
I revere your achievement and feel increasingly less complacent.
The culture which gave rise to you had everything you needed
Except the Wolfenden Report. You could design buildings,
Write sonnets in Italian, and when you painted a ceiling
It stayed painted. But above all, you could sculpt.
Michelangelo, *amico*, you once said
That you chipped away the marble until you found the statue inside.
As a poet I have been using the same technique for years, and wish
That I could be even less complacent than I am now. *Capito*?

P.S. Could you use a few bags of marble chips? I've
Got a garage full.

III

Now that I am Oxford Professor of Poetry, Wolfgang Amadeus
    Mozart,
The mere mention of your name brings me up short, wishing
That I had made better use of my time. At my age
You had been dead for years, yet look
At the stuff you turned out. *Figaro. Don Giovanni.* K488.
The Flute.
You never finished your Requiem, of course; and I try to take
Comfort from that. As a business brain, you were a non-starter
And freemasonry was a blind alley. You would never have made it
To the Oxford Chair of Poetry. But taken as a whole
Yours was a career that leaves a modern artist chastened.
My poem *Wildtrack* was influenced by the slow movement of your
    Fourth
Violin Concerto, although comparisons are odious. I bow.
Schlaf'wohl, Wolfgang – precursor of us all.

IV

Now that I am Oxford Professor of Poetry, Rainer Maria Rilke,
I think of your prodigious gift and quell my surge of pride.
What was it, three-quarters of the *Duinos* and all the *Sonnets
To Orpheus* written in two weeks? Not even *Wildtrack*
Came as such a protean outpouring. And you had connections,
    Bruder:
Contacts dwarfing anything of ours. Weekends
In a cloud-scraping Bavarian *Schloss* with aristocratic women!
*Aus dem besitz der Grafin-Königen Marie von Thurn-und-Taxis
    Hohenlohe*
You inscribed, while my lot dedicated stuff to Sadie Bloggs.
You make me feel small, Rainer, *mein Freund, Dichter.*
As do Wolfgang, Mike and Django.

Now that I am Oxford Professor of Poetry, Stephen Spender,
I would just like to say Tough Luck, Baby,
But that's the way the cookie crumbles. Someone has to lose,
So eat my dust.
The thirties haven't got it in the nuts any more. My turn, *padrone.*
But stick around. We haven't forgotten how you old guys
Opened up the rackets for the new ideas. Times have changed,
But we'll find some action that fits your style. Can you drive?

Symptoms of Self-Regard

As she lies there naked on the only hot
Day in a ruined August reading Hugo Williams,
She looks up at the window cleaner.
Who has hesitantly appeared.

Wishing that he were Hugo Williams
She luxuriates provocatively,
Her fantasy protected by the glass
Or so she thinks.

Would that this abrasive oaf
Were Hugo Williams, she muses –
Imagining the poet in a black Armani
Bomber jacket from *Miami Vice*,
His lips pursed to kiss.

Suddenly, convulsively, she draws
The sheet up over herself
And quivers, having at last realized
That it really *is* Hugo Williams.

He sinks out of sight,
His poem already written.
He signs it 'Hugo Williams'.
The blue overalls have come in handy.

He takes off his flat cap,
Letting his silken hair fall free.
Hugo Williams has gone back to being handsome.
The poet has come down to earth.

Richard Wilbur's Fabergé Egg Factory

If Occam's Razor gleams in Massachusetts
In time the Pitti Palace is unravelled:
An old moon re-arising as the new sets
To show the poet how much he has travelled.

Laforgue said missing trains was beautiful
But Wittgenstein said words should not seduce:
Small talk from him would at the best be dutiful –
And news of trains, from either man, no use.

Akhmatova finds echoes in Akhnaten.
The vocables they share *a fortiori*
Twin-yolk them in the selfsame kindergarten
Though Alekhine might tell a different story.

All mentioned populate a limpid lyric
Where learning deftly intromits precision:
The shots are Parthian, the victories Pyrrhic,
Piccarda's ghost was not so pale a vision,

But still you must admit this boy's got class –
His riddles lead through vacuums to a space
Where skill leans on the parapet of farce
And sees Narcissus making up his face.

Godfrey in Paradise

Admirers of Godfrey Smith's *Sunday Times* column, one of whose principal concerns is the various promotional free meals to which he is invited, were not surprised to learn, from a recent feature article by him in the same newspaper, that lunch is his idea of heaven.

When Godfrey Smith goes up to Heaven
He'll see more cream teas than in Devon
And angels in McDonald's hats
Ladling chips from golden vats.

Because he has been very good
Godfrey will smell all kinds of grub:
Lancashire hotpot, Yorkshire pud,
Saddle of lamb and syllabub.

When Godfrey breasts the pearly gates
Fat cherubs will bang spoons on plates,
Filling the air with chubby singing.
The gong for dinner will be ringing.

But dinner, Godfrey will intuit,
Leads on to breakfast, thence to brunch.
In Heaven there's no limit to it.
The whole thing's one enormous lunch.

Brie, Stilton, Roquefort and Caerphilly,
Banana splits *avec* Chantilly,
Petits fours, wafers, halva, toffee
Come with, if not before, the coffee.

The scoff in Heaven's done just right.
The chocolate sauce is not too thick.
They do not beat the mousse all night
Nor oversteam the spotted dick.

When Godfrey dines with his Creator
He'll bung five quid to the head waiter
And compliment his beaming host
On the aroma of the roast.

The Koran promises its readers
Heaven's one endless copulation.
Godfrey will pity the poor bleeders
From his eternity of gustation.

What proper man would plump for bints
Ahead of After Eight thin mints?
True pleasure for a man of parts
Is tarts in him, not him in tarts.

When Godfrey Smith finds Paradise
He'll sniff that spread both long and broad
And start by eating it all twice –
The Lord's perpetual smorgasbord.

The Wasted Land

T. S. Tambiguiti

April is a very unkind month, I am telling you.
Oh yes. And summer was surprising us very much,
Coming over the Tottenham Court Road.
What are the roots that grab around you,
What are the branches that grow, actually,
Out of all this? Can't you tell me that?
You know only a heap of images all broken up.
Under the brown fog of a winter dawn,
A crowd was flowing over London Bridge, so many,
So many people there were crossing that bridge
It was looking like Calcutta.
There I was seeing somebody I knew and crying out
Rhanji! Rhanji! You who were with me
In that correspondence course they were giving
About how to repair railway engines
At home. Did you pass? But that was
A long time ago, oh yes, a long time ago.
Oh the moon shone very brightly on Mrs Murray
Who lived in Surrey.
She washed her feet in chicken curry.
Twit twit twit twit
Jug jug jug jug
Moo
It is unreal, this place, I am telling you that.
Do you listen to what I am telling you?
Burning burning burning burning burning
The whole vindaloo is burning, Ghita,
While you are talking to that silly Mrs Chatterjee.
These fragments I have shored against my ruins.
Hurry up please, you must be going home now.
Hurry up please, please hurry up.
Good night Rhanji. Good night Satyajit.
Good night Rabindranath. Good night Assistant
District Commissioner Cunningham-Price-Alyston.

Good night. Oh yes. It's good night that I am saying.
Good night. Good night. Tambiguiti is mad again.
Good night.
Shantih shantih shantih.
It's only a shantih in old
Shantih town.

After Such Knowledge

Great Tom: Notes Towards the Definition of T. S. Eliot
by T. S. Matthews

I saw him when distaste had turned to nightmare
    Near the end of this interminable book:
    As if the terraced cloudscape were a staircase
And he himself yet palpable, his sandals,
    Achillean by asphodel uplifted,
    Propelled their burden's effortless ascent –
A tuft of candid feathers at each shoulder
    Proclaiming him apprentice, cherished fledgling
    To overhanging galleries of angels.
And so, the poet first and I behind him,
    But only he a freedman hieing homeward,
    My quarry turned towards me. I cried 'Master!
We all knew you could make it!' and embraced him –
    Since, being both Sordello and Odysseus,
    I forgot my teacher's substance was a shadow,
And gathered uselessly the empty air.
    'Just passing through?' he chuckled as I teetered,
    Perhaps to ease the anguish of my gesture.
'If I were you I wouldn't plan on staying,
    Unless you don't mind falling through the scenery.'
    His smile, admonitory yet seraphic,
Suggested Pentecost, the truce of Advent,
    The prior taste unspeakably assuaging
    Of the ineluctable apotheosis.
'You remember T. S. Matthews, Sir?' I asked.
    'T. S. Who?' 'He's written your biography.'
    'Matthews . . . I suppose I knew him vaguely.
A *Time* man. Is it awful?' A platoon
    Of cherubim flashed past us on the banister,
    Posteriors illumined by the marble:
The welcoming committee for Stravinsky,
    As yet some years below but toiling skyward.
    'Not quite as bad as most have said, but still

A pretty odious effort.' Here I wavered.
    Around his neck, the excalfactive Order
    Of Merit infumated, argentine,
But the gaze above, both placent and unsleeping,
    Entlastende without tergiversation,
    Compelled the apprehension it prevented.
And I: 'It hasn't got that many facts
    Which can't be found in places more reputed –
    Notably your widow's thoughtful preface
To the MS of *The Waste Land.* That aside,
    The speculative content can add little
    To the cairn of innuendo stacked already
By Sencourt's *T. S. Eliot: A Memoir.'*
    I paused. And he: 'Poor Robert was a pest,
    I'm sad to say. Well, all right: what's the fuss then?'
I caught a sudden flicker of impatience,
    Familiar yet ineffable. 'Sir, nothing;
    For nothing can come of nothing. Matthews puzzles
Repellently about those thousand letters
    You wrote to Emily Hale, but has no answers.'
    And he, diverted: 'Nor will anybody,
For another fifty years. I can't believe, though,
    A full-blown book enshrines no more than these
    Incursions void of judgement. Therefore speak.'
And I: 'He rates his chances as a critic –
    Allowing you your gift, he dares to offer
    Conjectures that your ear verged on the faulty.
You said, for instance, of St Magnus Martyr,
    Its walls contained inexplicable splendour.
    He calls that adjective cacophonous.'
'He calls it *what*?' 'Cacophonous.' 'I see.'
    And I: 'The strictures go beyond irreverence.
    His animus is manifest. Your consort
He terms "robust" at one point; elsewhere, "ample";
    Yet cravenly endorses in his foreword
    Her telling him in such a forthright manner
To render himself scarce.' A gust of laughter,
    Subversive of his sanctity, perturbed him.
    He conjured from the gold strings of his harp

An autoschediastic lilt of love
    Which might have once been whistled by Ravel.
    And he: 'She did that, did she? Excellent.'
I said, 'The pride you feel is not misplaced:
    Your wish that no biography be written
    Will not be lightly flouted. Forced to yield,
Your wife will choose her author with great scruple
    Yet most of us who wish your memory well
    By now share the opinion that permission
To undertake the task must soon be granted
    Lest unofficial books like this gain ground,
    Besmirching the achievement of a lifetime.'
And he: 'I'm sure the lass will do what's best.
    One's not allowed to give advice from here
    And care for earthly fame is hard to summon.
It may, perhaps, however, please Another
    To whisper in her ear.' He turned away,
    Declaring as he faded 'It's surprising,
But this place isn't quite as Dante said –
    It's like the escalator at High Holborn,
    Except there's no way down.' So he departed,
Dissolving like a snowflake in the sun,
    A Sibyl's sentence in the leaves lost –
    Yet seemed like one who ends the race triumphant.

What About You? Asks Kingsley Amis

When Mrs Taflan Gruffydd-Lewis left Dai's flat
She gave her coiffe a pat
Having straightened carefully those nylon seams
Adopted to fulfil Dai's wicked dreams.
Evans didn't like tights.
He liked plump white thighs pulsing under thin skirts in packed
    pubs on warm nights.

That's that, then, thought Evans, hearing her Jag start,
And test-flew a fart.
Stuffing the wives of these industrial shags may be all
Very well, and *this* one was an embassy barroom brawl
With Madame Nhu.
Grade A. But give them that fatal twelfth inch and they'll soon
    take their cue

To grab a yard of your large intestine or include your glans
Penis in their plans
For that Rich, Full Emotional Life you'd thus far ducked
So successfully.
Yes, Evans was feeling . . . Mucked-
up sheets recalled their scrap.
Thinking barbed thoughts in stanza form after shafting's a right
    sweat. Time for a nap.

The North Window

To stay, as Mr Larkin stays, back late
Checking accessions in the Brynmor Jones
Library (the clapped date-stamp, punch-drunk, rattling,
The sea-green tinted windows turning slate,
The so-called Reading Room deserted) seems
A picnic at first blush. No Rolling Stones
Manqués or Pink Floyd simulacra battling
Their way to low-slung pass-marks head in hands:
Instead, unpeopled silence. Which demands

Reverence, and calls nightly like bad dreams
To make sure that that happens. Here he keeps
Elected frith, his thanedom undespited,
Ensconced against the mating-mandrill screams
Of this week's Students' Union Gang-Bang Sit-in,
As wet winds scour the Wolds. The moon-cold deeps
Are cod-thronged for the trawlers now benighted,
North. The inland cousin to the sail-maker
Can still bestride the boundaries of the way-acre,

The barley-ground and furzle-field unwritten
Fee simple failed to guard from Marks & Spencer's
Stock depot some time back. (Ten years, was it?)
Gull, lapwing, redshank, oyster-catcher, bittern
(Yet further out: sheerwater, fulmar, gannet)
Police his mud-and-cloud-ashlared defences.
Intangible revetments! On deposit,
Chalk thick below prevents the Humber seeping
Upward to where he could be sitting sleeping,

So motionless he lowers. Screwed, the planet
Swerves towards its distant, death-dark pocket.
He opens out his notebook at a would-be
Poem, ashamed by now that he began it.
Grave-skinned with grief, such Hardy-hyphened diction,
Tight-crammed as pack ice, grates. What keys unlock it?

It's all gone wrong. Fame isn't as it should be –
No, nothing like. 'The town's not been the same',
He's heard slags whine, 'since Mr Larkin came.'

Sir John arriving with those science-fiction
Broadcasting pricks and bitches didn't help.
And those Jap PhDs, their questionnaires!
(Replying 'Sod off, Slant-Eyes' led to friction.)
He conjures envied livings less like dying:
Sharp cat-house stomp and tart-toned, gate-mouthed yelp
Of Satchmo surge undulled, dispersing cares
Thought reconvenes. In that way She would kiss,
The Wanted One. But other lives than this – .

Fantastic. Pages spread their blankness. Sighing,
He knuckles down to force-feed epithets.
Would Love have eased the joints of his iambs?
He can't guess, and by now it's no use trying.
A sweet ache spreads from cramp-gripped pen to limb:
The stanza next to last coheres and sets.
As rhyme and rhythm, tame tonight like lambs,
Entice him to the standard whirlwind finish,
The only cry no distances diminish

Comes hurtling soundless from Creation's rim
Earthward – the harsh *recitativo secco*
Of spaces between stars. He hears it sing,
That voice of utmost emptiness. To him.
Declaring he has always moved too late,
And hinting, its each long-lost blaze's echo
Lack-lustre as a Hell-bent angel's wing,
That what – as if he needed telling twice –
Comes next makes this lot look like Paradise.

VERSE LETTERS
AND OCCASIONAL VERSE

To Russell Davies: a letter from Cardiff

Dear Dai: I'm writing to you from location
For the new McKenzie film, in which I play
A role that would have filled me with elation
When I used to drink two-handed every day,
But as things are, it fills me with dismay –
With me no more than three weeks on the wagon
They're handing me free Foster's by the flagon.

I'm meant to be, you see, a drunken critic
Arrived in Europe from the Great South Land:
The least articulate, most paralytic
Plug-ugly in McKenzie's merry band,
Escorting that chaste hero on a grand
Excursion through the more arcane and zanier
Interstices of deepest Transylvania.

Which place we double here, in Cardiff (Wales),
Whose Burges follies neatly fill the bill:
They've even got the right-sized drawbridge nails.
Cold Castle Coch, perched darkly on a hill,
And Cardiff Castle in the city, will,
When cut together, serve as a spectacular
Surround for a larf riot spoofing Dracula.

Oh Cardiff! Dai, your homeland's sovereign seat,
This city of arcades and . . . more arcades,
I've hardly seen yet. Is there a main street?
No time for galleries or bookshop raids:
When precious shooting-time at evening fades
We shuttle back in vans to our hotel
And thank God that at least the beds work well

For nothing else there operates at all.
You risk your reason when you take your key.
They never wake you if you leave a call,
Do when you don't, refuse to give you tea

In bed unless asked not to – but get me.
I'm dining every evening in the presence
Of clown Dick Bentley, clever Donald Pleasence

And crazy Barry Humphries: no regrets.
On top of that, of course, I watch them work
Their wonders from sunrise until it sets –
A feast of practised talent which I lurk
In awe to ogle, feeling like a berk.
I think, my friend, our highest common factor
The certainty we share that I'm no actor.

Whereas, of course, you are – about the best
I met at Cambridge. Have you given up
That gift to spend more effort on the rest?
Your dispositions overflow the cup.
No matter. Early days. The night's a pup.
Though there be times you'd like to see the back of
A few of all those trades you're such a Jack of

It's too soon to be certain what's dispensable.
You're bound to write more, draw more, play more jazz:
The man who brands your output reprehensible
You'll know to be a monomorph like Bazz,
Whose one-track mind's the only knack he has.
I fear our purist friends find nothing seedier
Than the way we spread ourselves around the Media,

But we both know you are, with all your bents,
As much compelled as I am with my few
To make from art and life some kind of sense
That leaves room for enjoying what we do.
Hermetic rhetoric aside, what's new
In serving more than one urge to excel
Like Michelangelo or Keith Michell?

Now I myself, though full-time a pop lyricist,
Have found the odd stint as a strict-form poet
Has rendered me less trusting, more empiricist,
Concerning technique and the need to know it.

This stuff you must make work or else you blow it.
Sincere intent alone is not enough:
For though the tone is light, the rules are tough.

The obstacle, says Gianfranco Contini,
Is what brings creativity to birth.
(His mind unlocks a problem like Houdini.
The best-equipped philologist on Earth,
Contini, in my view – for what that's worth –
Was sent by providence to heal the schism
That sunders scholarship from criticism.)

The obstacle for Dante, claims the Prof.,
Lay in the strictness of the *terza rima*.
The old New Style perforce was written off,
Or rather, written up: the lyric dreamer
Got sharper with his tongue, became a schemer
Co-opting dozens of vocabularies
Into a language that forever varies

Yet in its forward pressure never falters –
A rhythmic pulse that somehow stays the same
For all its concrete detail always alters.
A form he would, when young, have thought a game
Had now the status of a sacred flame,
A fertile self-renewing holy trinity
Designed to give his Comedy divinity.

It worked, too, as I'm sure you have detected
Now that you're trained to read the Eyetie tongue.
At least I hope you have. If you've neglected
Your Dante when like mine your wife's among
His foremost female fans, you should be hung,
Or hanged. At getting grammar through to students
Your Judy's letter perfect, like my Prudence,

Who's perfect in all ways . . . but I digress.
However true, it's crass to call one's spouse
A paragon of loving comeliness
Who yet rates alpha double plus for nous

While still remaining keen to clean the house.
A paradox worth pondering upon:
We each loathed Academe, yet wed a don.

I don't know what my wife's at, half the time:
Locked up with microfilms of some frail text
Once copied from a copy's copy. I'm
Dead chuffed as well as miffed to be perplexed,
Contented neither of us has annexed
The other's field. Though it's conceited-sounding,
We Jameses think each other quite astounding.

I'd like to be back there at home right now,
Receiving from my helpmeet a fond look.
But here we Aussies are, rehearsing how
To quell with every cheap trick in the book
The Castle's evil Oriental cook –
A role played by a lithe and slightly spooky
Karate-ka 5th Dan, Meijii Suzuki.

He is (ah, but you twigged!) a Japanese.
I've never seen a man more fit or fleeter.
That guy can pull your teeth out with his knees
And kick the whiskers off a passing cheetah.
To Bazza's pals (me, Scrotum, Tazz and Skeeter)
Whom Meijii smites (the script says) hip and thigh,
He looks like at least seven samurai.

Perhaps propelled by an electric motor
His flying feet can draw blood like a knife.
His brain by Sony, body by Toyota,
This bloke's the Yellow Peril to the life:
And yet, a man of peace. In place of strife
He puts a focused force of meditation
That transcendentalizes aggravation.

A day of learning not to get too near him
Can leave you breathless. Think I'll hit the sack.
I'd like to tell the lad that, while I fear him,
I love the way he works; but there's a lack

In our communication. Keeping track
Of when he plans to lash out without warning
Has knackered me for now. More in the morning.

*   *   *

Another day since I began composing
These verses in spare moments has now passed,
And here's a whole free hour I can't spend dozing:
A chance to see the gallery at last.
It's early closing, though: so, breathing fast,
I sprint to the museum, pay 10p,
Race up the stairs, and Pow! Guess what I see:

Enough to make a man burst into tears.
Renoir's 'Parisian Girl'. A lilting dream
He painted, to the year, one hundred years
Ago. Deep storm-cloud blue and double cream,
Her clothes and skin are eddies in a stream
Of brush-strokes on a shawl of pastel silk,
A peacock-feather spectrum drowned in milk.

These rhapsodies in blue are his best things,
The style in which he really gets it on.
The Jeu de Paume has one that fairly sings –
A portrait of his kids, including Jean,
The boy who, when Pierre-Auguste was gone,
Became Renoir – whose pictures, as it proved,
Were just as human, just as great, and moved.

Even unto the second generation
Sheer genius descended, fully fashioned.
A transference that rates as a sensation:
That kind of baton-change is strictly rationed.
For which our gratitude should be impassioned –
If artistry, like money, ran in bloodlines
You very soon would find those bloodlines dud lines

Or dead lines. But we ought to leave to P. B.
Medawar the Nature–Nurture number:

I'm sure he's in the right. I'd get the heebie-
Jeebies reading Eysenck, except slumber
Has always supervened. They're loads of lumber,
Those figures meant to prove genetic strains
Determine your inheritance of brains,

For nobody escapes the play of chance.
The contract's binding: you have got the part.
You have to mime and juggle, sing and dance,
And when you think you've got the role by heart
Some idiot rewrites it from the start.
Nor is there, when your scenes run into trouble,
A volunteer prepared to be your double.

Tomorrow we're to film the kung-fu brawl.
Its imminence has got me feeling cagey,
Not least because I'm due to take a fall.
I'm worried (a) my acting might look stagey,
And (b) I'll have my head caved in by Meijii.
Cavorting with delight at making flicks
He'll get his thrills, but I might get his kicks.

The fight-arranger is my chum Alf Joint,
The Stuntman King (he did *Where Eagles Dare*,
The caper on the cable car). The point,
Says Alf, in flying safely through the air
Is landing with some energy to spare
So as to ease the shock of logs and boulders
By smart use of one's padded arms and shoulders.

'You're falling about two foot six,' they've said.
When put like that it doesn't sound like much.
The catch, though, is I'm landing on my head.
My first film role will need the tumbler's touch
Or else end on a stretcher or a crutch.
From Alf, who's done an eighty-times-as-high dive,
I can't expect much sympathy when *I* dive.

This could be the last stanza of my poem.
I'll scrawl a coda if I come up smiling,

But now I have to get out there and show 'em.
I find the idea nowhere near beguiling:
Suzuki's leg looks like a concrete piling.
But Hell, let's go. What's coping with a killer
To someone who wrote monthly for Karl Miller?

* * *

Per ardua ad astra. I survived!
The scrap went perfectly. In Panavision
It should seem like the Day of Wrath's arrived.
My nose and Meijii's toe faked their collision
And I, without a second's indecision,
Collapsed. I toast (in Coke) success (comparative)
And him who wrote my role into the narrative,

Bruce Beresford. From birth, my oldest mate
Was destined to call 'Action', 'Cut' and 'Print'
And 'Stop' and 'What went wrong? You fainted late,'
'You died too soon,' 'No good, I saw you squint,'
And (this to me) 'You're mugging. Make like Clint
Or Kirk or Burt. Don't even bat an eyelid:
Then, when the kick comes, crumple the way I did.'

That we would see in letters five feet high
His name one day spread shining in the gloom
Preceded with the words 'Directed by' –
To doubt that prospect there was never room.
He had the screenplay ready in the womb.
He was (he'll know I say it without unction)
By nature built for one creative function.

Alas, not true for us. We're several sided;
I to a certain, you to a large, degree.
The age is vanished when we might have prided
Ourselves on that. Karl Marx said history
Will get a re-run, but as parody.
The Universal Man won't be returning.
Too bad. But as I write, the castle's burning:

Our week in Wales will finish with this shot.
The clapperboard has clapped its final clap.
Sighs. Tears. Farewells. You know the bit. The lot.
We'll soon hear, barring unforeseen mishap,
The first assistant calling, 'It's a wrap.'
Of our last day, this is the day's last light
When darkest daylight shades to lightest night –

The time the film crew calls the golden hour.
The castle quakes. The FX flames leap higher.
We rescue Edna Everage from the tower
And super the end titles on the fire.
The heavy croaks. Our triumph is entire.
It's time to say, 'Nuff said.' You don't mind, do you?
I'll post this now, then try to beat it to you.

To Martin Amis: a letter from Indianapolis

Dear Mart, I write you from a magic spot.
The dullsville capital of Indiana
At this one point, for this one day, has got
Intensity in every nut and spanner.
Soon now the cars will sing their vast Hosanna
And pressure will produce amazing grace.
Drake-Offenhauser! A. J. Foyt's bandanna!
Velazquez painting Philip at the chase
Saw something like these colours, nothing like this race.

Ten thirty. Half an hour before the start.
The press-box at the Brickyard is up high.
We sit here safely, emperors set apart,
And kibbitz down as those about to die
Cry *Morituri* . . . Yes, but so am I,
And so are you, though not now. When we're older.
Where death will be the last thing we defy,
These madmen feel it perching on their shoulder:
The tremble of the heat is tinged with something colder.

But that's enough of talk about the weather.
To rail against the climate's not good form.
My subject ought to be the latest feather
Protruding from your cap. I mean the Maugham.
I offer you, through gritted teeth, my warm
Congratulations on another coup.
Success for you's so soon become the norm,
Your fresh young ego might be knocked askew.
A widespread fear, I find. Your father thinks so too.

The prize's terms dictate an expedition
To distant lands. That makes you Captain Kirk
Of Starship *Enterprise*. Your Five-Year Mission:
To Boldly Go etcetera. You can't shirk
The challenge. This award's not just a perk:
Queer Maugham's £500 are meant to send

Your mind in search of fodder for your work
Through any far-flung way you care to wend.
Which means, at present rates, a fortnight in Southend,

So choosing Andalusia took nerve.
It's certainly some kind of foreign part.
A bit close-flung, perhaps, but it will serve
To show you the left knee, if not the heart,
Of European Culture. It's a start.
Like Chesterfield advising his young son
(Who didn't, I imagine, give a fart)
I'm keen to see your life correctly run.
You can't just arse around forever having fun.

The day's work here began at 6 a.m.
The first car they pumped full of gasoline
And wheeled out looked unworldly, like a LEM.
A Mass was said. 'The Lord is King.' The scene
Grew crammed with every kind of clean machine.
An Offenhauser woke with shrieks and yells.
The heart-throb Dayglo pulse and Duco preen
Of decals filled the view with charms and spells
As densely drawn and brilliant as the Book of Kells.

BORG WARNER. BARDAHL. 'Let the Earth rejoice.'
'May Christ have mercy.' LODESTAR. OLSONITE.
America exults with sponsored voice
From Kitty Hawk to ultra-Lunar flight.
RAYBESTOS. GULF. Uptight and out of sight!
The Cape. BELL HELMETS. Gemini. Apollo!
Jay Gatsby put his faith in the green light.
Behold his dream, and who shall call it hollow?
What genius they have, what destinies they follow!

The big pre-race parade comes down the straight
While hardened press-men lecherously dote
On schoolgirl majorettes all looking great
In boots and spangled swimsuits. Flags denote
Their provenance. The band from Terre Haute
Is called the Marching Patriots. Purdue

Has got a drum so big it needs a float.
And now the Dancing Bears come prancing through,
Their derrières starred white and striped with red and blue.

From Tucson, Kokomo and Tuscaloosa,
From over the state line and far away,
Purveying the complete John Philip Sousa
The kids have come for this one day in May
To show the watching world the USA
Survives and thrives and still knows how to cock its
Snoot. Old Uncle Sam is A-OK –
He's strutting with bright buttons and high pockets.
Hail, Tiger Band from Circleville! Broad Ripple Rockets!

Objectively, perhaps, they do look tatty.
This continent's original invaders
Were not, however, notably less ratty.
Torpedoes in tin hats and leather waders,
Hard bastards handing beads around like traders –
Grand larceny in every squeak and rattle.
The whole deal was a nightmare of Ralph Nader's,
A corporate racket dressed up as a battle:
The locals kissed the Spaniard's foot or died like cattle.

The choice between the New World and the Old
I've never found that clear, to tell the truth.
Tradition? Yes indeed, to that I hold:
These bouncing brats from Des Moines and Duluth
Seem short of every virtue except youth.
But really, was there that much more appeal
In stout Cortez's lack of ruth and couth
Simply because it bore the papal seal?
It's art that makes the difference, and Art means the Ideal:

Velazquez (*vide supra*) for example.
You're visiting the Prado, I presume?
Well, when you do, you'll find a healthy sample
Abstracted from his *oeuvre* from womb to tomb.
The key works line one giant, stunning room:
Group portraits done in and around the Court

Whose brilliance cleans your brains out like a broom.
Bravura, yes. But products, too, of thought:
An inner world in which the Kings ruled as they ought,

Not as they did. His purpose wasn't flattery
Or cravenly to kiss the royal rod.
He just depicted the assault and battery
Of Habsburg policies as acts of God,
Whose earthly incarnation was the clod
That currently inhabited the throne.
He deified the whole lot on his tod,
Each royal no-no, nincompoop and crone.
Great Titian was long gone. Velazquez was alone.

Alone, and hemmed about by mediocrities
(Except for once when Rubens came to town),
He must have felt as singular as Socrates
But didn't let the pressure get him down.
He slyly banked his credit with the Crown
Until he was allowed a year abroad
(In Rome, of course. In Venice he might drown.)
To raise his sights by study. An award
The King well knew would be a hundredfold restored.

Conquistadores in their *armadura*
The drivers now are standing by their cars.
Unholy soldiers (but in purpose purer),
They look as if they're shipping out for Mars.
It's hard to tell the rookies from the stars:
When suited-up and masked, they seem the same.
White skin grafts are the veteran's battle scars.
For A. J. Foyt the searing price of fame
Was branded round his mouth the day he ate the flame.

A year back young Swede Savage swallowed fire.
He took six months to die. It goes to show
How hot it is inside a funeral pyre
And just how hard a row the drivers hoe.
I can't believe they're in this for the dough.
The secret's not beyond, but in, the fear:

A focal point of grief they get to know
Some other place a million miles from here –
The dream Hart Crane once had, to travel in a tear.

Eleven on the dot. The zoo gets hit
By lightning. Lions whelp and panthers panic.
The fastest qualifiers quit the pit
No more than hipbone-high to a mechanic
And take the track. The uproar is Satanic.
By now the less exalted have departed,
But still the sound is monumental, manic.
Librarians would hear it broken-hearted.
And this lap's just for lining up. They haven't started.

Around the speedway cruising on the ton
(Which means for Indy cars, they're nearly stalling)
They blaze away like spaceships round the Sun –
A shout of thunder like Valhalla falling.
(I'm running out of epithets: it's galling.
I've never heard a noise like this before.)
They're coming round again. And it's appalling –
The moment when you can't stand any more,
The green light goes! Geronimo! Excelsior!

It's gangway for the new apocalypse!
They're racing at two hundred miles an hour!
The likelier contenders get to grips
Like heavy cavalry berserk with power
And three-time-winner Foyt already rips
Away to lead the field by half a mile
As up the ante goes. Down go the chips.
No one but Rutherford can match that style,
And he starts too far back. I'll tell you in a while

The way it all comes out, but now I've got
To set this screed aside and keep a check
From lap to lap on who, while driving what,
Gets hits by whom or ends up in a wreck.
A half a thousand miles is quite a trek –
Though even as I'm jotting down this line

A. J.'s got someone breathing down his neck . . .
Yes, Rutherford's MacLaren, from row nine,
Has moved up more than twenty places. Heady wine!

Since Johnny Rutherford is from Fort Worth
And Foyt from Houston, they are Texans twain:
The both of them behind the wheel since birth,
The both of them straight-arrow as John Wayne.
This thing they're doing's technically insane
And yet there's no denying it's a thrill:
For something fundamental in the brain
Rejoices in the daring and the skill.
The heart is lifted, even though the blood may chill.

It's SOME TIME LATER. On the victory dais
Glad Rutherford gets kissed and plied with drink.
It looks a bit like supper at Emmaus.
Unceasing worship's damaging, I think:
One's standards of self-knowledge tend to sink.
I'd like to try it, though, I must confess.
Perhaps a little bit. Not to the brink.
Nor would that heap of lolly cause distress:
Three hundred thousand dollars – not a penny less.

Until halfway, the prize belonged to Foyt.
His pretty GILMORE RACING ketchup-red
Coyote skated flatter than a quoit,
The maestro lying down as if in bed.
He only led by inches, but he led –
Until his turbo-charger coughed white smoke.
The car kept running quickly while it bled,
But finally – black flag. For Foyt, no joke:
Unless he had his money on the other bloke.

The Coming Boy on his eleventh try
At winning the '500' finished first.
A perfect journey. No one had to die.
On looking back, I think about the worst
Catastrophe was that an engine burst.
The empty Brickyard bakes in silent heat,

The quarter-million race-fans have dispersed,
And I have got a deadline I must meet:
I have to tell the story of the champion's defeat.

Velazquez was ennobled in the end.
(Old Philip, fading fast, could not refuse
The final accolade to such a friend.)
His background was examined for loose screws
(Against the blood of craftsmen, Moors or Jews
Bureaucracy imposed a strict embargo)
And in a year or so came the good news,
Together with the robes and wealthy cargo
They used to hang around a Knight of Santiago.

Encumbered thus, he sank into the grave.
The man is dead. The artist is alive.
For lonely are the brilliant, like the brave –
Exactly like, except their deeds survive.
My point (it's taken ages to arrive)
Is simply this: enjoy the adulation,
But meanwhile take a tip from Uncle Clive
And amplify your general education.
There's more than literature involved in cultivation.

Tomorrow in the London afternoon
I'll miss your stubby, Jaggerish appearance
And wish you back in Fleet Street very soon.
Among the foremost ranks of your adherents
I'm vocal to the point of incoherence
When totting up your qualities of mind.
You've even got the rarest: perseverance.
A wise adviser ought to be resigned,
Unless he keeps the pace hot, to being left behind.

'We're given Art in order not to perish
Faced with the Truth.' Or words to that effect.
An apophthegm of Nietzsche's which I cherish:
He sees how these two areas connect
Without conceding that they intersect.

Enough for now. Go easy, I implore you.
It all abides your questing intellect.
The Heritage of Culture, I assure you,
Like everything, you lucky sod, is all before you.

To Pete Atkin: a letter from Paris

Trapped here in Paris, Pete, to shoot some scenes
Which end a film that's tied me up for weeks,
I've lost track of what what I'm doing means.
The streets of the Étoile are filled like creeks
By driving rain that blinds our fine machines.
We squat indoors, unprepossessing freaks
Made up as rough-cast hoboes of both sexes,
Surrounded by sun-guns and Panaflexes.

Our schedule's gone to Hades. Meanwhile you
Have gone to Scotland, there to make the rounds
Of clubs and halls to introduce our new
Collection of low-down yet highbrow sounds –
A sacrifice I hail. And so, in lieu
Of calls that would be tricky and cost pounds,
I'm scrawling you this missive in *ottava*,
A form I like like Fields liked Mocha-Java.

That Byron incarnates Don Juan in it
Should make it suicide to use again.
This note would end before I could begin it
Were I to dwell on that least pinched of men
(Who turned these stanzas out at two a minute)
And bring to mind the splendour of his pen,
The sheer *élan*, the lift, the loose-limbed jollity –
Yes, blue – but true blue, right? Legit. Star quality.

A strength that helps to prove these verse-form shapes
(Homespun or else, like this one now, imported)
Are far from being decorative drapes
Deployed to prettify some ill-assorted
Conceptions best half hidden: the gap gapes
Between the thought and deed (and drawn and quartered
Lies your result) if that's your estimation.
These strict schemes are a kind of cogitation

In their own right. Without them, no real thinking
Beyond the surface flotsam in the skull
Can happen. It takes more than steady drinking
To stop creative writers being dull.
Their gifts they'll soon find upside down and sinking
If discipline has not first keeled the hull.
For all true poets rhyme must equal reason
And formlessness be just a form of treason.

So no surprise you were the man for me,
Though others sang with much more cute a voice.
Approval was no matter of degree
But absolute. There was no other choice.
Our linking up was pure necessity,
As certainly as Rolls had need of Royce.
I viewed you, while the Footlights shouted Encore,
The way one Goncourt viewed the other Goncourt.

This kid, I mused, knows how to grasp the nettle.
With him the formal urge is automatic.
He's lamped the fact that only heat moulds metal
Or pressure makes the lyrical dramatic.
One's syllables would soon attain fine fettle
If tethered to his notes, be less erratic;
One's lexical pizzazz avoid fatuity
Attached to that melodic perspicuity.

We met, we talked of Bean and Brute and Bird
And Rabbit. You were full of praise for Trane.
We both thought early Miles had had the word
But (now I know this went against the grain)
I thought he later lost it. Had I heard
Of Archie Shepp? Yes. Good? No. Right: inane.
Our views were close, and on one salient thing
Inseparably united – Duke was King.

Of 'Main Stem', ' "C" Jam Blues' and 'Cottontail',
Of 'Take the "A" Train', 'In a Mellotone'
And 'Harlem Air Shaft' we took turns to wail

The solos so definitively blown
By sidemen somewhere in the age of sail –
The pre-war Forties, when Duke stood alone,
His every disc a miniature immensity,
The acme of schooled ease and spacious density.

It soon turned out you thought post-Presley pop
As real as jazz. This wheeze was new to me
And caught my sense of fitness on the hop:
I loved the stuff, but come now, seriously . . .
Hold on, though. My beliefs howled to a stop
And chose reverse. With one bound, Jack was free.
If rock struck me as fruitful, lively, good –
Why not get in and gain a livelihood?

The Broadway partnership of words and tune
Had been dissolved by pop, which then reverted
In all good faith to rhyming moon with June,
Well pleased with the banalities it blurted.
Those speech defects would need attention soon.
Gillespie and Kildare, in aim concerted,
We got started . . . but enough now in that strain:
The whole a.m. has just gone down the drain.

I'm sure the cost of sitting here is frightening
And days ago it ceased to be much fun.
Though, as we lunch, the sky might just be lightening:
This afternoon we could get something done.
And now the outlook's definitely brightening,
So more from the location. I must run.
We've just been told to grab a cab and ride out
To some guy called Quatorze's country hideout.

* * *

The weather's cleared. We're filming at Versailles,
Palatial residence of Sun King Louis,
Where everything is landscaped save the sky
And even that seems strangely free of *pluie*

For this one day at least. I find that I
Am sneakily inclined to murmur 'phooey'
When faced with all this Classical giganticism:
In fact it almost makes me like Romanticism.

Proportion, yes: the joint's got that to burn.
Sa regularity of window arch,
Ses ranks of cornucopia and urn.
Those balustrades like soldiers on the march!
Those gardens, haunt of robot coot and hern!
The whole confection fairly reeks of starch:
A dude ranch frozen with neurotic tension,
It chills the very notion of dissension.

And that was what *le Roi Soleil* was after,
Without a doubt. His absolutist frown
Is there in every pediment and rafter,
A stare of disapproval beating down
Propensities to any form of laughter
Beyond the courtly hollow kind. The Crown
Made sure to keep this four-star barracks filled
With dupes who thought they danced but really drilled.

Grim-jawed solemnity may have its worth
But geniality is just as serious
And *gravitas* is half deaf without mirth.
I don't mean one should roll around delirious
But art must take the air, not hug the earth –
Authoritative needn't mean imperious.
To preach cold concepts like the golden section
Is over-mightily to seek perfection.

We should be glad, then, that we work in rock
Whose mark for ordered symmetry is zero.
Its *cognoscenti*, talking total cock
Concerning slack-mouthed bitch or dildoed hero,
Combine the thickness of a mental block
With all the musicality of Nero:
And yet despite their IQs in two figures
They've sussed out where the only decent gig is.

In liking anti-intellectualism
They're wrong, but right to value simple verve.
A long way gone in pale eclecticism,
Like all those nostrums that no longer serve
(Vedanta, Social Credit, Pelmanism)
The classical succession's lost its nerve –
Or else it shrieks an avant-gardist foolery
That makes the average rock song shine like joolery.

But here the shine's gone off a hard half-day:
We're wrapping up with no shots left to do.
Inside a camera car I'm borne away
Along a six-lane speedway to St Cloud,
Where signboards set to lead non-Frogs astray
Now send us back Versailles-wards. Sacray bloo.
Our pub will keep a meal, though . . . Bloody Hell!
No food: we have to work tonight as well.

*   *   *

Throughout the evening's shooting in Pigalle
I marvel, as the red lights glow infernally,
That they can pull down places like Les Halles
When (rain or shine, nocturnally, diurnally,
Uncaring if you snigger, sneer or snarl)
Grim tat and tit dance cheek by jowl eternally
In *this* dump. What a drag! But its survival
Is no surprise if taste's its only rival.

Alone at last, I'm much too tired to sleep
(A hemistitch from Lorenz Hart. You tumbled?)
The drapes down-soft, the wall-to-wall knee-deep,
My hotel bedroom ought to leave me humbled.
By rights I should conk out without a peep,
But can't. The boys who did the decor fumbled:
It's just too scrumptious to be borne, too peachy.
They've ladled on an acre too much chichi.

The Gauche and not the Droite's the Rive for me.
To kip beneath plush quilts is not the same

As gazing *sur les toits* of that Paree
They fly behind the garret window frame,
Heraldic as France Ancient's fleur-de-lys,
To charm you through Act I of *La Bohème* –
Unless I've got Parnasse mixed up with Martre.
(You know I still can't tell those Monts apartre?)

So much for taste, then, and the same goes double
For those more recent phantoms, such as Youth.
As clear and brilliant as the tiny bubble
That canopies a baby's first front tooth,
There swells through times of sloth and troughs of trouble
The artist's one eternal, guiding truth –
Ars longa, vita brevis. Is that Horace?
It could be someone weird, like William Morris.

* * *

I'm writing halfway up the Eiffel Tower
While knocking back a rich *café au lait.*
We've been at work this high about an hour
And here my part will end, at noon today.
It gives a heady, Zeus-like sense of power
To watch, from *au-dessus de la mêlée,*
The myriad formiculant mere mortals
Who circumvest this crazy structure's portals.

Much earlier, and lovely in the dawn,
The gardens of the Louvre were full of mist.
The Tuileries lay like a smoking lawn
As I, my trusty notebook in my fist,
Saw Paris come unfolded like a fawn
And glitter like a powdered amethyst –
Whereat I felt, involved in her fragility,
A thumping streak of tough bitch durability.

We're all aware of how the continuity
Of Western culture's frazzled to a thread.
It doesn't take a soothsayer's acuity
To see the whole shebang might wind up dead.

One's sorely tempted to, in perpetuity,
Give up the struggle and go back to bed:
And yet Tradition, though we can't renew it,
Demands we add our certain something to it

No matter what. I leave from Charles de Gaulle
At Roissy this p.m. S-F HQ!
The planes feed in a cluster, like a shoal
Of mutant carp stuck nose to nose with glue
Around a doughnut in whose abstract hole
Aphasic humans escalating through
Translucent pipelines linking zones to domes
Seem pastel genes in giant chromosomes.

And that's the future, baby. Like the past
It's flowing, but unlike it it flows faster.
Ici Paris, below me. Will it last?
A heap of ageing bricks and wood and plaster –
Bombe glacée with one atomic blast.
A single finger's tremble from disaster.
But then, who isn't? So what else is new?
See you in London: there's a lot to do.

To Prue Shaw: a letter from Cambridge

I miss you. As I settle down to write,
    Creating for my forearm room to rest,
    I see the hard grey winter evening light
Is scribbled on with lipstick in the west
    As just another drowsy Cambridge day
    Discreetly shines and shyly looks its best
Before, with eyeballs glazed, it slides away
    And slips into a night's sleep deeper still,
    Where Morpheus holds undisputed sway
Throughout the weary academic mill –
    An atmosphere of cosy somnolence
    I hope that I can summon up the will
To counteract. I'm striving to condense
    Within the *terza rima* my ideas
    Concerning us, the arts and world events.
I shake my skull, which for the moment clears,
    And shape a line to say that minus you
    I'm lonelier than Hell and bored to tears:
Then slumber paints my eyelids thick with glue.
    Uncertainty bemuses. Somewhere round
    Lake Garda you've got lost and left no clue.
The post is void of cards, the phone of sound.
    If you were elsewhere than in Italy
    I'd start a hue and cry to get you found,
But as things are I think it best to be
    More circumspect. The blower's on the blink
    Across the strike-bound north from sea to sea,
And Heaven only knows the waste of ink
    Involved in trusting letters to the mail.
    The ship of state is getting set to sink
Again. (The poor thing never learned to sail.)
    Italia! Poverina! Yes, and yet
    The place's old enchantments never fail
To work their subtle wiles. You'll not forget,
    I'm sure, when passing ice-cold Sirmione,
    The way we used to swim and not get wet

In water soft and warm as *zabaglione.*
> The titles to the olive groves and palaces
> Catullus walked with courtesan and crony
In our time were Onassis's and Callas's,
> But as you stood hip-deep in liquid air
> I thought the moment sweet past all analysis
And thanked the pagan gods I knew were there
> (The sunset stretched a ladder of gold chains
> Across the lake) that they'd been so unfair
In handing you the beauty *and* the brains.
> An egocentric monster then as now
> I graciously resolved to keep my gains
By staying near you, never thinking how
> You might not co-divide that deep esteem.
> Unwarrantedly dry of palm and brow
I wed you, in due course. Today I dream
> Of what I would, if I had missed the boat
> Undoubtedly have undergone. A scream
Of retroactive anguish rends my throat.
> That physicist from Stockholm you refused,
> The one who tried to buy you a fur coat:
To think of the affection I abused!
> Now here was this attractive, well-heeled bloke,
> Whose talk of synchrotrons kept you amused,
Whose china-white Mercedes – Holy smoke!
> What made me certain he should get the grief
> And I the joy? I swear I almost croak
From apprehension mingled with relief
> Recalling how I flirted with defeat.
> It's only now I think myself a thief –
Of his luck and your time. You were to meet
> Yet brighter prospects later. I still won.
> I had a system nobody could beat.
I flailed about and called my folly fun
> For years and even then was not too late:
> The threads that joined us were as strongly spun
As your forgivingness of me was great.
> I wonder that your heart has not grown numb,
> So long you've had (or felt you've had) to wait

For my unthinking fondness to become
    A love for you like yours for me. The fault
    Is all mine if it has, for being dumb.
I'd have no comeback under Heaven's vault
    – my only plea could be *è colpa mia,*
    A hanging head, and tears that tasted salt –
If you should fade from my life like *la Pia.*
    But you have not, so I shall for the nonce
    Eschew this droning form of logorrhoea
Which feeds upon what might have happened once
    And hasten to give thanks that you and I,
    Like Verdi and Strepponi or the Lunts,
Seem apt, so far at least, to give the lie
    To notions that all order falls apart –
    Though giving them as one who would defy
The gods, yet feels a flutter in his heart.
    Has something happened? Down there, so much can.
    The right-wing terrorists are acting smart.
They've thought hard and have come up with a plan:
    To bomb the innocent. Earmarked for death
    Are woman, daughter, child and unarmed man.
From now on no one draws an easy breath.
    Your train ride down to Florence will be like
    Accepting a night's lodging from Macbeth.
I wonder if you'd rather hire a bike?
    Except the roads aren't safe. Well, why not walk?
    You'd thrive on a four-hundred-mile hike . . .
But no, all this is fearful husband's talk:
    What-might-be acting like what-might-have-been
    To turn my knees to jelly, cheeks to chalk.
No matter how infernal the machine
    Prepared to blow our sheltered lives to bits,
    It would be less than just, indeed obscene,
To harbour the suspicion murder fits
    The Italian national character. Not so.
    As always, most of them live by their wits
Amidst – as, to your cost, you've come to know –
    Administrative chaos. It's a wonder
    That utter barbarism's been so slow

In gaining ground from brouhaha and blunder,
    Yet even when *Fascismo* had its hour
    The blood was always upstaged by the thunder.
They held pyjama parties with their power
    Forgetting to wipe out a single race.
    Some blockhead said a bomb was like a flower,
Some communists got booted in the face,
    But no one calls that lapse a Holocaust –
    More like a farce that ended in disgrace,
When men yelled like a racing car's exhaust
    In uniforms adorned with a toy dagger;
    A time when word and meaning were divorced,
Divided by a verbal strut and swagger
    As pompous as a moose's mating call,
    Bombastic as a war dance by Mick Jagger.
But we both know it's not like that at all,
    The eternal Italy, the one that matters.
    The blue-chinned heavies at the costume ball
Whose togs inept explosions blow to tatters
    Are just the international tribe of jerks
    That crop up anywhere, as mad as hatters,
To pistol-whip the poor and cop the perks.
    The real Italians, far from on the make,
    Are makers. Ye shall know them by their works –
To which the guide who brought me wide awake
    Was you, ten years ago. You were my tutor.
    At times you must have thought this a mistake
And wished me elsewhere, or at least astuter.
    I paced our tiny rented room in Rome,
    I crackled like an overtaxed computer
And used my nerve-wracked fingers for a comb,
    Attempting to construe *Inferno* Five.
    It took so long I wanted to go home
But comprehension started to arrive
    At last. I saw the lovers ride the storm
    And felt the pulse which brought the dead alive.
For sheer intensity of lyric form
    I'd never read that stretch of verse's peer.
    You said such things, with Dante, were the norm.

You proved it, as we read on for a year.
    And so it was our Galahad, that book,
    As well as one ordained to make it clear
How art and intellect are king and rook
    And not just man and wife and guest and host –
    They link together like an eye and hook
While each moves through the other like a ghost.
    Both interpenetrate inside the mind
    And, in creation, nothing matters most –
By Dante these great facts are underlined,
    Made incandescent like a sunlit rose.
    My clenched fist thumped my forehead. I'd been blind!
Awaking from a Rip Van Winkle doze
    I realized I'd been groping in the gloom,
    Not even good at following my nose.
A knowing bride had schooled a clumsy groom:
    Belated, crude, but strong, his urge to learn
    Began there, in that shoebox of a room –
A classic eager dimwit doomed to burn
    The candle at both ends while, head in hands,
    He mouths what he can only just discern
And paragraphs twice read half understands.
    To Petrarch's verses and to Croce's thought
    We moved on later. Etiquette demands
I don't go on about the books we bought
    In all those second-hand shops we infested.
    I've never mastered grammar as I ought.
My scraps of erudition aren't digested.
    But still I've grown, drawn out by what I've read,
    More cosmopolitan – well, less sequestered.
(Our old friend Goethe, writing in his head,
    Would tap out stresses on his girlfriend's spine.
    Gorblimey, talk about Technique in Bed!
Urbanity on *that* scale's not my line.
    I must admit, however, that at times
    I found my brain, as well as fogged with wine,
Inopportunely chattering with rhymes.)
    And then there were the canvases and frescoes,
    Cascading like a visual change of chimes

Or stacked ten-deep like racks of tins in Tesco's
    All over Rome and Naples, Florence, Venice . . .
    I felt like a research group of UNESCO's
Investigating some microbic menace:
    To sort it out, life wasn't long enough.
    It just went on like Rosewall playing tennis.
There wasn't any end to all that stuff.
    An early Raphael, or late Perugino?
    (I haven't got a clue. I'll have to bluff.)
Who sculpted this, Verrocchio or Mino?
    (But who the heck was Mino?) No doubt what
    The banquet would have soon become (a beano
With sickness as the sequel) had you not
    Been there to function as my dietitian;
    Ensuring I'd not try to scoff the lot
But merely taste each phase at its fruition,
    Assimilating gradually, and thus
    Catch up with Europe's civilized tradition –
Which wasn't really a departing bus,
    You argued, but a spirit all around me
    I'd get attuned to if I didn't fuss.
From that time forward every summer found me
    In Florence, where you studied all year long.
    Your diligence continued to astound me.
I went on getting attributions wrong,
    But bit by bit I gained perceptiveness
    As day by day I keenly helped to throng
The galleries, exalted – nothing less –
    By how those fancy lads all worked like slaves
    To make their age so howling a success
Before they rolled, fulfilled, into their graves.
    In Cambridge, night wears on. The evening ending
    Will soon dictate the sleep my system craves.
I'll close. These lines might just be worth the sending
    To Florence, care of Rita at her flat.
    Supposing they get through, they'll wait there, pending
Your safe arrival – and amen to that.
    That city is a place where we were poor.
    In furnished dungeons blacker than your hat

We slept, or failed to, on the concrete floor
    And met the morning's heat chilled to the bone –
    Yet each day we felt better than before
Forgetting what it meant to be alone.
    Well, this is what it means: distracting games
    With tricky rhyme schemes and – wait, there's the phone.
'Will you accept a call from Mrs James?'
    P.S. You've made this letter obsolete
    But rather than consign it to the flames
I'll send it. For you must admit, my sweet,
    A triple-rhyming verse communication,
    While scarcely ranking as an epic feat,
Deserves perusal by its inspiration.

To Tom Stoppard: a letter from London

To catch your eye in Paris, Tom,
I choose a show-off stanza from
    Some Thirties play
Forgotten now like Rin Tin Tin.
Was it *The Dog Beneath the Skin*?
    Well, anyway

Its tone survives. The metres move
Through time like paintings in the Louvre
    (Say loov, not loover):
Coherent in their verbal jazz,
They're confident of tenure as
    J. Edgar Hoover.

Pink fairies of the sixth-form Left,
Those Ruined Boys at least were deft
    At the actual writing.
Though history scorns all they thought,
The nifty artefacts they wrought
    Still sound exciting.

Distinguishing the higher fliers
Remorselessly from plodding triers
    Who haven't got it,
Such phonic zip bespeaks a knack
Of which no labour hides the lack:
    A child could spot it.

And boy, you've got the stuff in bales –
A Lubitsch-touch that never fails.
    The other guys
Compared to you write lines that float
With all the grace of what gets wrote
    By Ernest Wise.

The Stoppard dramaturgic moxie
Unnerves the priests of orthodoxy:
    We still hear thicks
Who broadcast the opinion freely
Your plays are only sketches really –
    Just bags of tricks.

If dramas do not hammer themes
Like pub bores telling you their dreams
    The dense don't twig.
They want the things they know already
Reiterated loud and steady –
    Drilled through the wig.

From all frivolity aloof,
Those positivist killjoys goof
    Two ways at once:
They sell skill short, and then ignore
The way your works are so much more
    Than clever stunts.

So frictionless a *jeu d'esprit,*
Like Wittgenstein's philosophy,
    Appears to leave
Things as they are, but at the last
The future flowing to the past
    Without reprieve

Endorses everything you've done.
As Einstein puts it, The Old One
    Does not play dice,
And though your gift might smack of luck
Laws guide it, like the hockey puck
    Across the ice.

Deterministic you are not,
However, even by a jot.
    Your sense of form
Derives its casual power to thrill
From operating at the still
    Heart of the storm.

For how could someone lack concern
Who cared that gentle Guildenstern
    And Rosencrantz
(Or else the same names rearranged
Should those two men be interchanged)
    Were sent by chance

To meet a death at Hamlet's whim
Less grand than lay in store for him,
    But still a death:
A more appalling death, in fact
Than any king's in the Fifth Act –
    Even Macbeth?

In south-east Asia as I type
The carbuncle is growing ripe
    Around Saigon.
The citadels are soon reduced.
The chickens have come home to roost.
    The heat is on,

And we shall see a sickness cured
Which virulently has endured
    These thirty years:
The torturers ran out of jails,
The coffin-makers out of nails,
    Mothers of tears,

While all the Furies and the Fates
Unleashed by the United States
    In Freedom's name
Gave evidence that moral error
Returns in tumult and in terror
    The way it came.

But now the conquerors bring peace.
When everyone is in the police
    There's no unrest.
Except for those who disappear
The People grin from ear to ear –
    Not like the West.

Rejecting both kinds of belief
(Believing only in the grief
   Their clash must bring)
We find to use the words we feel
Adhere most closely to the real
   Means everything.

I like the kind of jokes you tell
And what's more you like mine as well –
   Clear proof of nous.
I like your stylish way of life.
I've thought of kidnapping your wife.
   I like your house.

Success appeals to my sweet tooth:
But finally it's to the truth
   That you defer –
And that's the thing I like the best.
My love to Miri. Get some rest.
   A tout à l'heure.

To Peter Porter: a letter to Sydney

To reach you in the You-Beaut Country, Peter,
Perforce I choose that scheme of rhyme and metre
Most favoured by your master spirit, Pope –
Whose pumiced forms make mine look like soft soap,
Despite the fact that this last fiscal year
Two thousand of my couplets, pretty near,
Have been read out in public – a clear token
The classical tradition's not yet broken,
Just mangled and left twitching in a ditch
By Aussies apt to scratch the fatal itch
That Juvenal and Dr Johnson dubbed
Cacoethes scribendi and well drubbed.
Your friends in London miss you something fierce:
You are the crux of talk like Mildred Pierce.
At Mille Pini or in Bertorelli's
We scriveners still meet to stoke our bellies
And with red wine we toast you *in absentia*
From soup to nuts and so on to dementia.
The grape juice flowing in across our dentures,
Tall tales flow out concerning your adventures.
As fleet of foot and fearless as Phidippides
You are our pioneer in the Antipodes,
A latter-day but no less dauntless Jason
Or Flying Dutchman as played by James Mason.
Vespucci, Tasman, Drake, Cook, Scott, John Glenn –
To those you left behind you're all these men:
The Town's not heard such daydreams of bravado
Since Raleigh sailed in search of El Dorado.
One rumour says that cheap drinks on the plane
Had detrimental impact on your brain:
It's said you smiled a smile like Nat King Cole's
While trying to take over the controls.
Another rumour graphically describes
The shameless way they're plying you with bribes
(A Philistine approach we're sure you'll spurn)
To make your trip a permanent return.

They've offered you £10,000 a year,
We're told, to dwell out there instead of here –
Plus car, two yachts, a house at Double Bay
And Mrs Whitlam in a negligée.
Temptation! You'd not only soon get rich,
Your kids would scarcely need to wear a stitch –
They'd be as brown as berries in two shakes.
Perhaps you ought to up stakes for *their* sakes . . .
To let them share the unexampled wealth
Australia's young are given free – good health.
Good health (i.e. preventive pediatrics)
Provides the punch behind Jeff Thomson's hat-tricks.
Good health ensures the Ashes stay down under.
It lends John Newcombe's smashes extra thunder.
Good health is what puts beefcake on Rod Taylor –
It makes Rolf Harris sound like a loudhailer.
Good health helps Eddie Charlton score like Bradman
And Sidney Nolan sling paint like a madman.
But vitamins and body-building cereals
Are only some among the raw materials
That go to stuff the bulging cornucopia
Which all wise men now know to be Utopia –
Though once none but the hopeless ever went there
And death was preferable to being sent there.
The tables are well turned. The biter's bitten.
The pit of desperation now is Britain –
Where soon must fall a dark night of the soul
With (HEALEY WARNS) three million on the dole
Unless some pin is found to pierce inflation
And thereby save the pound and thus the nation.
For their own chances loath to give you tuppence,
The British seem concussed by their comeuppance:
Like fearful Pooh and Piglet they keep humming,
But few believe a cure will be forthcoming
That won't make their poor country even poorer –
A bald man getting drunk on hair restorer.
To say 'So much the better' would be base
As well as out of key and not my place.
And yet, though some might deem the pause a pity,
The slump seems to have saved our favourite city

From being hacked to pieces like King Priam's –
Here by Joe Levy, there by Harry Hyams.
May wasting assets pauperize them both:
They made a graveyard and they called it Growth.
But now it's clear (thank Heaven for small mercies)
The land boom was a siren-song like Circe's
That sapped the system's last remaining vigour
By crooning, 'You must go on getting bigger.'
To which thought there can only be one answer –
A flagrant Harvey Smith, for so must cancer.
Forgive me if that reference to pathology
Offends your deep concern with eschatology –
The Last Things are for you no laughing matter
And there I go reducing them to patter.
You think of death, you've told me, all the time,
And not as a quietus but a crime.
You think of death, you've told me, as a curse
That caps a life of pain with something worse.
You think of death, you've told me, as obscene,
And all your poems show me what you mean,
For your horrific vision would make Goya
Plead mental cruelty and phone his lawyer –
And even Dürer's 'Ritter, Tod und Teufel'
Beside what you evoke looks almost joyful.
A paradox, in view of this, that you,
Of all the London literary crew,
Are much the most authentically elated
By everything great artists have created.
I miss your talk not just because of savouring
Its bracing lack of artificial flavouring,
But also for the way that Grub Street scandal
Is spiced by you with thoughts on Bach and Handel,
And whether the true high point of humanity
Was Mozart's innocence or Haydn's sanity.
For though your calling's poetry, your passion
Is Music – and I'm cast in the same fashion,
Believing that man's fate, if hardly cherishable,
Through Music may partake of the imperishable.
(A sacrament, I fear, which smacks of heresy
To some of our close friends among the clerisy,

Who can't conceive of anybody needing it –
And stick to writing verse, while rarely reading it.)
Enough. Since this must reach you through the 'Staggers'
Claire Tomalin will look askance and daggers
At claims for space beyond a second column,
So I shall close. Perhaps with something solemn?
Alas, I'm ill-equipped for sounding cryptic.
Besides, I just don't feel apocalyptic!
For all her empty coffers ring like cisterns,
For all her strength now lies with Sonny Liston's,
For all her looming future looks appalling,
Great Britain must for always be enthralling
To anyone who speaks her native tongue.
Turn back, and leave Australia to the young!
Turn back, and push a pencil as you ought!
Turn back! The times are right for rhymed report!
We need you here to help us face the crunch
(Or, failing that, to face the bill for lunch),
Lest in these islands folly govern men
Until the day King Arthur comes again –
And finds, no doubt, his advent greeted warmly
By Jack Jones, Arthur Scargill and Joe Gormley.

To Michael Frayn: a letter from Leningrad

I

Dear Michael, here in Leningrad
The wind unseasonably chill
For April ought to make me sad,
And yet I feel a heady thrill
To see the white rice in the air
Blown every which way round the square
Before the Winter Palace. Cold
Grey sky sets off the flourished gold
And whipped-cream plaster rococo
Embellishments that help to make
The place look such a birthday cake –
I only wish there were more snow.
Despite the risk of frozen feet
I'd like to see the dream complete.

II

Speaking of feet: they're killing me.
I've walked around the city now
For ages, there's so much to see.
Already I can well see how
Poets, composers, every kind
Of artist thought this town designed
Exclusively so that they might
Be stimulated day and night
To works of genius. I shan't
Pretend to be quite in their league.
Indeed I'd rather plead fatigue
And shirk the challenge, but I can't:
The ghosts of all those gifted men
Are sneering as I suck my pen.

III

The greatest of them all, of course,
Was Pushkin. I'm just halfway through
His masterpiece, but the full force
Of inspiration's only too
Apparent. In all literature
There's no fecundity so pure
As his. Through him the gods gave tongue
And made damned certain he died young.
So multifarious a voice,
So disciplined a formal sense –
His talent was just too immense.
He had to go. There was no choice.
Like Mozart he was Heaven-sent
And back to Heaven he soon went.

IV

Eugene Onegin! In an hour
I read one stanza. Such compression
Demands all one's attentive power.
Besides, I must make a confession:
My Russian, after months of sweat,
Is really not so hot as yet.
In fact it's pretty poor. As well
As being envious as Hell
Of all your other attributes,
I wish my army hitch had taught
Me tricks of a more taxing sort.
I studied how to polish boots
With spit and spoon. *You* got to know
The lingo of the dreaded foe.

V

We neither of us won the war.
I'm told it sort of went away

When both sides settled for a draw.
Lord Chalfont still has lots to say
About the imminent Red Threat,
But nothing much has happened yet
In global terms. The Warsaw Pact
Intractably remains a fact.
It's hard to see how they could lose,
Our experts warn, should they advance.
Poor NATO wouldn't stand a chance.
They've got more tanks than they can use.
By midday on D-Day Plus One
They'd be in Budleigh Salterton.

VI

But will they risk annihilation?
I don't think anybody knows.
The thought of total devastation
If ever harsh words come to blows
Still keeps the Super Powers in check.
Better to wring each other's neck
At second hand, on battlegrounds
Where losses can be kept in bounds.
When ideologies collide
They tend to choose exotic places
Where folk with ethnic-looking faces
Don't mind committing suicide,
Or anyway don't seem to. Thus
It's all thrashed out without much fuss.

VII

Meanwhile the vast USSR
Grows ever stronger and more bored.
The ceaseless struggle rages far
Away, in little lands abroad.
The Marxist-Leninist ideal
At home long since became as real

As it could ever be. The State
Takes charge of everybody's fate
From womb to tomb. Complete control
Is exercised on all resources.
The harnessing of natural forces
By now includes the human soul.
What you may do or even dream
Is all laid down by the regime,

VIII

Which should have no more use for terror.
The People now are too well drilled
To contemplate embracing error.
Assent's so thoroughly instilled
That new directives are obeyed
Before they've even been displayed
On all those billboards and red flags
Beneath which every building sags.
Nobody sane could see the need
For harsher methods than this thick
Miasma of bad rhetoric.
The masses long ago agreed
That inner freedom makes no sense.
Which only leaves the Dissidents –

IX

Who go through several kinds of Hell
In special clinics where the drugs
That make them ill instead of well
Are forced upon them, not by thugs,
But qualified psychiatrists.
It's one of history's little twists:
The sane are classified insane
And rather than relieving pain
The doctors cause it. Strange, but true –
When those with preternatural guts

Are first of all defined as nuts,
Then made so – but that's Marx for you:
To put the future beyond doubt
What must be must be brought about.

X

The common run of folk, meanwhile,
Can feel comparatively safe
From decimation Stalin-style.
Their bonds, though still strong, do not chafe
As proudly they with one accord
March asymptotically toward
That feast of dubious delights
Zinoviev calls the Yawning Heights –
A Workers' Paradise on Earth
Which has no use for abstract thought.
Fantastically good at sport
A new mankind has come to birth,
A race that stands a whole head taller –
Except the head's a trifle smaller.

XI

Useless to ask what might have been
Had things stayed roughly as they were.
October 1917
Made certain nothing could occur
Save transformation. History's tide –
Which Spengler said we have to ride
Or else go under – ran its course
With hypermetamorphic force
Until no links were left to sever.
All ties were broken with the past.
No going back. The die was cast
And everything was changed for ever.
How strange, in that case, we should feel
Those days to be so much more real

XII

Than these. Yet really not so strange,
For nothing dates like human dreams
Of Heaven. Terrified of change,
The Russia of the present seems
An embolism. Time forgot
To flow, and stopped, and formed a clot.
There's next to nowt in the whole place –
Including rockets aimed at space –
That wouldn't be there anyway
Had Lenin failed to catch his train.
Suppose he'd chosen to remain
In Zurich, who can really say
His country would not now be strong?
Perhaps he got the whole thing wrong

XIII

And simply blasted in the bud
What might have been a brilliant flower.
Perhaps in shedding so much blood
To gain unchallengeable power
He stopped what was just getting started
And left his country broken-hearted,
With what result we now all know –
The Gulag Archipelago.
Too black a thought with which to end
This letter, and besides, I'm too
Aware that I'm addressing you –
A master of the light touch. Friend,
Forgive my solemn voice of doom.
I aimed at gaiety, not gloom,

XIV

But somehow lost my mirth. Mistake.
It's boorish to parade one's grief

And weep for a whole country's sake,
Assuming it's lost all belief
In human decency. The fact
Remains that, though the deck is stacked
Against them, none the less the just
Are born and win each other's trust.
Nadezhda Mandelstam has said
The truth still comes back from the grave
And she should know. I think I'll waive
What rights I have to mourn the dead.
I'm better at the kind of tears
I cried when seeing *Donkey's Years*.

XV

Besides, I like it here, I've seen
The Peter-Paul and the Tsars' tombs.
I've stared at the Bronze Horseman, been
Through all the Hermitage's rooms.
I've seen the Empress Catherine's clock –
A ten-foot wingspan gold peacock
Some Grand Duke thought the kind of gift
That might convey his general drift.
I've seen ... But there seems little point,
Here in this Window on the West,
In telling you what you know best.
You've been here and you've cased the joint,
Liking to know whereof you speak.
Good principle. See you next week.

To Craig Raine: a letter from Biarritz

Dear Craig, I've brought your books down to the sea
In order to catch up with what you've done
Since first I gasped at your facility
For writing Martian postcards home. The sun
Illuminates *The Onion, Memory*
Two pages at a time. The beach girls run
With naked bosoms on my low horizon
And yet yours are the lines I've got my eyes on.

Not all the time perhaps, but none the less
It's fair to say I'm utterly drawn in.
When praising your alchemical prowess
One hardly knows the best place to begin.
Your similes are struck with such success
At least one bard has called your gift a sin.
You spot resemblances with a precision
Not normally conferred by human vision.

What I admire and envy most, however,
Is your unflinching hunger for the real.
Proportionate you are but pallid never.
With strength of knee unknown to the genteel
You push on with your passionate endeavour
To sweep aside the veil of the ideal
And view the actual world on a straight footing
In every aspect, even the off-putting.

'Your stomach's got no eyes,' a man once said
Who'd guessed I didn't like how oysters look.
For you I'd stand that saying on its head:
Your eyes have got no stomach. They can brook,
Nay revel in, sights that would strike me dead
And make me queasy even in a book.
I'd like to call it sorcery or knavery
But all too clearly it's a kind of bravery.

You'd need it, too, if you were here today,
I think I might just mention at this point.
For every sweet young curved hip on display
There squeaks a fearsomely arthritic joint.
Those oiled old hands will never smooth away
The cellulite and wrinkles they anoint,
And many of the bare breasts on parade
Sensationally fail to make the grade.

Squeezed flat and creased like empty toothpaste tubes
Or else inflated to degrees grotesque –
To sum up this array of has-been boobs
The only adjective is Düreresque.
That woman sports a pair of Rubik's cubes.
That woman there could use hers as a desk.
At these exhausted sources of lactation
Words can't convey my lack of fascination.

But back again to literary matters.
One or two critics, I have lately noted,
Are showing signs of going mad as hatters
At hearing you so often praised and quoted.
The strictest of them taciturnly natters
Of how you could well find yourself demoted:
You are too popular and should tread warily.
Also, he says, your lines end arbitrarily.

I always thought *his* ended when the bell
Rang on his Olivetti. Never mind.
Your stanza forms still check out pretty well,
Even if arbitrarily inclined.
They break no rules as far as I can tell.
There are no wasted words that I can find.
In later works your rhythm grows less striking
But that might mean strong rhythm's to my liking.

Speaking of form and rhythm, incidentally,
Two water nymphs so beautiful I bet
The sight of them would paralyse you mentally
Are playing tennis. It seems I'm the net.

They must be highly privileged parentally:
Such clear skins and fine bones you only get
When there's a solid family tradition
Of no-expense-spared, well-thought-out nutrition.

Needless to say that with these two the breasts
From every viewpoint seem in A1 shape,
Though no doubt if it came to tactile tests
There'd be a yielding, as with a ripe grape.
Praise God that they've got those where we've got chests
I muse, while being careful not to gape –
A bald and overweight old coot from Sydney
Who cops a Frog tart's let ball in the kidney.

Now they've pranced off and plunged into a wave
Which warmly fondles them as who would not.
Their gaiety of mood has left mine grave,
Preoccupied with man and his brief lot.
I think of time's hourglass and bladed stave,
Of how we waste the few days that we've got,
Of how my youth is gone and shan't return.
I must turn over or my back will burn.

I'm writing now in the supine position,
A posture more conducive to high thoughts
Of Culture and the means of its transmission.
From here on in I think you'll find all sorts
Of pundits prophesying the perdition
Awaiting you, complete with boils and warts,
If you should go on proving so appealing
To the unclean, unthinking and unfeeling.

I don't imply, I hasten to assure you,
Your fate's to be a pop star like Kate Bush.
Though seas of spellbound faces stretch before you
The bodies underneath won't pee or push.
I know the more you're buttered up the more you
Will stay as untouched as the Hindu Kush.
Endowed with inspiration of such purity
You'd gladly follow it back to obscurity.

It's obvious that you're a heavyweight:
Your harshest critics can't say otherwise.
Your status would remain inviolate
Though Jeff Nuttall should praise you to the skies.
In that regard you've got it on a plate,
Whence comes the shamrock tinge of certain eyes.
While hitting the jackpot in all essentials
You've managed to hang on to your credentials.

You write intensely *and* you're entertaining.
For those of us less apt to do the first,
Apart from silence there's one course remaining –
Which is to do the second. At the worst
(And when this happens it's no use complaining)
The public clamours to be reimbursed,
But on the whole there's some cause to be proud
If what one writes makes people laugh aloud.

Or so I think when critics in terms drastic
Inform the world my feet are half trochaic.
It seems my scansion's absolutely spastic.
Even my best iambics are spondaic.
The poor fool's sense of rhythm is elastic!
His diction is archaic Aramaic!
As for his rhymes, let's send him back to Kogarah! Hell,
The stuff he drivels isn't even dogarahhell!

It's useless to invoke the semi-vowel
And point out 'bevel' *is* a rhyme for 'Devil'.
The cloth-eared scribes who write prose with a trowel
Will smugly wonder if I'm on the level.
One really might as well throw in the towel.
Fulke Greville's brother was called Neville Greville . . .
No, let the critics stew in their pale juice:
A joke's a joke and it needs no excuse.

Far out on their twin-fin potato chips
The young star surfers sprint to climb astride
A wave as smooth as spit feels on your lips
And when it breaks you see them there inside –

Born acrobats trained to their fingertips.
Meanwhile here at the thin edge of the tide
A man pretending he's a submarine
To please his children's also in the scene.

A Boudin painted by Tiepolo,
A beige and azure fresco two miles long;
The sky brushed pink, the *sable d'or* aglow,
The plump swell dimpled like a silver gong;
The beach lit by *le ciel*, laved by *les flots*,
An airy glittering shantung sarong,
Unfolds into the south where with a stain
Of Monet nenuphars France turns to Spain.

And though down there the Basques will bomb your car,
Up here they are a people touched with grace.
They know the sweet years only go so far
And life is more than just a pretty face.
However poor and sick and old they are
The sun shines for them, too. They have a place.
A fact which would provoke me to deep thinking
Were not the sun now on the point of sinking.

Clear plum juice simmers in the solar disc.
The soft light off the pale blue water stipples
With gold the green cliff-clothing tamarisk.
The breathing sea sends in its silken ripples.
High on the sea wall the last odalisque
Looks down with mute approval at her nipples.
La mer, la mer, toujours recommencée.
But that's enough of versing for one day.

I'll get up now and put on thongs and hat.
I'll gather up your books and these few pages.
I'll shake and roll my tatty rattan mat
And up the cliff *trottoir* by easy stages
I'll dawdle with a feeling of that's that –
Great talents may write poems for the ages,
But poetasters with their tongues in fetters
When all else fails at least can still write letters.

To Gore Vidal at Fifty

To Gore Vidal at – how should I commence?
The trick is to strike sparks and still make sense.
To Gore Vidal at fifty – sounds a lot.
Should I be flippant about that, or not?
To Gore Vidal at fifty years of age –
That slights the sprite, though it salutes the sage.
To Gore Vidal at fifty years of youth –
A trifle twee, but closer to the truth,
Since you (I speak in awe, not animosity)
Remain the incarnation of precocity,
A marvellous boy whose man-sized aureola
Still scintillates like fresh-poured Pepsi-Cola
(If I can mention safe from repercussions
The formula that Nixon sold the Russians),
Whose promise is renewed in the fulfilling,
A teenage thrill that goes on being thrilling,
A pledge kept firm with no recourse to perjury
Save incidental, mainly dental, surgery.
And yet you will admit you are no chicken.
Admit? Insist. The Peter Panic-stricken
Might cling to childhood out of self-delusion,
But that or any similar confusion
You've always held in absolute contempt –
The only absolute that you exempt
From your unwearyingly edifying
Assault on mankind's thirst to be undying:
A hope you've never ceased to make a mock of
Or boldly nominate what it's a crock of.
Small wonder you admire that far-off era
The clear lens of your style brings that much nearer,
In which, as Flaubert wrote (and here I quote,
Or, rather, quote what you said Flaubert wrote)
The gods were dead and Christ was not yet born,
A quick, cold night dividing dusk from dawn,
When man was quite alone, with nothing holier
To call his own than clear-eyed melancholia –

That penetrating gaze into infinity
Revealing it devoid of all divinity
And transcendental only in its endless
Detachment from our dread of feeling friendless –
A universe which neither plans our grief
Nor pampers us in payment for belief,
But rings its changes utterly unheeding
Though sadist die in bed or saint lie bleeding.
Committed in its course beyond retrieval,
Indifferent to all talk of good and evil,
Unreachable by prayer, untouched by curses,
It tirelessly assembles and disperses,
Created and destroyed and recreated –
Reduced, reprocessed and repristinated;
Its victories defeats, retreats advances,
Its triumphs tragedies, disasters dances,
Its involuted curves of time and distance
All adding up to one fierce, flat insistence –
That its immensities will still be there
When we are not. It simply doesn't *care.*
This is the void that you with the cool grace
Of your prose style help teach us how to face.
This is the pit from which none can escape
Your wit lights up that we might see its shape.
But to convince the world the soul of Marcus
Aurelius must perish with his carcass
Was hard even for him. Most men prefer
To hide their heads in warm sand and not stir.
That public probity, not sexuality,
Is really the foundation of morality –
That justice plays no active part in fate,
Not even when fate leads to Watergate –
That all the prayers and powers of the Kennedys
Buy not one moment's rest from the Eumenides –
That Caesar is not God, nor the good Lord
Someone who walks and talks like Gerald Ford –
With facts like these we find it hard to grapple,
And much prefer to think Eve plucked the apple
Specifically so that redemptive love,
Beamed down on her descendants from above,

Could ease the pangs of her initial blunder
And make us grateful as we knuckle under.
My own view is that mankind would be worse
Than ever should that cloud of dreams disperse,
But your view is the one we're here to praise
For how it penetrates the wishful haze
Which forms when all-too-human self-delusion
Allied with solipsism breeds confusion –
A mist that men call vision as they grope
And choking on it give the name of hope.
So dense a fog will be a long time thinning
So let's call your work thus far a beginning,
And for our own sake wish your life that too –
And, friends before, years more be friends to you.

To Anthony Thwaite at Fifty

Great folly is it to be afraid of death, since all of us alike
must pay that debt.

                         – Aristophanes

Well, Anthony, by now the secret's out
Of what this book is really all about.
The heavyweights have weighed in in your praise
With mighty line and lapidary phrase
Whereby both life and death are shown to be
Imbued with enigmatic majesty.
To celebrate your fifty years of life
The top scribes have been lined up by your wife
To send in something serious, hard-bitten,
Heart-felt and (with a good nib, please) handwritten,
These separate contributions to be sewn
Into a book which for its names alone
Should leave the average *Festschrift* looking bleak
And knocked into the middle of next week,
A synergistic *donativum* that
Should knock all others into a cocked hat.
With such wits to evoke the stern advance
Of Kronos I don't think I stand much chance
Of adding anything in *that* respect.
Monuments of unageing intellect
Have doubtless flooded in, all calculated
To leave you feeling slightly devastated
At how your trim form must perforce disperse
Eventually into the universe,
With random fragments of the quondam you
Attached to wisps of mist and drops of dew.
This leaves me feeling somewhat overparted
And vaguely wondering how to get started,
As well as worried that I've made a gaffe
By using this clapped-out Rapidograph
Instead of the italic pen or quill
Appropriate to orthographic skill:

The marks that this thing makes look thin and pale
And all in all I feel I'm doomed to fail.
For deep thoughts and grave words I have no touch.
Qu'allais-je faire dans cette galère? Not much.
But why feign fear at what one does not see?
There might be virtue in necessity.
The grim view, though it must be the initial one,
Needs complementing from the superficial one.
Even to echo Horace's *Eheu*
Fugaces I would have to find it true
And I just don't. I *like* the way the years
Elapse, or anyway I shed few tears.
Perhaps I lack the mental wherewithal
To face the fact that one day night must fall.
Perhaps in smiling at it I'm ignoring it
When what I should be doing is deploring it.
But is one owning up to a soft head
Merely because one's not consumed by dread,
And even finds a strange kind of relief
In hearing, far off, surf roar on that reef
To which, Lucretius says, all things must tend,
Exhausted by the flow of time? We end,
Said Pushkin, to make way for a fresh start
By others: let the newborn give us heart.
'They crowd us from the world,' he wrote, but not
As one who, scared of losing what he's got,
Has really nothing very much to say
Beyond *timor mortis conturbat me* –
He simply found it just, and not just certain,
The play of life should have a final curtain.
(In his case it fell on him like a ton
Of bricks right in the middle of Act One,
Which put the mockers on his flood of song –
But still I think he was more right than wrong.)
'Death joins us to the great majority,'
Droned Edward Young. No quarrel there from me.
'Age', Bacon burbled, 'will not be defied.'
A boring thought that will not be denied,
For fatalism, even as a platitude,
Remains the only reasonable attitude,

While if compounded with inventive verve
Its realism thrills your every nerve,
And has done since the *Iliad* was composed
(In braille – a fact not commonly disclosed).
Some thug on one of Homer's battlefields
Lifts up his voice above the bonging shields
And what he bellows takes away your breath –
And when you get it back you laugh at death.
'The race of men', he half exults, half grieves,
'Is like the generations of the leaves:
They fall in autumn to return in spring.'
A sentiment I find most heartening –
As did, no doubt, the chaps he yelled it to,
And dropped their guard. (And *then* he ran them through.)
The duty you called 'valuing the dust'
In your fine book *Inscriptions* (which I must
Say makes some of our newer bards look tired
Before their time, as well as uninspired)
Remains plain. As that Irish fellow says,
Man is in love and loves what vanishes –
Except he left out one important thing:
A wise man learns to love the vanishing.
Good humour is the mark of those who do,
A virtue highly manifest in you –
Which might sound like an insult to all those
Who think a poet should write about crows
In tones undeviatingly devoid
Of any hint that life's to be enjoyed.
So, Anthony: grow old along with me
And all your friends. The best is yet to be,
Simply because it hasn't happened yet,
And what's to come we never can forget.
It stays sweet till we get to it, at least;
The only wonder that has never ceased –
And that's a fact as certain as my name's
(This line I'll have to pad a bit) Clive James.

To Margaret Olley on the Occasion of her
Retrospective Exhibition in Sydney, October 1996

Margaret, the Jeu de paume
As it used to be back when
All the painters of light
In that lilting dawn patrol
Gathered and felt at home
Is in your mind and art –
A dream-time pleasure dome
With the decor done just right
In a Tuileries born again
As a fairground for the heart,
A health farm for the soul:
Montparnasse and Montmartre
Rolled into one *venue*
With dancing every night –
That's how we think of you.

Bonnard, Degas, Derain,
Matisse, Renoir, Manet,
Monet, Vuillard, Cézanne –
They're all there in your frame,
But you have drawn on them all
For something beyond themselves:
A multiple interplay
No American football game
Could match for complexity –
Or rainbow's swirling veil
Backed up by its waterfall
For tensile frailty
Spun off from inner steel.

The crockery on your shelves,
The posters on every wall
Of that magic Paddington house,
On your canvas shift around

In a permanent minuet
Of colour arranged like sound,
Keeping their essences
While giving themselves away
In a blissful synthesis –
A fusing of separateness
Delicious as a kiss.

There's alchemy in your hands
The way Toulouse-Lautrec
At an artists' ball one night
Played barman and mixed tall drinks
Of every colour combined:
Pure spirits in vivid bands,
Striped towers of pigments and inks,
Their effect was dynamite.
A poet went out of his mind,
A collector died of fright,
The hostess is still a wreck –
The evening, nevertheless,
For exalting the sense of sight,
Was hailed as a success.

We love the Impressionists.
Well, Goering loved them too,
But acted out the desire
Differently from you.
He ticked them off on lists,
He loaded them on to trains,
He buried them down salt mines –
Yet in one way you and he,
Though he lacked your manners and brains,
Thought on the same lines:
You both saw that entire
Upsurge of human joy
In its timeless unity,
And couldn't repress the urge
To make the whole thing yours.
A greedy boy with a gun,
An art-struck bum in a rush,

He did it, but not for long.
You did it for keeps with a brush
And the patience that waits like a nun
Behind her life's closed doors
For the love of God to emerge
From a bowl of fruit like a song.

Margaret, with you the quest
For a National Identity
Uniquely Australia's own
Stands at last for all to see
Revealed as a mare's nest.
By going it alone
With not one home-grown theme –
Except our feeling free,
Even if we offend,
To hold ourselves apart
And choose what we may dream –
Your representational art
That represents us all
Reminds us, in the swell
Of our millennial pride
And its raucous picture books,
That nothing counts in the end
But the individual,
Whose eternal right it is
To swim against the tide
With strokes specifically hers –
Spectral ripples that blend
Intoxicatingly
Into something that looks
Wonderful on the wall.

A Paean for Peter Porter:

to mark his seventieth birthday

The sound of breaking glass in Germany
Was still ten years ahead when he was born.
In Brisbane the mass threat to sanity
Was white ants trekking in across the lawn
To bring the house down very gradually
As elves might masticate the Matterhorn –
Yet somehow that small noise of steady chewing
Served to forewarn him something big was brewing.

He grew up in a little world elsewhere
By weeks at sea from Europe torn apart,
And yet by some strange process he was there:
That distant anguish helped to form his heart.
The endless damage no prayers could repair
Was his to mourn, and thus in his own art,
Which would evoke the wealth of what was lost,
Assess its value and so count the cost.

The armies of Japan were brought up short
A few hours north while he did well at school
In English but did not excel at sport.
Bronzed Aussies brilliant in the swimming pool,
Gods of the cricket pitch and tennis court,
Marvelled at one who, clearly not a fool,
Rather than limping home thick-lipped and bleeding
From rugger could prefer to waste time *reading*.

For him the books in an unbroken line
Stretched from the *Iliad* to Auden's new
Slim volume, title vertical on the spine.
He wolfed the whole lot down as bright boys do.
Even of Christendom the grand design
Was what men wrote and painted. In his view
Art outranked faith and of all arts above
Stood music, his first-found and life-long love.

Most of the paintings he had not yet seen
Except in reproduction. The far side
Of the planet still held poems that would mean
A great deal to him but would stay tongue-tied
Until he got there. Music, though, came clean:
There were no secrets it knew how to hide.
The records spun unfazed save by the fluff
That choked the needle. Music was enough –

Enough to tell him that no national dream
Cancels the universal yesterday.
There are no fresh beginnings. Even the scream
Of rampant Lucifer can't scrape away
That stateless stateliness, that seamless seam
Of treasure all may share yet none can pay
Into a bank or claim for ideology
Save through poor taste backed up by bad psychology.

Like Thomas Mann in exile, every night
He would be drawn back through the gramophone
Into a culture at its blazing height,
A forge with a blast-furnace set in stone
Whose double flame of *Schwung* and *Sauberkeit*
Yet burned, but by this afterglow alone:
The Architect of Pandemonium
Had blown the whole shebang to Kingdom Come.

All too aware the Schubert string quintet
In C's *adagio* moving him to tears
Had done the same for Mengele, he yet
Grasped with a strength of mind beyond his years
The salient fact doomsayers still forget:
Great music has no morals. He who hears
And weeps, though he might be a lunatic,
Comes sick to it, is not by it made sick.

That the arts made sense but had no sense of duty
Save to themselves was not a cosy notion
In a nation feeling its raw natural beauty
Could use a touch of home-brewed body lotion.

Così fan tutte through to *Tutti Frutti,*
Too much had been brought in across the ocean:
Cringing Australia ought to stand up straight.
He saw their point but could not fight his fate.

For some are born to stay and some to go,
And some of those who go will stay away
Always, and even then will never know
Quite why the urge came over them that day
To up stakes. Though in those days Room to Grow
Remained a good excuse, still we can say
When a man thinks even Paradise can't hold him
The inner voice lies very deep that told him.

The world he sailed to was already gone.
He was a spaceman travelling to a star
That had gone nova. Bits of it still shone
When he arrived, but only showed how far
And wide the old coherent synchrotron
Had flung its shards. He was an avatar
Cast as a revenant sent to reveal
Die Welt von Gestern ruined but still real.

In London he wrote poems whose modernity
(Trendies in Chelsea boots, blondes in fast cars)
Was peppered with the pet names of eternity:
Gluck, Goethe, Goya, all the Eurostars –
The list long but he didn't need to learn it. He
Saw Botticelli's Venus eat Mars Bars
In his mind's eye, and heard the Tyburn axeman
Sharpen his tool in letters from the tax man.

And through this *macédoine* lurched his persona
Choked by a suit too cheap and loved too little –
Beside the merest Morris Minor-owner
Unpropertied, prospects of tenure brittle.
Half Mr Hulot, half Hancock's Blood Donor,
In the King's Road not a jot of well-born tittle
Bobbed near enough to defuse the intense
Desire made worse by his aesthetic sense.

Strange to relate, it was that very store
Of learning that his Grub Street denigrators
Pounced on. An upstart from the fatal shore
Was welcome to complain how the bomb craters
And tower blocks by Wimpey and Charles Clore
Had made a Horlicks of the gas and gaiters,
But dragging in Van Gogh, Van Eyck, Van Dyke . . .
Vans by the van-load! That they didn't like.

His range of reference struck them as pretension,
A nervous self-display of erudition
Designed to give a scholarly dimension
To the insecurity of his position.
The most he could expect was a suspension
Of sentence pending clear signs of contrition:
An anxious misfit self-taught Outback highbrow
To whom the best response was a raised eyebrow.

True lovers of his work, though, recognized
A man not up on stilts but on his knees
In thanks for how tradition civilized
An age of overpaid performing fleas.
The background noise his critics patronized
Was just the murmur of fond memories:
For him the great things that had been achieved in
The past were what he lived by and believed in.

Collections multiplied, his fame increased,
His place in serious verse was undisputed,
But even as in England carping ceased,
Back in Australia it was scarcely muted.
He stood accused of, at the very least,
The floating loyalty of the uprooted.
'The Poms have conned the bastard,' they droned chippily,
'The way they've conned us ever since Gallipoli.'

The truth, of course, was the exact reverse.
He'd helped to give his country what it craved:
National Identity, which is a curse
When tubs are thumped and any flag that's waved

Must first be redesigned to spite our nurse.
It could be said, if pride needs to be saved,
Expatriates are proof Australia Fair
Advances with exuberance to spare.

The Australian Spirit, if there's such a thing,
Stays with our envoys who abide abroad.
Melba could swear as well as she could sing
And Errol Flynn made fun of his drawn sword.
Bradman did not kowtow to meet the King,
Nor bridle, but just struck the common chord.
Bred in the bone, that unassuming ease
Has always done things for us Overseas.

Mark Philippoussis serves a Mach 1 ace.
Dame Edna stars again in the West End.
Kylie Minogue with her new sultry face
Is still the girl next door or her best friend.
All are ambassadors for the Good Place
Where birth means nothing and to buck the trend
Of history is a man's God-given right,
Like getting rat-arsed drunk on Friday night.

That national cast of mind helps him endure,
Though often in his poems he denies
Its force and plays a character less pure –
Racked by cupidity, stabbed through the eyes
By sexy promises of a quick cure
For envy's canker. So the poet lies
About himself to tell a greater truth
About an age uncultured and uncouth.

The man behind the mask through which the voice
Talks like a Tragic chorus has a soul
Less fearful. He does what he does from choice:
It is by self-denial he stays whole.
Though BMW may buy Rolls-Royce
And any goalkeeper may sell his goal,
This man, albeit that the cost is grim,
Lives for his art, as his art lives through him.

The land on whose cold shore he burned his boats
Decrees a Cool Britannia pleasure dome.
Schools have no place for anyone who quotes
Latin, or knows why all roads led to Rome.
The Princess on her raft of flowers floats
To Avalon, the only fitting home
For beauty in an era whose salacity
He guessed would outstrip even its rapacity.

Less fraught with danger than weighed down with tat,
Ours was an epoch ripe for mordant wit
Like his, but he's done so much more than that:
Through his *epistulae ex ponto* flit
The singing ghosts who leave us sounding flat.
His fugue grows sad, but there's no help for it –
The play-out music of a patriarch
Is often Bach but seldom Offenbach.

It's time. What he won't say himself let's say
On his behalf, though he blush at our boast:
His friends love him, and none, home or away,
Would not be proud as Punch to play the host
At this world-girdling feast for his birthday,
Thus to propose a heartfelt double toast –
God bless a man who had so much to show us
We should thank God he found the time to know us.

The Backstroke Swimmer Rolf Harris:

to mark his seventieth birthday

When young he was a backstroke champion,
Even to fans a fact not widely known.
Backstrokers lie down, look up at the sun
And must get used to being on their own.

Backstrokers squint to ward off the bright sky
And at the most they see where they have been.
His future lay behind him, how he'd fly
One day to great fame on a little screen.

The beard, the felt-tips and the wobble-board,
The task of tying down a kangaroo –
These things the children of the world adored.
Small injured animals admire him too.

Kittens up trees, dogs trapped in microwaves
Are grateful for his friendly, nasal drawl:
Tots lower hamsters into tiny graves
Sure that his tender heart sustains them all.

He was, is still, the incarnation of
The Australian spirit, spry yet down to earth:
Raw energy that taught itself to love
The strange life in the vast land of its birth.

The world has learned from him, and I likewise.
For me, however, what he has to teach
Starts where the spine-basher screwed up his eyes:
The loose, long-footed kick, the easy reach –

Signs of true power, which lies in power to spare.
The strength behind all useful gentleness
Is gained by seeing that the past is there
And what comes next a man can only guess.

He stretched, he yawned, and woke up to world fame.
He grinned, and children by the million grew
To adulthood still smiling at his name,
His laugh lines hard-earned from the harsh but true

Sting of chlorine, the flame that bleached the blue.

The Great Wrasse: for Les Murray at sixty

Mask wet and snorkel dry, I'm lying loose
On the glass roof of time, and forty years
Straight down I see it teeming, the bombora
Of Manning House. Tables like staghorn coral
Chewed at by schools of poets. Frensham girls
(Remember Xanthe Small and Joanne Williamson,
Those blouses and tight skirts? *You little beaut*
We breathed into our fried rice. God, what dreams:
By now they must be grandmothers) glide by
Like semicircle angelfish. Psychologists
With teeth like wahoos turn their heads as one,
Torn from discussion of the Individual,
Their Watch Committee late-lunch seminar
Prorogued *pro tem.*
                    Poised Andersonian squid
Explain to freshettes peeping from their shells
If dualism allows no real division
There can be no real connection. Fusiliers,
Trevallies, sweetlips, damselfish, hussars
Patrol in Balbos, split up, feed, re-form,
Waved at by worshipping anemones.
The food chain and the mating dance, the mass
Manoeuvring, the shape-up and the shake-out,
The pretty faces pumping pain through spines:
It's all there, displayed in liquid crystal,
No further than my fingertips adrift
(A year in time is just an inch in space) –
And there *you* are, and I can see you now
For what you were, most brilliant of the bunch,
The Great Wrasse.
                    But to know that, I had first
To see the thing itself, in all its glory,
Five years ago. Sleeping on Lizard Island,
My family was recovering its strength
From too long in the cold. On the second day
We woke at noon and rolled into the water

To join the turtles feeding on the seagrass
Between the beach and sandbar. Serious fish
Were just around the point, at the big bommie.
We drifted off the platform at the back
Of the launch and let the current take us over
A chunk of reef that came up to arm's length:
Just what the doctor ordered. We could see
The whole aquarium in action, hear
The parrotfish at work on the hard coral
Like journalists around the Doric porch
Of some beer-froth tycoon whose time had come
To be cast out of Toorak.
                    Then it was there –
Beside us, as if to share our view:
Materializing, as is its marvellous way,
With no preliminary fanfare,
Like an air-dropped marching band that opens up
Full blast around your bed. *Lord, I can see,*
I said in silence, smiling around my rubber
Dummy like a baby. Powered by pearls
On fire inside its emerald envelope,
The Wrasse comes on like a space invader
In docking mode, filling the vision full:
The shock of its appearance stops the swimmer
Dead in the water, flippers frozen solid,
Stunned by a sudden nearness so aloof.
As if the Inca, walking his lion's walk
In soft shoes, were to pass by from behind
Preoccupied by his divinity,
So with this big fish and its quiet storm,
Its mute Magnificat.
                 Bigger fish yet
Plumb deep holes of the Outer Barrier –
Potato cod in mottled camouflage
Like Japanese Army Kawasaki fighters
Parked in the palms, *franc-tireur* Tiger sharks
With Kerry Packer smiles, the last few marlin
To keep their swords – but nothing quite as massive
As the daddy of all wrasses, the Daimyo number,
Shows up at the bombora, and nothing as bright

Is known the whole reef over.
                              Over the reef,
You realize, is where this fish belongs –
Above it and not of it. Nothing is written there,
Enjoyed or cherished. Even the beautiful,
There in abundance, does not know itself.
'Sex is a Nazi' you once wrote, and so
It is here. Killing to grow up so they can screw,
Things eat, are eaten, and the crown-of-thorns
Starfish that eats everything looks like
A rail map of the Final Solution,
But all it adds to universal horror
Is its lack of colour.
                        Even in full bloom
The reef is a *jardin des supplices*:
The frills, the fronds, the fans, the powder puffs
Soften the razor's edge, the reign of terror.
Lulled by the moon snail and the Spanish dancer
With choreography by Carlos Saura,
By feathery platoons of *poules de luxe*
Cute as the kick-line of the Tropicana,
The tourist feels this is the show for him –
Atlantis in an atrium, a rumpus room
For slo-mo willy-willies of loose chips
From bombed casinos, a warehouse arcade
For love seats, swansdown pouffes and stuffed banquettes
That he could snuggle up to like a prayer
Of Hasidim against the Wailing Wall
And soothe his fevered brow in yielding plush –
But only an expert should ever touch it
Even with rubber gloves.
                          Buyer beware,
The forms of death are not just for each other
But for us too, and not all are as ugly
As the stonefish, toadfish, puffer and striped Toby
In his leather jacket. Even a child can see
That these are kitted out for bio war:
They pull the face of neurotoxic venom.
But the cone shells that beg to be picked up
By writers are like antique fountain pens

Proust might have held except he would have written
A short book, and that dreamboat with the sulk
Like Michelle Pfeiffer lolling in the glass
Elevator in *Scarface* is a breed
Of butterfly whose class would set you raving
At closer quarters, anguish cloaked in floating
Come-hither chiffon veils that spell curtains
At the first kiss.
            Rising above it all,
A benign airship poised over New York –
The *Hindenburg* without the *Hakenkreuz*
Or parking problems – just by its repose
The dawdling Wrasse siphons up Hell's Kitchen
And turns it to serenity, the spectrum
Of helium in Rutherford's radon tube,
The clear, blue light of pure polonium,
The green, fused sand of Trinity, the silent
Summary, the peaceful aftermath.
Something, someone, must be the focal emblem,
The stately bearer of the synthesis
To make our griefs make sense, if not worthwhile.
That the young you, in a red-striped sloppy joe
Like Sidney Greenstreet cast as Ginger Meggs
Progressing through the Quad the very year
Of the first Opera House Lottery draw,
Would be the Great Wrasse, few could guess
But now all know, glad that the time it took
Was in their lives, and what you made of it –
Those new and strange and lovely living things,
Your poems – theirs to goggle at when born:
Born from your mouth.
            Born fit to breathe our sea,
Which is the air I surface to drink in
(My mask a nifty hat by Schiaparelli)
Having seen wonders – how our lives once were,
Nature's indifference, time's transparency,
Fame's cloud of pigment, fortune's blood-tipped needles,
And finally, most fabulous of all,
A monumental fish that speaks in colours,
Offering solace from within itself.

To Leonie Kramer, Chancellor of Sydney University: A Report on My Discipline, on the Eve of My Receiving an Honorary Degree, 1999

The brief is to report on what's been done –
Or, if it hasn't, to report on that –
In my field over twenty years. The gun
Is to my head and I will eat my hat
Sooner than flinch, but my job's too much fun,
Too fissile, for a *précis* to get at.
Leonie, let's be frank. My discipline
Is serious like Jack Benny's violin.

Mine is no academic bailiwick:
In fact it is defined by being not one.
Gowned bigwigs might well find it a bit thick
To see my name among theirs. 'That's a hot one,'
They'll mutinously mutter. '*This* Osric
Fronting a field of study: has he got one?'
They're right, I haven't; but I do this stuff
On the assumption they aren't right enough.

My territory's the chattering hedgerow
Between the neat fields forming the landscape
Of proper scholarship. By now we know
The ecosystem winds up out of shape
When too much science grabs the soil to grow
The *pouffe*-sized pumpkin and the pre-shrunk grape.
We've organized the land to serve society
So thoroughly we've wiped out its variety.

Too bad, some say. We can't eat singing birds –
You see the way my metaphor is tending –
Or cope with hedgehogs roaming round in herds:
The cost of feeding them would be mind-bending.
The same goes double for the world of words:

The era of the ragged edge is ending.
The kind of writing we can't classify
Might fairly soon have barely room to die.

I mourn its passing, and guess you do too,
Or A. D. Hope would not have dedicated
His Roman letter to you. Knowing you
Would get a kick from being celebrated
In such a *jeu d'esprit*, a tiramisu
Designed to leave you nothing but elated,
Our mightiest poet tossed off something lightweight,
Not doubting that that weight would be the right weight.

Of all Hope's poetry I found that letter
The most amazing thing he'd written, ever.
Had Byron ever done the same thing better?
Had even Auden been so clearly clever?
From then on I was Hope's eternal debtor,
Convinced, despite the times, the time is never
To let one's literary ambition stifle
The urge to squander talent on a trifle.

Always supposing talent's what one's got –
But let's take that for now as a *donnée*
And ask if those of us who, on the spot,
Can put a phrase together in a way
That gets attention ought to, or ought not,
Feel so responsible for what we say
We don't say anything, however witty,
That might not please the Nobel Prize committee.

I think not. Literature is out of hand.
With so much genius jostling for position
Shakespeare would have to fight for room to stand,
Dante to kneel and pray. A mass emission
Of deathless texts leaves nothing *an den Rand
Geschrieben*. All's composed on the condition
We read it with the awe-struck, furrowed brow
We'd read the classics with if we knew how.

None of which means, of course, I want books burned.
Heine foresaw the bonfire in Berlin.
Men who burn books burn men: that much we learned
Sifting the ashes of the loony bin.
Now that some form of sanity's returned
We should be glad the age we're living in
Accords great writers every accolade
From the T-shirt to the ticker-tape parade.

The only problem is, no other kind
Of writer *except* great's thought worth attention.
This attitude, in matters of the mind,
To my mind robs us of a whole dimension.
Intelligence just isn't that refined:
It's less a distillate than a suspension,
An absinthe we'd knock back in half a minute
Without the cloud of particles within it.

Just so, a living culture is a swarm
Of moments that provide its tang and tingle:
Unless it's fuelled by every minor form
From dirty joke to advertising jingle
It ends up like Dame Edna's husband, Norm,
Stiff as a post. I think John Douglas Pringle
Was first to spot our language, at its core,
Owed its *élan* to how a wharfie swore.

Shifting that notion further up the scale
We soon discover it applies worldwide.
The casual jotting priced for a quick sale
Can be a bridesmaid that outshines the bride.
There is a vantage point beyond the pale:
To pull the inside job from the outside
Confers on essayist or rogue reviewer
The plus of knowing where to put the skewer.

Nor need he specialize in kicking ass
(*Pro tem* to speak *à la Americaine*).
In fact a gadfly's likely to sound crass
If all he ever does is dish out pain,

Just as to pump the anaesthetic gas
Of adulation backfires on the brain –
Dooming the sycophant to a sclerosis
Off-putting as the cynic's halitosis.

The voice I favour questions *and* enjoys.
No pushover, it's ready to submit.
It homes on a clear signal through the noise
Kicked up by the tumultuous cockpit
We call the Arts, and from the girls and boys
It separates the men and women. Wit,
When true, well knows a show of cleverness
Means least when it is most meant to impress,

And yet a comprehensive lack of flair
By no means guarantees the truly serious.
It takes a cool, hard head to be aware
How art is in its essence a mysterious
Compound engendered by a gift as rare
As hen's teeth of the base and the imperious.
It takes an artist, though that appellation
Seldom adorns his dodgy reputation.

Just such an artist was my most revered
Role model from the old world Hitler wrecked,
Alfred Polgar, who, as the menace neared,
Focused despair to such a fine effect
His *feuilletons* teem with all that disappeared.
Schatzkammer snow-domes of the intellect,
Polgar's packed paragraphs reintegrate
A time bomb getting set to detonate.

He and the other refugees who scattered
To the Earth's four corners not excluding ours
Personified the unity left shattered
Where once they had devoted first-rate powers
To the ephemeral as if it mattered.
Their fate proved that it had. The topless towers
Of Ilium arise from the hubbub
Of the bazaar, the throb of the nightclub.

It is the wasted talents that I sing,
The ones that might have climbed to high renown,
Have done great things, had they done the done thing
And steered clear of the *demi-monde* downtown.
A nation needs them the same way a king
Lost on the heath should listen to his clown,
Lest literature withdraw to a top shelf
And vivid language serve only itself.

Australia Felix, sea-girt land most fair –
Fair go, fair suck, fair prospects of success
For all – there's an equality more rare
Even than these, though it be cherished less:
A mental life that everyone may share.
Its secret lies in the receptiveness
Of how we speak, our tongue that makes a poet
In two weeks of a taxi-driving Croat.

Whole cultures in our time razed to the ground
Enriched us with their homeless destitute,
A thriving proof the Promised Land is found
Where all is hallowed save the absolute.
That thought revives my hopes as, with one bound,
Like Emile Mercier's Wocko the Beaut,
I fly to my reward at your fair hand.
Lady, I'm blushing. Will there be a band?

EARLIER VERSE

As I See You

As I see you
Crystals grow
Leaves chime
Roses flow

As I touch you
Tables turn
Towers lean
Witches burn

As I leave you
Lenses shiver
Flags fall
Show's over

The Deep Six

Because the leaves relaxing on the water
Arrange themselves in attitudes of death
Like mannequins who practise languor
I know it must be autumn in the sea.

When the time comes for me to take you there
Through hanging gardens, and all colour trails away
To leave your eyes entirely my secret
And your hair like smoke rising

You will never learn from me about the winter
That will keep us locked at wrist and lips for ever
Like a broken clockwork model of a kiss
When everything is over, where we came from.

Berowra Waters, New South Wales

The seas of the moon are white on white towards evening
Kingfisher strikes head out on the deck for the trees
Veils of tulle are drawn by the dragonflies
The treetops shudder to silence like coins set spinning.

Fireships of cirrus assemble and ride in the west
Tracksuit trousers go on, and a second sweater
Baiting for low-level fish is like writing a letter
To someone whose last name you caught but whose first you missed.

The sun goes over the hill with a whole day's flames
The bottles fluoresce going down, like silver spiders
The old astronomers' animals graze the fields of stars
The guttering cirrus drops on the tide to the Sea of Dreams.

The Morning from Cremorne, Sydney Harbour

Someone sets it
Turning again,
Dumps of junk
Jewellery doing
Their slow burn:
Bonbons spill, and a
Rocket rips,
Pops, goes haywire
Inside the head
Of an emerald pit
Some con man sold
Who's dead, perhaps.

With each night showing
Your share less
You weep for the careless
Day's use:
A play of light
That folds each night
While the milkmen dress.

Con man, milkman,
Someone wires
The light traps,
Ice fires:
The hail-fall blazing
Trails to dawn
That will take the wraps
Of white glass wool
From the warships
Coming into their own
Cold steel.

The Lady in Mourning at Camelot

Before the tournament began
She walked abroad in sable sack:
Embattled knights rang hollow when
They tapped each other on the back
And pointed
(Get the one in black)

All plumage is but camouflage
To shapeliness, this lady knew,
And brilliants shame the lips and eyes:
Simplicity, not sadness, so
Became her
(Check. She stole the show)

Four Poems about Porpoises

I

Swallows in leotards
Burrowing holes
Submarine termites
Quicksilver moles

Dazzling galleries
Spiralling aisles
Daydreams in sunlight
Sinking for miles

Hurtling shuttles
Trip up and flee –
Porpoises, weaving
A shot-silk sea.

II

In Operation Silent Sails
For submarines at sea last night
The porpoises, on fire with fright
Blew every tube in Fylingdales.

III

I take one look and I know I'm dreaming –
Planing fins and the colour streaming
Boundary layers in the mind.

I take a breath and I'm sure I'm stalling –
Looping blades and the harvest falling:
Grain blown back like a bugle calling
Light brigades along the wind.

I take my ease and I'm scared I'm ageing –
Stunting jets and a war game raging;
Seas are riddled, undermined.

I take my leave and I know I'm crying
Tears I'll be a lifetime drying,
The tree house down and the peach tree dying
Home behind.

IV

Porpoises move
Through tunnels of love.

The Banishment

Ma fu' io solo, là dove sofferto
fu per ciascun di tòrre via Fiorenza,
colui che la difesi a viso aperto.

Blemishes age
The Arno tonight
The lamps on the bridges
Piledrive light

Kinky bright krisses
Bent new pin
Opal portcullises
Lychees in gin

Bean-rows of breakable
Stakes going in

Chinese brass burnishes.

Pearlshell caskets
Tumble plunder
Soft rose ledges
Give, go under

Bolts of lamé
Fray
Sunder.

If you open slowly
Eyes half crying
That whole flowing
Blurs like dying

Chi'en-Lung
Colours
Run.

Pinking scissors
Choke on velvet:
Cut-throat razors
Rust in claret.

The Crying Need for Snow

It's cold without the softness of a fall
Of snow to give these scenes a common bond
And though, besotted on a viewless rime,
The ducks can do their standing-on-the-pond
Routine that leaves you howling, all in all
We need some snow to hush the whole thing up.

The ducks can do their flatfoot-waterfool
Mad act that leaves you helpless, but in fine
We need their footprints in a higher field
Made pure powder, need their wig-wag line
Of little kites pressed in around the pool:
An afternoon of snow should cover that.

Some crystalline precipitate should throw
Its multifarious weightlessness around
For half a day and paint the whole place out,
Bring back a soft regime to bitter ground:
An instant plebiscite would vote for snow
So overwhelmingly if we could call it now.

An afternoon of snow should cover that
Milk-bottle neck bolt upright in the slime
Fast frozen at the pond's edge, brutal there:
We need to see junk muffled, whitewashed grime,
Lean brittle ice grown comfortably fat,
A world prepared to take our footprints in.

A world prepared to take our footprints in
Needs painting out, needs be a finer field:
So overwhelmingly, if we could call it now,
The fluffy stuff would prime it: it would yield
To lightest step, be webbed and toed and heeled,
Pushed flat, smoothed off, heaped high, pinched anyhow,
Yet be inviolable. Put like that,
Gently, the cold makes sense. Snow links things up.

The Glass Museum

In cabinets no longer clear, each master's exhibit
Of Murano-manufactured glass has the random look,
Chipped and dusty with eclectic descriptive cards,
Of the chemistry set the twelve-year-old abandons,
The test tubes cracked, the pipette choked solid with dirt:
A work-with-your-hands vocation that never took
And was boxed away near the bottom of the cupboard
Between the clockwork Hornby and the Coldstream Guards.

The supreme exemplars, Ferro, Bigaglia, Radi;
Their prize examples, goblet, bottle and dish;
These classical clearings overgrown in a lifetime
By a jungle of tabular triumphs and tendrilled fish,
Dummy ceramics tricked out with a hand-faked Guardi,
Tubular chandeliers like a mine of serpents:
Age in, age out, the demand was supplied for wonders,
And talent discovered bravura could pay like crime –
To the death of taste and the ruin of common sense.

So the few good things shine on in the junk museum –
A dish with a milk-white helix imprisoned inside,
Miniature polychrome craters and pocket amphoras
Flambeau-skinned like an oil slick slimmed by the tide –
While more global-minded than ever the buyers come
By the jet-load lot into Marco Polo to order
Solid glass sharks complete with sucking remoras
Or thigh-high vases certain to sell like a bomb
Whether north of Bering Strait or south of the Border,
As throughout the island the furnaces roar all day
And they crate the stuff in wood wool to barge it across
To Venice which flogs it direct or else ships it away
And must know by now these gains add up to a loss
But goes on steadily selling itself down the river.

In Sydney years ago when my eyes were wider
I would shuffle the midway sawdust at the Easter Show

As the wonder-boy from Murano rolled pipes of glass
In the furnace-glow underneath a sailcloth roof
And expelled his marvellous breath into gleaming spheres
Which abruptly assumed the shape of performing seals,
Silvered inside and no heavier than a moth –
Between the Hall of Mirrors and the Pygmy Princess
Across from the Ferris wheel and the Wall of Death.

The Young Australian Rider, P. G. Burman

Philip Burman bought an old five hundred
Side-valve BSA for twenty quid.
Unlicensed as they were, both it and him,
He poker-faced ecstatically rode home
In second gear, one of the two that worked,
And everything that subsequently could be done
To make 'her' powerful and bright, he did:
Inside a year she fled beneath the sun
Symphonically enamelled black and plated chrome.

At eighteen years of age he gave up food,
Beer and all but the casual cigarette
To lay his slim apprentice money out
On extra bits like a special needle jet
For a carb the makers never knew about.
Gradually the exhaust note waxed more lewd,
Compression soared, he fitted stiffer springs
To keep the valves from lagging at their duties.
The decibels edged up, the neighbours nearly sued,
Hand over fist that breathed-on bike grew wings
Until her peak lay in the naughty nineties.

Evenings after school I'd bolt my meal
And dive around to his place. In the back
Veranda where he slept and dressed he'd have
Her roaring with her back wheel off the floor
Apocalyptically – the noise killed flies –
Her uncased primary chain a singing blur.
His pet Alsatian hid behind a stack
Of extra wheels, and on the mantelpiece
A balsa Heinkel jiggled through imagined skies.

There was a weekend that we took her out
To Sutherland to sprint the flying mile
Against a mob of Tiger Hundreds. I
Sat wild-eyed and saw his style tell,

Streaming the corners like remembered trails.
They topped him, nearly all of them, but still
They stood around and got the story. 'What
It cost? No bull?' And when we thundered home
I sat the pillion, following his line
Through corners with the drag behind my back
Plucking and fluttering my shirt like sails,
Dreaming his dreams for him of Avus Track,
Of Spa, the Ring, the Isle of Man TT,
The Monza Autodromo and the magic words, Grand Prix.

Two years later, on my spine at Ingleburn
Just after I came back from leave, I thought
Out piece by piece what must have happened.
He was older, and the bike was new: I'd seen
It briefly the year before and heard the things
He planned to do to it. Another BSA,
Still a push-rod job but OHV at least;
One-lung three-fifty. Home-made swinging arm
Both front and rear, a red-hot shaven head,
Light piston, special rings – the heavy stuff.
We lost contact. I kept hearing off and on
How broke he was from racing and improving her.

One Saturday while I practised the Present
With Bayonet Fixed, a thousand entities
In bullring splendour of precision blaze
To gladden hearts of all who'd guard our shores,
He banked through Dunlop Corner at Mount Druitt
Leading a pack of AJ7Rs –
All camshaft jobs, but not a patch on him.
A fork collapsed. The bike kicked up and paused,
Her throttle stuck wide open, as he sprawled
With helpless hours to watch her pitch and toss
Like some slow-motion diver on a screen
Before the chain came down across his throat.

I had leave the evening after. Halfway down
The street a neighbour told me at her gate,
And then another neighbour – they were all

Ready and willing, full of homilies
And clucking hindsight. And, I'll give them this,
Of grief, too. He was noisy, but they'd liked him –
'Phil killed himself at Druitt yesterday.'

It's not that I felt nothing. I felt nothingness
Pluck at the armpits of my loose KDs
And balsa models jiggled on their shelves
While soaring roadways hurtled, shoulder high.
I had one thought before I turned away:

The trouble is, with us, we overreach ourselves.

A Line and a Theme from Noam Chomsky*

Furiously sleep; ideas green; colourless
Sweet dreams just lately ain't been had.
Sweat smells like the colour of the jungle.
Things looked bad then. They go on looking bad.

No question Charlie asked for what he got
Below from us, from up there by the jets;
Else their I D-ola G'd've prevailed,
They'd've swum here and stole our TV sets.

We lined 'em up, we knocked 'em down; we smoked.
We finished off what we'd been told to do.
Back stateside I expected to forget
How heads look when an M16 gets through.

Green nightmares; pillow strangled; sheets mussed up
By day a 'Go' light stops me in my tracks.
Shades don't help: they make the whole *works* green.
A night's sleep is a string of heart attacks.

Furiously sleep; ideas green, colourless
Sweet dreams just lately ain't been had.
That time our gunships hit us by mistake,
I was mad then, I mean angry. But this is mad.

---

* Noam Chomsky gave *furiously sleep ideas green colourless* as an example of a random
sequence of words which could have no meaning. It seemed possible that they could, if
the context were wide enough, and that their meaning might relate to the Vietnam War,
at that time Chomsky's main political concern.

The Outgoing Administration

The gods have eyes the colour of the sky.
They drink from crystal goblets full of cloud.
They laugh and sing a lot, but not aloud,
Since their appeal is mainly to the eye.

Their games become less hectic with the years,
Their wanton cries too feeble to deceive.
The very sight of them seems keen to leave:
It turns to powder like the salt of tears.

The vivid images are growing soft,
The purple robes are ceasing to wear well.
You see the azure through the muscatel
In all those grapes they've held so long aloft.

To think our children now will never know
How beautiful those creatures used to be,
How much more confident than you and me!
The reason why we had to let them go.

Neither One Thing Nor the Other

Sometimes I think perhaps I'm just obtuse.
Noon yesterday I took a turn through King's.
The crippled physicist came whirring by,
No doubt preoccupied with cosmic things.
I stepped aside. Above us in the sky
A burping biplane shook a glider loose
Whose pilot, swerving sunward, must have felt
As overwhelmingly at liberty
As this man felt pinned down. Was that right, though?
To lie still yet see all might feel more free
Than not to know quite why you're free to go.
The chair hummed off. The glider made no sound.
If I can't fly, why am I not profound?

Le Cirque imaginaire at Riverside Studios

In 'The Phantom of the Clouds' Apollinaire
Pretended to have gone downstairs to see
The acrobats, and found that when he tried
To drink in what he saw them do, it all
Turned bitter on the tongue. Pink pantaloons
Looked like decaying lungs. The fun was spoiled,
The family act more destitute than when
Picasso painted it. The War was on.
Apollinaire was in it, hence the dudgeon.

Without belittling him, you still might say
He needed horror to dilute delight,
Since childish joy to grown men feels like loss,
If only of childhood. There was a time,
Quite early in *Le Cirque imaginaire*,
When Vicky Chaplin walked on the tight wire
Inverted underneath it, that I thought
I'd just turned five. Her father in his film
The Circus did a stunt like that, but had
To fake it, though with good results. He died
The death in later life, became a bore
About his immortality, which was
No longer under his control. It lives again
When his thin daughter, blessed with Oona's looks,
Draped in sheet silver enters on all fours
High up on four tall stilts that look like six,
A basketballing insect from the depths
Of a benign nightmare.

                    Her husband makes
Surprises happen, just as, long ago,
With something of the same humility,
Her father could. A suitcase full of tricks
Yields up its secrets. Wherein lies the joke:
I mean the joke is that you *see* the way
It works. Except when the huge rabbit,

Which really *couldn't* be in that red box,
Emerges to remind you that this coy
Parade of diffidence is based on full
Mastery of white magic.

                              Now the stage
Is full of birds and bouncing animals,
Of which only a few do not excrete.
Silk-slippered on the bare boards pipped with mire,
The happy couple take their curtain calls
And we go back into the world, which has,
No doubt, produced, while we've been gone,
Plenty of stuff to cut this down to size –
Car bombs in day-care centres, *coups d'état*
In countries whose cash crop earns in a year
Less than *Evita* in a so-so week,
A torture farm in California
That takes all major credit cards.

                              Back in
Reality it needs Apollinaire
(Who went on being right about a war
That cost him half his head) to help retrieve
My reason from the most misleading evening
We spent at the imaginary circus –
Which children shouldn't see without a warning
Things might start looking different in the morning.

VERSE DIARIES

An Address to the Nation

Dear Britain, Merry Christmas! If I may
Presume on your attention for the space
Of one broadsheet, I'd simply like to say
How pleased I am to see your homely face
Perked up and looking forward to the day
When even the downcast are kissed by grace –
The day a perfect birth is celebrated
And we who are imperfect feel elated.

It's normally the Queen, I'm well aware,
Who takes upon herself the awesome onus
At each year's end of going on the air
And giving us our verbal Christmas bonus.
This year when we switch on she'll still be there,
A crumb of comfort History has thrown us,
Though some, and not the worst, think her the essence
Of suicidal social obsolescence.

But some things can't be said on television
Nor may the monarch speak of politics.
And thus it is I make the bold decision
In my role as a yokel from the sticks
To grasp the nettle and to court derision
And generally to kick against the pricks
By taking space in this great publication*
Wherewith most humbly to Address the Nation.

Three million out of work and work undone
Because nobody can afford to do it.
A monetarist engine that won't run.
Monetarists who say they always knew it.
A Government which hasn't yet begun
To reap the bitter harvest coming to it.
Next summer if the inner cities burn
Some dolt will say we spend more than we earn.

* *London Review of Books* (December 1981).

233

And over there the Loyal Opposition
Is catastrophically split between
Survivors who've long lost their sense of mission
And scolds who say exactly what they mean.
The former are in pitiable condition,
The latter even madder than they're keen.
The old brigade run on the spot like Alice.
The new boys want to storm the Winter Palace.

It's deadlock. Just to get the Tories out
Is no good reason to put Labour in.
One lot's got rabies and the other gout.
Whichever way it goes you just can't win.
The only proper state of mind is doubt
When Parliament sounds like a loony bin
With each side barracking the other's slogans –
Slogans with whiskers on like Terry Wogan's.

You've reached a turning point, that much is plain.
It's deeply felt by almost all of you.
The social fabric, if not under strain,
Is further stretched than it's accustomed to.
The body politic cries out in pain
And mere placebos will no longer do,
But just when it seems time to call for surgeons –
Behold! A peaceable solution burgeons!

They style themselves the Social Democrats.
It's their ambition to take centre stage.
On Labour's sinking ship they are called rats
By those who can't swim owing to old age.
Their leaders take an extra size in hats.
They grandly talk of turning a fresh page
In British politics and might well do so –
Or, hitting a new note, croak like Caruso.

The truth is no one can be sure as yet
How this third force will in the long term fare.
Both Labour loyalist and Tory Wet,
Though by their parties driven to despair,

Still say the SDP is a bad bet
And doubt the possibility is there
Of wooing anyone but floating voters –
Exotic types in flannels and straw boaters.

Meanwhile the Liberal half of the alliance
Looks puzzled like a dog wagged by its tail.
The pressure of events dictates compliance
Lest their declining star grow yet more pale.
But offered a back seat some breathe defiance
Preferring to stand on their own and fail.
They too seem to suspect something innately
Unsound about a Johnny come so lately.

What class can it be said to represent?
What ideology does it propose?
Pressed on these points the SDP is meant
To reel back clutching a disjointed nose.
But questions thus put are more eloquent
About the attitudes which they disclose.
The questioner defines his own condition:
A patient who pretends he's a physician.

You British are the only people left
In Europe who are still obsessed by class.
It sometimes seems you'd rather remain cleft
In twain than see the age-old hoodoo pass.
Without it the West End would be bereft
Of half its drama and of all its farce,
And think of all those books gone down the drain
By Amis, Amis, Bainbridge, Barnes, Bragg, Braine . . .

But artists of all kinds can be excused
For cherishing a stratified society.
Their privilege, which exists to be abused,
Is to lay hold of life in its variety.
Granted they do it well, we are amused
And readily forgive the note of piety
When Brideshead gets paid yet another visit.
It's no more daft than numismatics, is it?

That stanza was completed in some haste
Because I had to pack, sprint for a plane,
And fly here to this strip of shameless waste
Camped in the midst of the immense inane.
Las Vegas revels in its own bad taste
With neon waterfalls that soak the brain –
A full-tilt celebration of democracy
That makes you think more fondly of theocracy.

And yet despite the uproar of vulgarity,
As always in the US I relax.
Encouraged by the general social parity
Whose class divisions seem no more than cracks.
Notoriously a place that's short on charity
And long on shelters against federal tax,
Vegas breaks hearts and runs bums out of town.
Before you're out, though, you must first be down.

If you can pay, you play. No one excludes you –
A rule of thumb for the whole USA.
There may be a sweet life that still eludes you,
But no code word you don't know how to say,
No simple accident of birth denudes you
Of dignity. You're free to make your way,
And though one race gets held down by the other
At least they sometimes *talk* to one another.

Americans talk all the time, of course.
They use a lot of words while saying little.
They verbalize until they should be hoarse
Yet somehow don't run short of breath or spittle.
They'll plough on like a saga in Old Norse
And what they say won't mean a jot or tittle:
Semantically it's not much more than static.
It is, however, deeply democratic.

They speak a language everyone can speak,
Which means the tongue-tied aren't left in the cold.
The powerful talk bunkum like the weak,
The timorous talk loudly like the bold.

Even to strangers they all talk a streak.
They drone on while you stand there growing old.
E pluribus unum. Out of the many, one.
It means you'll hear the same mishmash from anyone.

There's no nuance because there is no rigour,
But in amongst the mush there's often verve.
One can be struck by a demotic vigour,
A heady access of linguistic nerve,
When someone suddenly lets loose a figure
Of speech that like a screwball or a curve
Will swerve around your bat and leave you flailing
Flat-footed, with a feeling that you're failing.

Just such a gift belongs to Melanie,
A neat blonde who deals blackjack at the Sands.
This week she's made a pauper out of me.
The cards that flow like water from her hands
Smoothly entice me into penury,
And yet I could embrace her where she stands
Because her riffles, shuffles, flicks and flutters
Turn pale beside the patter that she utters.

She tells me that I'll never beat the grind
Unless I bet big with the house's money
While I'm ahead. 'But don't pay me no mind.
You got a special style that's all yours, honey.'
In this light you can't tell her face is lined.
There was a day she was a Playboy Bunny,
And when it's time to take up a new trade
You can be sure that she won't be afraid.

Having your health bills paid from womb to tomb
Strikes Melanie as organized servility.
She claims she'd scream from lack of elbow room.
She cherishes her own adaptability.
She's certain that one welfare cheque spells doom
For any spark of spiritual agility.
She sounds, in other words, like Margaret Thatcher –
Though words are just where Thatcher couldn't match her.

It's easy for the Yanks to preach self-help:
There's so much protein they can help themselves.
In Britain we'd be feeding children kelp
And watching them grow up the size of elves
Were we to heed the age-old Tory yelp
That's heard when the tinned goods on the shop shelves
Are priced so as those people can afford them
Who'll only eat them when they ought to hoard them.

Our film on gambling is completely shot
So back we fly to where it's cold and poor.
There it was hot and rich but here it's not.
Yes, here now feels less nice than there before.
There is a lot that Britain has not got –
A fact it takes some effort to ignore.
(I fear this stanza's a bit elementary:
I'm shattered by the impact of re-entry.)

A newsflash. In the latest by-election
The Liberal William Pitt has won the seat.
His personal appeal defies detection.
At previous attempts he met defeat.
Clearly it is the SDP connection
Which has supplied the upsurge of white heat
That melts the Tory vote to a minority
And Labour's to abject inferiority.

This Pitt falls far short of so grand a name.
Long in the beard, he's less so in the legs.
He lacks the stature for his sudden fame.
It's plain that of the Pitts he is the dregs,
And yet he is a Titan all the same.
The great name lives again as sure as eggs:
For Mr Steel, Pitt *minimus* will function
To bless and sanctify the new conjunction.

With no more murmurs in the Liberal ranks
In Labour's there is total consternation.
If Michael Foot tore out his hair in hanks
He could not look more prone to perturbation.

The right wing loudly calls the left wing cranks
And no one stays calm in the altercation
Except for Tony Benn, who sucks contentedly
On his prop pipe and stares ahead dementedly.

What does he see there in the depths of space?
Still half defined, it sets his large heart beating.
The vision clarifies and lights his face.
He sees some vast canteen in which a meeting
Of Britain's workforce endlessly takes place
And no one minds the lack of central heating.
What lifts their spirits? Why are they ecstatic?
Because their chairman is so charismatic!

No, Destiny demands he try again
To wrest the Party from the Right's dead grip.
He stems from a long line of working men.
His fellow workers need his leadership.
Lord Stansgate walks the earth as Tony Benn.
He comes to cleanse the temple with his whip.
They've crucified him once. It felt quite nice.
No reason why it shouldn't happen twice ...

Healey, meanwhile, turns beetroot red with rage,
His jowls so vibrant he can hardly speak.
The right ideas, the right looks, the right age –
And yet his place is filled by an antique,
While fools ensure a once-proud heritage
Goes down a tube that comes out up the creek.
But he and Hattersley must grin and bear it:
The cap Benn gives them fits. They have to wear it.

The Labour Right's lip-service to Clause 4
Now stands revealed as outright atheism.
They simply don't believe it any more,
Hence the exultant rancour of the schism.
The heretics have nine points of the law.
The creed they preach is Fundamentalism.
They say the Right is Socialist no longer.
They say the truth, and so they must grow stronger.

But purified or not, the Labour cause
Within our time could dwindle to a rump.
Not for the sake of some outdated clause:
It's just that people tend to get the hump
When told too often that Behind Closed Doors
Ten million union votes cast in one lump
By some strange means have all made the same choice.
Whatever happened to the human voice?

The Tory version of it now seems camper
Than ever. Thatcher's condescending whine
Was always guaranteed to put a damper
On anybody's urge to rise and shine.
She made you want to pack a wicker hamper
And have a picnic down a disused mine,
But still the odd factotum like Jim Prior
At least seemed relatively a live wire.

Now Prior's gone and in comes a new broom
Named Twitchit. Rabbit? Sorry, I mean Hobbit.
His eyes like lasers penetrate the gloom.
He takes the nation's pulse like William Cobbett.
He paces, ponders, clears his throat of rheum
And in due course gives forth this juicy gobbet:
We must work harder. That's what we must do.
(No need to add that by 'we' he means you.)

That's the Employment Secretary's plan
For getting us out of our present mess.
One wonders if he's really the right man.
He should be tagging wildlife in Loch Ness.
The CBI are back where they began,
Frantically making signals of distress.
They said they wanted to be lean and mean
And now they are, and now they're not so keen.

Inflation slows but industry slows faster
And British Leyland might grind to a halt.
The strike looms like a nuclear disaster
Except no expertise can trace the fault.

The management's run out of sticking plaster.
The Cabinet might perform a somersault
Or else stand firm where previously it wouldn't,
Or would have done but as things stood it couldn't.

The policy said No Help For Lame Ducks.
Reality said big lame ducks must eat.
A lame duck that makes half our cars and trucks
Could put a million people on the street.
For such a bird the treatment is de luxe
Lest it should trip over those awkward feet.
Hence the webbed boots and plastic knee-protector
Paid for by cutting back the public sector.

Leaving the Mini Metros to their fate
I pack my bag again and take the air,
Progressing south-east at a dizzy rate
Until I look down and see Sydney there.
The Harbour Bridge looks like a paperweight,
The Opera House like fractured Tupperware.
It all shines like quicksilver in the dawn.
Cloud cuckoo land. The land where I was born.

Here when the young are forced to take the dole
It just means they spend more time at the beach.
Thinkers bemoan the country's lack of soul
While still contriving to own three cars each.
You scoop wealth up like opals from a hole.
All you can dream of is within arm's reach,
And no one mugs you, kidnaps you or taunts you –
Though sometimes you might find your conscience haunts you.

As our world goes this is an unreal land,
A paradise devoid of modern menaces,
A land where Eve and Adam hand in hand
Star in a rewrite of the book of Genesis.
Recumbent Adam gets his forehead fanned
While wooing Eve in verse like C. J. Dennis's.
They won't be asked to leave. They're set for ever.
They've got the freehold of the never-never.

I'm here to plug my book from town to town.
All day I'm either in the air or on it.
The first time I wrote that last stanza down
It came out three lines longer than a sonnet.
I'm having trouble telling verb from noun.
Quid verbis opus est? A plague upon it.
But after all it's just the flesh that's tired.
The spirit's willing, not to say inspired.

Inspired above all by the piercing twang
Of Austral voices flagrantly projected,
Astringent as the antiseptic tang
Of iodine upon the place infected.
It might not be the song the sirens sang.
You might wish that your ears were disconnected,
But still you must admit there's something stimulating
In how they have no notion of dissimulating.

They may lack subtlety who have no guile.
They often – it's their own word for it – whinge.
The open freckled face they call the dial
With injured pride adopts a purple tinge.
Often they bristle when they ought to smile,
But what you never see them do is cringe.
Would-be sophisticate or brute barbarian,
Your Aussie is a true egalitarian.

But now the demon bowler Dennis Lillee
By his behaviour starts a frightful barney.
Too much success too young has made him silly.
He kicks the shin of a small Pakistani.
Here and in Britain the press willy-nilly
Combines to sing a chorus from *Ernani*.
All are agreed that such obtuse aggression
Denotes the opposite of self-possession.

Perhaps they're right. No people should be praised
For confidence when they are so well fed.
Needless to say I'm suitably amazed
At how my native land has gone ahead,

But when one's had one's turn at looking dazed
Reluctantly it also must be said
That anywhere so prodigally blessed
Is ultimately short of interest.

Australia's cities remain safe and clean,
The public telephones unvandalized.
Like free advertisements the beach girls preen
In costumes overstressed and undersized.
Once more as I take off from Tullamarine
I feel to leave all this is ill-advised,
But also, floating over the Dead Heart,
Feel somehow not unhappy to depart.

Down there in that hot ocean of red rock
There is no history, only geography.
Some ethnic dance group may attempt to shock
With semi-nude formation choreography,
But basically this place has stopped the clock,
Made time a tableau like high-speed photography.
It's only at the fertile utmost fringes
The age we're living in even impinges.

Dante's Ulysses told his trembling crew
They should not stay like beasts where life was easy,
And Baudelaire, who sailed to find the new,
Best recognized it when it made him queasy.
Australians with a thirst for derring-do
Find modern Britain challengingly sleazy –
It's chill, dank, broke, pale, dirty, constipated,
But also tough, real, quirky, complicated.

Heathrow at dawn is cloud down to the ground,
Black taxis queue as if for the bereaved.
The body of a child has just been found.
It seems that British Leyland is reprieved.
One Aussie dollar buys almost a pound.
Welcome to Britain. Why am I relieved?
Because although life here is far less pleasant
Nevertheless it happens in the present.

Foot now at last and probably too late
Tells Benn to either belt up or get lost,
While Thatcher at an ever quickening rate –
As if there were some profit in the cost –
Unbolts large pieces of the welfare state
Which lying in the rain rust where they're tossed.
Good people in both parties look hag-ridden.
Small anguished cries come to their lips unbidden.

The Crosby by-election, shriek the polls,
Must go to Shirley Williams by a cable.
Should that occur the toiling Fleet Street trolls
Will find her shapelier than Betty Grable,
While making sure a solemn tocsin tolls
To tell Roy Jenkins he is not Clark Gable.
About the top spot there'll be much palaver
As some fans cry *bravo*! and others *brava*!

Someone will have to lead the SDP.
Ten Downing Street won't sleep a whole committee.
In all good time a choice there'll have to be
But making it too soon would be a pity,
Lest we, bombarded by publicity,
Lose touch with what should be the nitty-gritty –
That polite knock on the large door at the centre
Outside which common reason waits to enter.

Perhaps by now it's been too long outside,
Hat in one hand, the other with raw knuckles.
Perhaps by now it's gaunt and hollow-eyed,
Wearing a powdered wig and shoes with buckles.
Perhaps it will take one unsteady stride
Before dissolving into drunken chuckles,
But what most of us hope we will be seeing
Is just a reasonable human being.

The secret of the so-called common touch
Resides in its appeal to common sense.
Though simply to talk straight might not seem much
The consequences could just be immense.

Now that the country's choking in the clutch
Of toxic verbal fog at its most dense,
Merely to speak in terms that do not slight us
Might almost be enough to reunite us.

Which must be done *before* the long slow task
Of getting well again is undertaken.
The patient's lying there in a gauze mask,
Fed through a vein and feeling godforsaken.
He'll do the twenty press-ups that you ask
But first his will to live must reawaken.
He must hear in your voice the note of sanity
Struck by acknowledgment of shared humanity.

As long as the Alliance can talk sanely
It will not so much matter for the nonce
That when it moves it is a bit ungainly
And stumbles off six different ways at once.
Would-be hardbitten critics snipe inanely,
There's mockery from every hack and dunce,
But for most people that uncertain feeling
Is just what makes the new lot so appealing.

By now the big ideas have all been tried,
Become bad jokes we have grown sick of hearing.
The economic rough stuff on one side,
The other's dreams of social engineering,
Render the average punter gratified
That honest doubt at last is reappearing.
At least this bunch don't spout like know-it-alls
The usual load of patronizing balls.

Ideally they should stay unencumbered
With whopping programmes that they can't enforce.
It's still the classic way of getting lumbered.
The cart is meant to be *behind* the horse.
There is no need to feel our days are numbered,
Only to trace the power to its source:
The people's goodwill is what drives the nation
And holds the secret of regeneration.

Ms Williams wins. This time she caught the train.
But BL's Longbridge plant is still on strike.
From Ireland comes the daily scream of pain.
It's still the same old story if you like.
The deep-ingrained uncertainties remain.
The Way Ahead's a hell of a long hike.
You've not a jot in common but the weather.
The rain's the only thing you're in together.

The rain, the sleet and soon, no doubt, the snow.
Through autumn into winter I have scribbled
This crackerbarrel tract at which I know
The expert commentators will wax ribald.
This is a complex subject, they will crow,
A mountain range at which a mouse has nibbled –
But I still think the British within reason
Have reason to be glad this festive season.

Note: Not long after completing this poem, and not before time, I began to read Australian history in some depth, and soon reached the conclusion that I had made a drastic mistake in going along with the easy notion that the democratic achievements of my homeland were in some way the naive blessings of a benevolent fate, and therefore lacking in interest. My later work, including much of the poetry, has been dedicated to the proposition that Australia, far from lagging by world standards, actually sets them. The problem is: if freedom comes with the air you breathe, how can you tell that it is precious? In the year I wrote *An Address to the Nation*, I exemplified that conundrum. I had no idea that the confidence which had given rise to my pronouncement should have been my subject. Why does it take so much time to bring wisdom? Because you don't know your luck.

Poem of the Year (1982)

To C. L. Perowne and the Downhill Badger

Preface

Most narrative verse is written from hindsight. The reader doesn't know what happens next but the writer does. There has always been a place, however, for the kind of narrative verse which turns this relationship back to front, putting the reader in the know and the writer in the dark. In a verse chronicle of unfolding events, the writer can accurately predict very little, whereas the reader will judge from experience. The finest modern example is Louis MacNeice's *Autumn Journal*, a poem one starts off by admiring and then admires more deeply with advancing age. MacNeice could be fairly certain that the autumn of 1938 would bring the Second World War closer, but not of anything else. His personality declared itself along with the events, gaining coherence as they lost it. Rarely has apprehensiveness sounded more human or humanity so worth preserving.

A verse chronicle must be essentially self-revealing. The attitudes struck can easily look ridiculous, and never more so than when struck judiciously, so as to hedge all the bets. The temptation to go back and rewrite is hard to resist. I denied it to myself by publishing my efforts *pari passu* in five separate issues of the *London Review of Books*. The few stanzas which had to be taken out for production reasons I have here put back in. Also I have altered the prosody in several lines which the mother of the dedicatees thought were too much of a challenge to the jaw muscles. One couplet has been rewritten for the good reason that it struck even its author as two matched lengths of haematite. But otherwise the thing is as it was when it was growing in 1982, a year whose events turned out to be beyond anybody's calculations, including those of Nostradamus.

Nobody, certainly not the Foreign Office, knew that Britain would fight a war in the South Atlantic. If you believed in the State of Israel's right to exist, but doubted that Mr Begin was the ideal man to help exercise it, never in your worst memories of Deir Yassin would you have thought that he might let Christians murder Muslims while Israeli soldiers stood by. It was perhaps a fair bet that Mr Brezhnev would grunt his last, but the same bet had been fair for some time. And that Princess Grace would die too was outside the computations of any astrologer.

The only thing the narrator could be reasonably sure of, as the year began, was that the cause of the free Polish trade union Solidarity would be lost before it ended. But there was no telling quite how until it began happening, and then the telling of it was hard on the nerves. *Ottava rima* is not necessarily always a comic form, but it tends that way, and many a time, as the Zomos patrolled in Warsaw or the innocent died bloodily even in the streets of London, I wished I had chosen a stanza inherently more sonorous. But to keep it light was the original idea. Living from day to day, with the television screen bringing us the whole world's grief, we joke to stay sane. If we dwelt on every tragedy it would sound like ours as well as the victim's, and that would be presumptuous. The time to write the elegy is later on, looking back.

Looking back over my longer excursions in verse, I have good cause to thank the editors of those newspapers, magazines and literary periodicals who over the years have given up whole pages to them and sometimes whole issues. Some of these editors thought that what I was doing couldn't be called poetry but they ran it anyway. Their faith was an inspiration and the recipient would like to salute them all now, at the moment when he has convinced himself that he is at last, after so much practice, capable of setting down roughly what he means. Ian Hamilton, Claire Tomalin, Anthony Thwaite, Harold Evans, Donald Trelford and Robert Silvers have all, at one time or another, printed extensive concoctions which they knew would earn them letters from serious poets saying that there was a barbarian within the gates. Finally Karl Miller, when faced with the prospect of an entire year in verse, said yes instead of no. It was an instance, negligible on a world scale but looming large for his contributor, of how the individual can affect history. I would never have written this journal without his encouragement. Nor, it might be said, would John De Lorean have ever made that cocaine deal if someone hadn't told him it was a sure thing.

Unpredictability was what made the idea irresistible. It was also what threatened my dedicatees. They watched me scribbling and crossing out until the thing was finished, but in the end they accomplished something just as chancy. They had grown a year older, in a world where no man can be sure that his children will survive the night. In this age which is supposed to be modern, terror hasn't gone away, it has just spread out. Fear now is like gravity: weak but all pervasive. Reading back over what I have written, I think I can hear it everywhere, and don't know whether to congratulate myself or feel ashamed. But perhaps there are no ways left to take it easy, and all we can do is take it.

London, 1983

I

The old year ends with Cambridge under snow.
The world in winter like the moon in spring
Unyieldingly gives off a grey-blue glow.
An icy laminate caps everything.
Christmas looks merry if you wish it so.
One strives to hark the Herald Angels sing,
But at each brief hiatus in the feast
A bitter wind howls sadly from the east.

In Poland now the only Santa Claus
Is General Jaruzelski looking grim.
With Solidarity a brave lost cause
There is no father figure except him.
His overall demeanour gives one pause.
Nor are peace prospects really made less dim
By Ronald Reagan recommending firm
Measures that make his NATO allies squirm.

Snow falls again. The atmosphere turns white.
The airfields of East Anglia are socked in.
The atom bombers will not fly tonight.
Tonight the Third World War will not begin.
There's so much concentrated heat and light
Stored around here that if they pulled the pin
The British Isles would be volatilized.
Even the dons would be a bit surprised.

One theory says the Polish Army acted
Only to stop the Russians doing worse.

So clumsily to have a tooth extracted
By family friends calls forth a garbled curse,
But left too long the fang will get impacted
And you won't like the dentist or his nurse.
At least – the pun's not just weak but emetic –
Get the job done with *local* anaesthetic.

Such reasoning is comfortable like us
But soon there are dark rumours to belie it.
The fact the coup has led to far more fuss
Than they say, you can tell when they deny it.
Here in the West we have much to discuss
Beyond the danger to a healthy diet.
You like the thin mints? Try the orange sticks,
Has anybody seen the walnut picks?

Most of the Poles have not got much to eat.
Their democratic leaders have still less.
A cold and cruel and long-drawn-out defeat
Must be the price they pay for small success.
They bucked a system that they could not beat
Which reasserts itself through their distress.
White flakes may decorate the searchlight beams –
The barbed wire is exactly what it seems.

Those men and women braver than the brave
Penned in the open air are telling you
It's better to risk death than be a slave –
Something you thought that you already knew.
And yet to stick together till the grave –
Could we do that if that's what it came to?
One's rather glad one's not cast as a hero
Out there tonight at twenty below zero.

The turkey carcass and Brazil-nut shells
And mandarin rinds fill the pedal bin.
The ice-rimmed church and college chapel bells
Stiffly combine to call the New Year in.
The snow melts and in London the Thames swells
As once the lake lapped Tantalus's chin,

But as I leave the usual filthy train
I guess that the embankments took the strain,

Or else my book-lined eyrie near St Paul's
Would look down on a city rather like
Venice or Amsterdam plus waterfalls
Cascading over many a broken dyke.
There'd be ducks nesting in the choir stalls
Of Clement Dane's, and people would catch pike
(With suitably refined outbursts of joy)
From windows at the back of the Savoy.

But there is nothing underfoot save slush
Compounded from crushed ice, old snow and dirt.
Your wellies slurp and gurgle in the mush.
Spat by a taxi wheel the stuff can spurt
Up from the street in one exultant gush
To inundate you where you stand inert.
The cars and buses churn the rhubarb slurry
Until it darkens into cold beef curry.

Schmidt goes to Washington and tells the Yanks
That while his Germany might still be Jerry
The Russians are not Tom and have large tanks
Whose side effects it can take weeks to bury.
Therefore he is reluctant to give thanks
For Reagan's speeches, which to him seem very
Naive, as if designed to aggravate
The blind intransigence they castigate.

Congress is humbled by Schmidt's eloquence
Which makes the President sound like an actor
Who reads a script well but is slightly dense
If not as crass as Carter on his tractor.
The Chancellor's impact has been immense.
Intelligence emerges as a factor
In statesmanship and might well start a fashion
Of saying things with point and not just passion.

But whether he is right is hard to judge.
Meanwhile the snow which only last week went

Comes back as if it bore a lasting grudge
And whites the country out from Wales to Kent.
On the M4 the lorries do not budge.
The usual helicopters have been sent
To find the troops last seen the day before
Searching for lost birdwatchers on Broadmoor

In no time the whole country's ten feet deep:
Landscapes by Breughel, cityscapes by Lowry.
They're using sonar gear to find the sheep.
All Europeans get this as a dowry
But after twenty years I still could weep,
Feeling more foreign to it than a Maori.
I'm half delighted and I'm half disdainful –
It looks so lovely and it feels so painful.

Roy Jenkins will be standing at Hillhead
In Glasgow. The world wonders: is this wise?
Lose Warrington and it's a watershed:
Defeat there was a victory in disguise.
But this time if he doesn't win he's dead
With all his party sharing his demise.
The SDP, awed by its own audacity,
Strikes postures of unflappable sagacity.

But more of that – much more, no doubt – anon.
Meanwhile Mark Thatcher's managed to get lost
Somewhere in Africa. The hunt is on.
Airborne armadas at tremendous cost
Search all directions where he might have gone.
One tends to find one's fingers slightly crossed.
The days go by and soon it's not a joke.
He's even talked of as a nice young bloke.

Since he in fact is something of a prat
This sudden fondness constitutes a proof
The British heart still beats though lagged with fat.
His mother weeps who once was so aloof
But few there are who take delight in that.
Many who think her son a cocksure goof

And wish her and her politics in hell
Nevertheless in this case wish her well.

The boy is found and instantly reverts
To his accustomed status, that of jerk.
The next blow to the nation really hurts.
ASLEF the footplate union will stop work.
The papers tell us we'll all lose our shirts
Because train drivers can't forgo a perk.
The sum of Fleet Street's pitiless analysis
Presages chaos, followed by paralysis.

If Fleet Street takes so unified a view
We can be sure the truth must lie elsewhere.
The first train strike of 1982
Inspires more irritation than despair.
Unmotivated locos are not new.
What's fearsome is when planes fall from the air.
In Washington one does. Down on the bed
Of the ice-locked Potomac sit the dead.

The whole world tuning in through television
For once sees human nature at its best.
A man who might have lived makes the decision
To stay and try to save some of the rest.
Were this a movie, think of the derision
With which we'd greet such an absurd *beau geste*.
On that small screen the big hole in the ice
Frames the reality of sacrifice.

II

The feeling that there's grandeur in mankind
Is soon dispelled by fresh cause for lament.
A rapist is not jailed but merely fined
Because, it seems, the girl was 'negligent'.
Perhaps the judge has gone out of his mind,
Unless it's him that's straight and us that's bent.
He's set the price for screwing a hitch-hiker:
Two grand. Just toss her out if you don't like her.

Fleet Street, which always disapproved of rape
Despite provoking hot lust on page three,
This time gets on its high horse and goes ape.
In Scotland several men have been set free
Because the woman is in such bad shape
She can't be called on to give testimony.
The man in charge says it's an awkward case.
He's got a point, but no one likes his face.

So Nicky Fairbairn now gets pulled apart
Both in the House and by the public prints.
I must confess I'm not touched to the heart.
That 'style' of his has always made me wince.
I've never liked his haircut for a start,
Nor the sharp trews in which he's wont to mince.
His *Who's Who* entry puts the lid on it:
He has the hide to call himself a Wit.

That title's one which nobody can claim.
You have to wait for others to bestow it.
Not even Oscar Wilde assumed the name,
Who called himself both genius and poet.
That he was self-appointed to his fame –
A true wit wouldn't hint it, much less crow it.
Poor knackered Nicky thinks he's Alan Coren:
He's just a wee laird with a twitching sporran.

And yet it's wise to give conceit expression –
Within the limits set by the absurd.
A boast might be self-serving like confession
But similarly festers if unheard.
Much meekness stands revealed as self-obsession
When self finds a release too long deferred.
Beware the kind of people who don't flower
Until their shrivelled roots taste fame and power.

Take Henry Kissinger as an example.
The man personifies megalomania.
He's back in action with another sample
Of foreign policy from Ruritania.

On Poland Reagan's harsh words have been ample
But Henry hankers after something zanier.
Leave it to me, he seems to be implying,
And Russian fur will pretty soon be flying.

Suslov checks out. Unless he died of fright
At Henry's rhetoric, it's just old age
That now removes Stalin's last acolyte
And faithful killer gently from the stage.
The mental stature of potato blight
Left him unchallenged as the Party sage:
The perfect man to make sure Ideology
Maintained its power to torture by tautology.

They bury Suslov in the Kremlin wall:
A tribute to his cranial rigidity.
Propped up like that the bricks will never fall.
Meanwhile the intellectual aridity
He helped create still casts its stifling pall:
A dry red dust of cynical stupidity
Ensures the last trace of imagination
Is wept away in hot tears of frustration.

Frustration, but the trains do run on time –
Mainly because the drivers must keep driving
Since any form of strike would be a crime.
No doubt there are time-honoured forms of skiving.
Perhaps their trains, like ours, are sprayed with grime
Before they leave and once more on arriving.
They do, however, go. Without delay.
And what is more they do so every day.

Ours at the moment run five days a week
Or four days, subject to negotiation.
It might be three days even as I speak:
I've lost track of the inverse escalation.
The union leaders talk their usual Greek.
The matter must not go to arbitration.
The strike must bite. The strike days must be staggered.
Sir Peter Parker still smiles but looks haggard.

Sir Peter Parker picked a pickled peck
Of pepper when he took on British Rail.
With every kind of triumph at his beck
And call, perhaps he felt the need to fail.
His chance of saving something from the wreck
Equals his chance to find the Holy Grail.
You never know, though. He and Sidney Weighell
Might possibly cook up some sort of deighell.

If Buckton's ASLEF joined Weighell's NUR
Then BR's board plus ACAS minus VAT . . .
We might as well give up and go by car
Or coach, or on foot if it comes to that.
Some say the train lines should be paved with tar,
Which no doubt counts as talking through your hat,
But if it's true what's needed most is cash
Then stand aside and watch out for the crash.

It's no time to owe money at the bank,
A fact now underlined by Freddie Laker –
Although in part he has the banks to thank
His airline's laid out for the undertaker.
It seems they lent him dough as if they drank
Their lunch directly from the cocktail shaker,
But now the plugs are pulled and in mid-flight
His planes turn back as he gives up the fight.

Disconsolate the DC10s come home
To Gatwick, where in time someone will buy them.
An airliner is not a garden gnome.
They can't just sit there. Somebody will fly them.
Defeated legions coming home to Rome
Would choose new emperors and deify them,
But Freddie, though his hearty laugh rings hollow,
Is not an act just anyone can follow.

Sir Freddie, Thatcher's knight with shining wings,
Her favourite Private Sector buccaneer,
Seems to have made rather a mess of things.
Is this collapse the end of his career?

His air of loosely buckled swash still clings.
The cut-price flying public holds him dear.
They send pound notes to keep Skytrain in motion –
Straws in the wind although drops in the ocean.

Here's proof the people value enterprise
And overlook, in those they think have got it,
A Rolls like Freddie's of excessive size,
A house so big an astronaut could spot it.
Whatever shibboleth might galvanize
The public, public ownership is not it.
Despite the very real risk of fatalities
People identify with personalities.

Just when Sir Freddie masticates the dust
The civil servants get their indexed pensions.
Not only Thatcher fans express disgust
At this exposé of the inner tensions
Between what she would like to do and must.
It is an awkward fact she seldom mentions:
The spread she said she'd end of public spending
Increases, and the increase is unending.

She can't trim bureaucratic overmanning.
She cuts the social services instead.
You needn't be as wise as Pitt or Canning
To see how malnutrition lies ahead.
Conversely, Labour's universal planning
Is just the cure to leave the patient dead.
The Alliance must win if it has the nerve to.
At this rate if they don't they don't deserve to.

III

A thought to bear in mind as we now watch
The Labour Party tear at its own guts.
The Peace of Bishop's Stortford's a hotchpotch
Which to place faith in you must first be nuts.
With moulting mane Foot still attempts to scotch

All doubts by well-placed ha-has and tut-tuts,
But while he waffles wanly about unity
The toughs build up their beachhead with impunity.

The Peace of Bishop's Stortford lulls the press
Which now says it's the SDP that's split.
The lead of the Alliance has grown less,
The tabloids chortle, champing at the bit.
Alliance policies are in a mess
And all in all this new lot aren't quite it.
On Tebbit's union bill they show dissension –
Clear indication of internal tension.

De Lorean the glamour-puss tycoon
Whose gull-wing car is built with our tax money
Might lay at least a gull-sized egg quite soon.
He's suave and clever and his wife's a honey.
For Northern Ireland he has been a boon.
But still and all there's something slightly funny . . .
Or maybe I just find the car too dull,
Attractive only to another gull.

At any rate, the books are with Jim Prior,
Who must decide if we should drop De Lorean
And cut the loss or raise the ante higher.
De Lorean's first name should have been Dorian:
That ageless face of the *Playboy* high-flyer
Is decomposing like an ancient saurian.
I think he's guilty mainly of wild dreams
And now he sees them cracking at the seams.

Prior pronounces. Not another penny
Of public funds. De Lorean must raise
The cash himself. Has he himself got any?
His blink rate slows to a stunned mackerel glaze.
No doubt he has some rich friends but how many?
He has to find the moola in two days.
Meanwhile the bootlace leeches of Fleet Street
Come sucking up in search of easy meat.

De Lorean finds every well is dry
And Prior duly puts in the Receiver,
Who luckily is not just the one guy
Since lately he's been working like a beaver.
Times Newspapers might be the next to die,
Tossing and turning with the self-same fever.
A mighty panic's on to kill things off.
They're giving the last rites at the first cough.

To think the SDP is on the wane –
While Labour's somehow on the comeback trail –
Unless I am a Dutchman is insane.
I don't say the Alliance cannot fail.
I just say that they cannot fail to gain
If Labour puts itself beyond the pale
By dosing its venereal infection
With Valium until the next election.

The bubble's burst already. It's revealed
The Militants have plans by which the fate
Of all non-Marxist MPs would be sealed
And power would go leftward on a plate.
All bets are off and it's a battlefield.
Poor Foot is in a terrifying state,
While Benn's grin says with fathomless hypocrisy
That's what you get for holding down Democracy.

The Tendency's great plot, is it a fact?
It could be fake like the Zinoviev letter.
There's something phoney about this whole act.
When people plot red plots don't they plot better?
They can't be nincompoops as *well* as cracked.
You'd get a better plot from a red setter.
They should have signed it with the mark of Zorro.
Perhaps *The Times* will tell us all, tomorrow.

I go to buy my paper the next day
Feeling that every *Times* may be my last,
And meet Neil Kinnock making a *tournée*
Of St Paul's Yard. He's gleefully aghast

At the Red Plot. 'You'd think the CIA
Had written it!' But it was moved and passed
And signed, sealed and delivered through the post
By these dumb-clucks. They've served themselves on toast.

Brave Kinnock thinks his cause will by this blunder
Be further armoured in defence of sanity.
I'd hate to see good men like him go under:
So much charm rarely has so little vanity.
But why else is his party torn asunder
If not because the measure of humanity
He represents is deemed not just outdated
But doomed to be hacked down and extirpated?

For Benn's and Scargill's Labour I won't vote.
For Kinnock's I would think it churlish not to.
Foot knows most voters are like me and float
And that to win them he has simply got to
Keep down the ranters who get people's goat.
He must do something but does not know what to.
Frank Hooley booted out at Sheffield Heeley
And now Fred Mulley too! It's too much, really.

Foot's shuffling feet should be in carpet slippers
But clearly Kinnock remains loyal still.
As he and his nice wife and their two nippers
Pursue their half-term hike down Ludgate Hill,
Threading between the tourists and day trippers,
They seem to incarnate the People's Will.
I only wish that such a thing existed
And like a cherished building could be listed.

As Amersham achieves Privatization
And sells the way hot cakes do when dirt cheap
We realize with a sickening sensation,
As of a skier on a slope too steep,
That if the soundest firms owned by the nation
Are flogged, the duds are all we'll get to keep –
And when the auction ends they'll sell the hammer.
We're heading downhill faster than Franz Klammer.

On that one deal the public's out of pocket
Some umpteen million quid or thereabouts.
Thatcher gives everyone concerned a rocket
But re her policy betrays no doubts.
Around her neck she wears a heart-shaped locket
In which lie curled some undernourished sprouts
Of Milton Friedman's hair plucked from his head
Or elsewhere during hectic nights in bed.

I speak in metaphor, needless to say:
Milton and Maggie you could not call lovers
Save in the strictly intellectual way
By which they sleep beneath the same warm covers
And wake up side by side to face the day
Throbbing in concert like a pair of plovers –
Though Milty while he shaves sometimes talks tough
And tells her she's not being rough *enough*.

Monetarism as an orthodoxy
Is lethal preached by one like the PM,
Precisely *because* she's got so much moxie.
She burns deep like the hard flame from a gem,
Sticks to her guns like glutinous epoxy,
And views the dole queues others would condemn
As growing proof that cutting out dead wood
Can in the long run only lead to good.

No need to say those millions on the dole
Are there because the Government decrees it.
The contrary idea is a live coal,
A notion so dire that the mind can't seize it.
Suppose that unemployment on the whole
Would be the same no matter what . . . Stop! Cheese it!
Better believe that Maggie acts from malice,
Childishly spiteful like JR in *Dallas*.

An aircraft hijacked in Dar es Salaam
Arrives at Stansted full of Tanzanians.
The Immigration officers keep calm
Almost as if these folk were Europeans.

One wouldn't want to see them come to harm.
Stansted's a long way north of New Orleans.
But dash it all, eh what! What a kerfuffle
Just to sort out some minor tribal scuffle!

It seems these hijack chappies hate Nyerere
And think that Stansted's the best place to say it.
The SAS are on tap looking scary,
A mighty strong card if we have to play it.
As hijacks go, though, this one's airy-fairy.
The price they ask is vague and kind words pay it.
Believing that their cause is understood
They throw down weapons mostly carved from wood.

A mess on our own doorstep's thus averted.
What started it we fail to comprehend.
Once more we in the plush West have asserted
Our will that awkwardness must have an end.
And yet it's possible that we've just flirted
With some great hurt no words of ours can mend,
In which we might well once have had a hand –
A homing chicken coming in to land.

IV

Speaking of which, one fears that Mr Thorpe
Will not reign long as Amnesty's new chief.
Placed under stress he has been known to warp,
As David Astor points out with some grief.
I must say that Thorpe's nerve gives cause to gawp.
A decent silence should not be so brief.
One does feel he might wear more sober togs
And do things quietly in aid of dogs.

Marcus Aurelius said there's an age
Beyond which we should scorn the public eye,
Put down our seals of office, quit the stage,
Settle our business and prepare to die.
No one denies the Emperor was a sage:

His precepts, though, we nowadays defy.
Old Brezhnev, for example, will stay there
As long as there's enough dye for his hair.

Perhaps he's dead already and controlled
Remotely by a powerful transmitter.
Another waxwork poured in the same mould
Might stir up protest or at least a titter.
His chassis, valves and circuits have grown old.
The struggle to replace them could be bitter.
At checking-out time for the ape-faced gremlin
Try to avoid the front desk of the Kremlin.

But just as I write this the rumour's rife
That Brezhnev's had it and the fight is on
For who'll be next to taste immortal life
As General Secretary when he's gone.
Silent arrests and kindred signs of strife
Compose the usual deaf-mute telethon.
One man scores points for standing near another
But drops out when denounced by his own mother.

How droll these thugs would be if not so sad,
Watching their backs and also the main chance.
Most aren't insane or even mildly mad.
Each owns a blue suit with two pairs of pants.
By now they think Marxism was a fad
But still they hold that men should live like ants
While they themselves adorn the doll museum
Standing on top of Lenin's mausoleum.

Blue-jawed top dogs of the *Nomenklatura*,
They loom while squads of workers toting spanners
Come stomping by like Nazis past the Führer
Except the signs are different on the banners.
The *idée fixe* is still that a bravura
Performance turns this comedy of manners
Into some species of impressive drama
Instead of just a childish diorama.

According to the *Sunday Times*, Pat Wall,
Prospective Labour MP (Militant),
Has risen on hirsute hind legs to bawl
A vintage load of Jacobinist cant,
Insisting that the monarch, Lords and all
Such privileged figures strangely yet extant,
Must forthwith holus-bolus be abolished
Or strictly speaking physically demolished.

Wild Wall includes the judges in his fury,
Which indicates that when he comes to power
As well as MP he'll be judge and jury –
A prospect at which even saints might cower.
The Party handles him as Madame Curie
Handled her radium hour after hour,
Unmindful that the steady radiation
In her own blood and bones worked devastation.

But now South Africa becomes the focus
Of every cricket lover's expert gaze,
While those who think the great game hocus-pocus,
A ritual rain dance that goes on for days
Until the grey clouds open up and soak us,
This time can only look on in amaze
As British cricketers receive abuse
For being not just tiresome but obtuse.

Boycott, we hear, should live up to his name,
And not be one by whom sanctions are busted.
He and his mates of almost equal fame
Could well prove to have been falsely entrusted
With their credentials in the holy game.
Students of sport pronounce themselves disgusted
Since segregated cricket, in a sense,
Is like denying blacks the sacraments.

Apartheid has not much to recommend it.
What else can it engender except hate?
One day the blacks will find a way to end it
Their masters will not spot until too late.

Meanwhile the sole good reason to defend it
Somebody should be brave enough to state:
With all of the appropriate delights
Top-level cricket is reserved for whites.

You must be white to wear the proper cap
And have a drink while you watch Boycott bat
And during lunch go down and meet the chap
And slap him on the back and have a chat
And go back up and take a little nap
And finally he's run out and that's that.
Yes, that was Boycott's finest innings yet:
Those fifteen runs that took three days to get.

Boycott was born to give the Wisden bores
The perfect subject for their lucubrations.
He is the average oaf whose average scores
Are averaged out in their long computations,
Reducing you to helpless yawns and snores.
Like small boys spotting trains in railway stations,
They fall into the deep trance of the mystic
Merely by contemplating some statistic.

The Thunderer survives. To celebrate
It seems the editor must walk the plank.
You'd think that Gray's Inn Road was Watergate.
If driving there you should go in a tank.
The building's angled walls of armour plate
Look harder to bust open than a bank,
But in the corridors strong men now stagger
Their shoulders having grown the sudden dagger.

By having Rupert Murdoch as proprietor
Printing House Square hoped for some meed of peace,
But even if at first the storms grew quieter
From disputation there was no release.
And now your average *Times* man thinks a rioter
Is lucky to be fighting just the police,
Such is the measure of the relaxation
Achieved under the Murdoch dispensation.

When I dispraise my great compatriot
It's not just out of envy for his loot,
Though if it's good he should have such a lot
Still tends to strike me as a point that's moot.
For how his influence sends things to pot,
However, one's concern must be acute.
The centre cannot hold, things fall apart
And everybody ends up in the cart.

Howe's Budget pacifies the Tory Wets,
And at the same time seems fine to the Drys.
In other words, the PM's hedged her bets
If only for the breathing space it buys
While everyone who's got a job forgets
Roy Jenkins once was roughly twice as wise
A Chancellor as is Sir Geoffrey Howe –
A fact she'd rather like suppressed just now.

The Peace of Bishop's Stortford and Howe's Budget –
In each case the effect might not be meant,
But if it's by the outcome that you judge it
You must ascribe it to the one intent:
Don't rock the party boat or even nudge it,
Bail as a team until the squall is spent,
And when the central threat has blown away
We'll fight among ourselves another day.

At Hillhead Jenkins slips back in the polls,
The press rehearses doom for the Alliance.
Great play is made with the electoral rolls.
Psephology is cried up as a science.
E'en as the cookie crumbles the bell tolls.
The gaff is blown and fate brooks no defiance.
One question, though, if anybody cares:
How often do *you* answer questionnaires?

Never, of course, because you are too bright,
As most Hillheaders are cracked up to be.
Which could just mean, if I am guessing right,
There's still a vote there for the SDP,

Though if it will be all right on the night
We'll simply have to wait ten days and see,
While Jenkins stands increasingly alone
On those cold concave doorsteps of grey stone.

V

Supposedly a media creation,
The SDP's now patronized in print
From all sides as a hollow aberration,
A candy zero like a Polo Mint.
At best such lofty talk's an irritation,
At worst it sets the heart as hard as flint,
But summed up it must prove, if Jenkins conquers,
That stuff about the media was bonkers.

Columbia flames spaceward from the Cape,
Aboard it a glass box of moths and bees.
As Jenkins makes a last lunge for the tape
The press and pollsters are in agonies.
The free-fall moths still buzz in tip-top shape.
The bees just hang there looking hard to please.
Both moths and bees go nowhere in a hurry,
Bees in a sulk and moths in a fine flurry.

So what's the point of effort in that case?
Why didn't old Roy stay home and write books
Instead of pounding through this paper chase,
The sweat of which does little for his looks?
The bees have got the right approach to space:
The moths flap uselessly like fish on hooks . . .
The tension's fearful and one feels no better for
Committing such a thoroughly mixed metaphor.

The die is cast but does not yet lie still
And while it rolls it's hard to count the dots.
The shape of politics for good or ill
Lies in the gift of a few thousand Scots
Of whom a certain element will fill

Their ballot papers in with jokes and blots –
But that's Democracy and worth preserving
Although at times incredibly unnerving.

Roy Jenkins wins and history is made
Or if not made at least it's modified.
The dingbats straight away are on parade
With Benn at his most foam-flecked and pop-eyed,
Saying the SDP has overplayed
Its hand and now must go out with the tide.
Thus King Canute spake as his feet got wetter,
But further up the beach his court knew better.

But now a comic opera interlude
Wins our attention from cosmetic cares.
The generals in the Argentine, though rude
And cruel and prone to giving themselves airs,
Have in the foreign field so far been shrewd,
Confining lunacy to home affairs.
Their latest coup arouses less admonishment
Than universal open-mouthed astonishment.

The Falkland Islands taken by invasion?
So what's there to invade excepting sheep?
It's no great wonder that on this occasion
The Foreign Office got caught half asleep.
Deuced awkward that the natives are Caucasian
And what is more, we're told, resolved to keep,
Though so far-flung in crude terms of locality,
All ties intact of British nationality.

Storms in a teacup are a sign of spring
And few can take the Falkland business seriously.
Wavers of flags will have their little fling,
Diehard imperialists will speak imperiously,
And one sincerely trusts that the whole thing
Will fade away the way it came, mysteriously.
Meanwhile by long tradition Oxford's won
The boat race and there's been whole hours of sun.

Dick Saunders at the age of forty-eight
Wins the Grand National. Excellent result.
We raddled crocks excitedly spectate
Dismissing youth as no more than a cult.
The horses nosedive at a frightful rate.
It's carnage yet one can't help but exult
As David Coleman, fiftyish and cocky,
Congratulates 'the oldest winning jockey'.

Nobody wants to be a fading power
And countries are like men in that regard.
A nation brushed aside as past its hour
Even if that is true will take it hard.
The sceptic courts a sojourn in the Tower
Of London with a yeoman as a guard.
War fever mounts. All one can do is watch it
And hope that this time our side doesn't botch it.

The Secretary of Defence, John Nott,
Has made a whopping balls-up in the House.
The Foreign Secretary's on the spot,
Loudly accused of being short of nous.
The top gunboat exponent of the lot,
A prancing lion where once crouched a mouse,
Is Michael Foot, who now speaks for the nation
In this alleged Hour of Humiliation.

Lord Carrington presents the dazed PM
With his own head upon a point of honour.
The nitwit Nott stays at his post *pro tem*
Though in the long term he must be a goner.
Poor Thatcher makes a mighty show of phlegm
At all the bad luck that's been heaped upon her,
Announcing, as the Fleet prepares to sail,
We must not even *think* that we might fail.

Such rhetoric is brave if weirdly phrased,
Though fustian it's backed up by legality,
Yet what can't help but leave you slightly fazed
Is the persistent air of unreality.

Those china eyes of hers were always glazed
But now have the glaucoma of fatality,
As if what happened on the field of Mars
Could somehow be predicted by the stars.

Proud ancient Athens sent a sure-fire mission
So strong it could not fail to overawe.
Its name was the Sicilian Expedition.
It lost them the Peloponnesian War.
Ill fortune and long distance worked attrition
Not even the most timorous foresaw.
Thucydides was there and for posterity
Wrote down the consequences of temerity.

As those Greeks at Piraeus in the dawn
Cheered when the galleys raced towards Aegina,
Our patriots now lean on the car horn.
The little motor boats from the marina
Are teeming in each other's wash like spawn.
All wish the Fleet fair winds for Argentina.
Invincible looks worthy of its name.
The battleship *Repulse* once looked the same.

I don't doubt our atomic submarines
Can sink their diesel ones in nothing flat.
We sold them all our second-best machines
And man to man should put them on the mat.
But time and place are with the Argentines:
Say what you like there is no blinking that.
We'll take two weeks to get to where we're going –
Which means that until then there's just no knowing.

Two weeks of spring in England, with the hedges
Acquiring flowering hawthorn like dried snow.
The lawns with rows of daffodils at the edges
In Cambridge look too succulent to mow.
I'm told at night they jack them up on wedges
And pull the grass down slightly from below.
Millions of tourists sip at a serenity
Made all the sweeter by the world's obscenity.

Two weeks in the museum and the garden
That some say bitterly Britain's become.
They say Dutch elm disease is rife in Arden.
Britannia's teeth have grown loose in the gum.
The brain gets softer as the arteries harden.
There's too much store set by detached aplomb . . .
So think the vitalists and spoil for action,
Finding in hesitation no attraction.

Two weeks go by and there's no other news
Except what centres on the vexed Malvinas.
If UN Resolution 502's
To mean a thing the next move's Argentina's.
The Yanks, alas, are either short of clues
Or scared of being taken to the cleaners.
Al Haig, while six quacks monitor his ticker,
Sits on the fence through which his allies bicker.

South Georgia falls to us with no life lost.
Our Fleet is justly proud but Fleet Street's prouder.
The jingo hacks want war at any cost:
Abaft cleared desks they perch on kegs of powder.
At last the US gets its wires uncrossed.
Sighs of relief are heaved but somewhat louder
The first bombs fall. It may or may not suit you,
But those who are about to die salute you.

VI

As fifty thousand people in Warsaw
March for Walesa and for Solidarity,
They rate, beside the South Atlantic war,
The same space as a fun run staged for charity.
The Falklands dwarf even El Salvador,
Which ought to be a ludicrous disparity,
But clear-cut issues fought out to a finish
Have sex appeal no slaughter can diminish.

Port Stanley's airstrip is the first thing hurt,
Bombed by a Vulcan and a pack of Harriers.
No skin and hair fly with the grass and dirt.
Unharmed back to Ascension and the carriers
Go all the planes. This war seems snugly girt,
Like some Grand Prix, with crash-proof safety barriers.
It would be fun to watch it on TV
Instead of that chap from the MOD.

You couldn't call the way he talks laconic,
Which mainly means not to be too effusive.
What few words come from this guy are subsonic.
While waiting for the point you grow abusive.
And yet it adds up to a national tonic
For reasons which to my mind prove elusive,
Unless based on a firm belief that God
Speaks to one people and spares them the rod.

Indeed the other side is first to find
Even a sand-tray war costs full-sized lives.
Summoned by noise of a familiar kind
The Exterminating Angel now arrives.
Perhaps, although like Justice he is blind,
It riles him that the gauchos fight with knives:
At any rate, they are the ones he picks
To prove that punctured ships go down like bricks.

Their cruiser the *Belgrano* takes a hit
Opening up her side to the cold sea,
Which enters in and there's an end of it.
Hundreds of sailors either can't swim free
Or can but freeze, and prayers don't help a bit,
Nor raise the temperature by one degree.
The fire is just to burn those who don't drown
As too full of young voices she goes down.

This is the finest hour of *Mail* and *Star*.
The *Sun* especially is cock-a-hoop,
Shouting commands as if at Trafalgar.
Swab out the trunnion cleats and caulk that poop!

What terrifying warriors they are,
These slewed slop-slingers of the slipshod sloop
El Vino, which each lunchtime takes them south
Into the raging gales of the loud mouth.

A scrivener myself, I should not gripe.
The natural consequence of a free press
Must be that hacks are well paid to write tripe.
One normally feels more scorn than distress
At clichés ready set in slugs of type,
But this exceeds the usual heartlessness:
Faced with a raucous clamour so mind-bending
You wonder if free speech is worth defending.

The war dance falters. Foam dries on the lips
As word by drawn-out word the news comes through:
The *Sheffield*, one of our most modern ships,
A spanking, Sea Dart-armed type 42
Destroyer built to wipe out radar blips,
A Space Invaders expert's dream come true,
Is hit. With what's so far an untold cost
In lives. Has burned. Is given up for lost.

An Etendard released an Exocet
Which duly skimmed the waves as advertised.
Our tabloids wring what mileage they can get
Out of French perfidy, but undisguised
Is their amazement such a classy jet
Flown by these dagos that they've patronized
Should leave the runway, let alone deliver
This thing so clever that it makes you shiver.

Imagination, if it slept before,
Is now awake and fully occupied
By what's occurred and still might be in store.
With closed eyes you can see the way they died:
The bulkheads hot as a reactor core,
The air the same to breathe as cyanide.
And now that the grim news has got us thinking,
Think of the *Canberra* broken-backed and sinking.

With all at risk there is a pause for thought,
But lest the nation's troubled heart grow faint
El Vino without ever leaving port
Fires paper salvoes that confer the taint
Of Traitor on the doubtful. All those caught
Equivocating must dodge yellow paint
Which flies in dollops like wet chamois leathers
Whilst air-burst cardboard shells disgorge white feathers.

My own view is we ought to go ahead
Even though press support brings only shame.
But my view's that of one with a warm bed
While others face the shrapnel and the flame.
What can you do except note with due dread
The other side in this case are to blame
And would, unless constrained to go away,
Keep what they took though talking till Doomsday?

Such elementary thoughts make me feel dull.
Rarely is it so simple to be right.
But for the nonce there is a blessed lull.
It's possible the UN still just might
Ensure we've seen the last cracked-open hull
And fighter plane turned to a fire in flight.
The mind, robbed of its surfeit of raw action,
Spoiled for the real now searches for distraction.

Snooker on television is the moral
Equivalent of war. Man against man,
It is a pitiless yet bloodless quarrel
Racking the nerves behind the deadened pan.
Slowly a break accumulates like coral
Yet has the logic of a battle plan.
Fought out on a flat sea within four walls
Well has this conflict been called chess with balls.

This year the final's between two ex-champs.
Veteran Ray Reardon's cool, calm and collected,
While Alex Higgins twitches and gets cramps
Whenever from his headlong rush deflected.

I'd like to keep a foot in both these camps,
Believing the two styles, deep down, connected.
They fight it to a finish frame by frame
And no one doubts it's more than just a game.

Higgins has won and as the fuss subsides
We realize that a game is all it is:
A fish-tank show of strength by fortune's tides,
A showcase for old smoothness and young fizz,
Where Reardon's neatly brushed short back and sides
Bow out with good grace to a lank-haired whizz,
And from the Crucible, their battlefield,
Nobody needs to go home on a shield.

But now on Friday, 21st of May
We hear what happens in a proper fight.
Eight thousand miles south in San Carlos Bay
The invasion has been going on all night.
Men on both sides have really died today.
The bridgehead's been wide open since first light.
Out in the Sound our gun-line ships pump flak
Through which their planes fly low to the attack.

I'm speaking as an armchair strategist
Who's been through every scrap since Marathon
When I suggest (some colleagues would insist)
Amphibious assaults are just not on
Unless you've got the air clasped in your fist.
This is the biggest gamble since Inchon,
And there the Yanks had more planes than they knew
Quite what to do with. We've got precious few.

Not that the Harrier falls short of being
A modern miracle of engineering.
When it performs you can't grasp what you're seeing:
A frisbee fork-lift truck with power steering,
It floats, flies backwards, stem-turns as if skiing –
The thing's a runabout for Wilma Deering.
The Argentines are suitably outclassed
But still get through by going low and fast.

No pictures except those in the mind's eye
Exist to give some inkling of the scene.
The Skyhawks and Mirages come mast-high,
We're told, but must suppose what those words mean.
Our rockets rush to burst them as they fly
Like thrown milk bottles full of kerosene,
But back along their line of flight the bay
Seeded by bombs grows tall white trees of spray.

So it goes on but can't go on for ever
Without ships hit by something worse than spume.
Brave pilots die in swarms but their endeavour
Is part rewarded when a bomb finds room
Inside the frigate *Ardent*, there to sever
Her spinal column like a lowered boom.
We're also told they've hit the *Antelope*
But that bomb was a dud and she can cope.

VII

It wasn't. Twenty hours from being struck
The *Antelope* erupts in the dark night.
Having no pictures might be our good luck:
Without doubt it's a mesmerizing sight.
The mere sound is enough to make you duck,
But what might really make us choke with fright
Would be to see the troopships the next morning
Still looming there in spite of that grim warning.

Ashore in strength, our soldiers now advance.
The Pope's at Gatwick with the same intention.
It could be said he's taking the same chance
Of getting shot, but let's not even mention
That possibility as the slow dance
Of ritual opens with his condescension
To kiss the tarmac, which this osculation
No doubt excites to transubstantiation.

The Popemobile moves off on its campaign
Of conquest, firing fusillades of prayer.
Appropriate response I find a strain,
Suspecting that this pontiff talks hot air
And only got the part when Michael Caine
Turned cold on the long frocks he'd have to wear.
But thousands of young Catholics seem delighted
As if he were the Beatles reunited.

Without fail every rock-concert-sized crowd
Goes mad while the old boy lays down the law.
It seems that birth control's still not allowed.
Also he deeply disapproves of war.
His fans are all too busy being wowed
To search these propositions for a flaw.
He might as well be singing 'Love me tender'.
They shout and put their hands up in surrender.

Soon now the Argentines will do that too.
Their Skyhawks still punch large holes in our fleet
But in Port Stanley they must know they're through.
The paras and marines slog through the peat
Towards them looking too tough to be true.
A chilling enough spectre of defeat
To make those poor young hungry conscripts wary
About the last stand promised by Galtieri.

Reminding us that it's not over yet
The *Coventry* is lost, and in Bluff Cove
The prospect that has always made one sweat
Comes true. The Skyhawks find their treasure trove:
A loaded troopship, which they promptly set
Ablaze like a defective petrol stove.
We're given just the name, *Sir Galahad*.
No figures, which suggests they might be bad.

That was the nightmare from the very start,
The sea full of drowned soldiers, but the dread
Is dulled by distance to a thing apart.
Israel's ambassador is left for dead

In London, which one tends to take to heart.
He lies there with a bullet in the head.
Israel strikes north into the Lebanon
And instantly another war is on.

Reagan rides into London looking grey
Around the gills at how the world is going.
By this, of course, I do not mean to say
His make-up's worn off and the real skin's showing:
Just that the outer pancake's flaked away
To show the thick foundation wanly glowing,
Cracked by his smile of disbelief at meeting
Lord Hailsham dressed for the official greeting.

If Reagan's jet-black hair seems slightly strange,
What about Hailsham's wig, sword, socks and cape?
The President when dressed to ride the range
Looks odd, but not as weird as a square grape.
For Reagan it must make at least a change
Wondering how they let this nut escape,
As backwards Hailsham goes with a low bow
Showing him where the boys sit down to chow.

The Falklands War ends and Galtieri falls:
His hawk-like features drawn as a wet sheet,
He takes a minimum of curtain calls
And finds, outside the stage door in the street,
That though his mouth continues to spout balls
His tears have made mud pies of his clay feet,
And so he has to crawl instead of walk
Home to a house full of his empty talk.

One counts the hundreds dead in the Atlantic
And feels regretful at the very least,
But as wars go it rated as romantic
Beside the shambles in the Middle East,
Where thousands are dead, maimed or driven frantic
As round Beirut the steel squeeze is increased.
Some say the Jews have been transmogrified
To Nazis, and that this is genocide.

One doesn't have to be a Zionist
To spot the weakness in this parallel.
Begin strikes me as still the terrorist
He started off as and a fool as well,
But bad though things now look, one must insist
That war is war. The Holocaust was Hell.
For Begin, children's deaths seem incidental.
For Adolf Hitler they were fundamental.

The Nazis sought complete obliteration,
Women and children being top priority.
The PLO's a warlike armed formation
Whose goal – we have it on their own authority –
Is Israel's disappearance as a nation.
No nonsense about rights for the minority,
Just dumb insistence that the hated state
Should make its mind up to evaporate.

The Jews won't sit still twice for being slaughtered.
The Palestinians will fight to live.
Justice and mercy will be drawn and quartered.
Things will be done a saint could not forgive.
The towns and cities will be bombed and mortared
Until like hot sand they fall through a sieve,
And on the day that blood turns into wine
There will be peace again in Palestine.

My biblical locutions you'll excuse:
The Royal Birth, if not a new Nativity,
Is everywhere regarded as Good News
Except by those of levelling proclivity,
Who think the common folk do not enthuse
At such shows of elitist exclusivity
From choice, but somehow cheer because they've got to,
Being by glamour too bedazzled not to.

War-leader Thatcher, having proved her nerve,
Now rants of a new spirit sweeping Britain,
But peace is not war and high talk won't serve
For long to stop the biter getting bitten.

Let's hope the lorries don't run short of derv:
Even as this last couplet's being written
The London Tube strike's trumped by British Rail,
Which stops dead too but on a larger scale.

A Borgless Wimbledon soaks up the rain
Which falls like a monsoon arriving late.
Al Haig resigns with every sign of strain:
Someone called Shultz is now in charge at State.
The new prince is named William. The odd train
Starts up again as if to celebrate,
But ASLEF thinks a moving train just fosters
Flexible notions with regard to rosters.

Ray Buckton therefore plans a whole new strike.
Meanwhile the members of the SDP
Mark ballot slips to name the man they'd like
To lead them on the stroll to destiny.
The polls and press say Roy will need a bike:
Young Owen's gone too far ahead to see.
Fuelled by the Falklands Factor Owen's flowered
And left Roy looking rather underpowered.

Most members of the SDP, however,
Joined in the first place to see Roy PM.
No question Dr Owen's very clever:
The elder statesman's still the man for them.
They vote to prove the Falklands business never
Made hazy the true *terminus ad quem*.
The thing that matters is the next election,
Not smart young David's feelings of rejection.

Though disappointed, Owen takes it well.
One might just say the same for McEnroe.
Outplayed by Connors he does not raise hell
But mainly hangs his head in silent woe.
He lurks like a sick crab in a dull shell.
His only tantrum is to drag his toe,
And when a cross-court drive goes nowhere near it
Say 'Fuck it' where the umpire cannot hear it.

Jimbo I've always thought was mighty good.
It's nice to see a champion come back.
But McEnroe, we're told, is such a hood
That when he can't run haywire he goes slack.
He should have smashed his racket to matchwood
And used the jagged handle to attack
The umpire, linesmen, ballboys, Duke of Kent
And so on till his bottled wrath was spent.

For McEnroe, Release of Pent-up Tension
(I quote Mark Cox, player turned commentator)
Is fundamental to the whole dimension
Of polished touch akin to Walter Pater
Which makes John's game so marvellous the mere mention
Of his resemblance to an alligator
Can only mean that genius is beyond us –
Unless, of course, the little bastard's conned us.

VIII

Off home flies McEnroe in deep dejection,
His face a sweet potato cooked in steam.
But this time his behaviour bore inspection,
The usual nightmare merely a bad dream.
One looks upon him almost with affection
And hopes the England World Cup football team
Will similarly take the setback stoically
If it transpires they don't do so heroically.

A goalless draw with Spain wipes out the chance
England was in with. Miffed at how we muffed it,
The British fans, deprived now of romance,
Regain the sad hotels in which they've roughed it
And ponder at great length the fact that France
Was the one team to whom we really stuffed it.
Many a fan's bald head shows the deep crease
Made by the impact of the Spanish police.

Young men of Britain sleep now at Goose Green
In plastic bags lined up in a long grave.
Large speeches were engendered by that scene
Of how our Comprehensive lads were brave.
But now, as if the war had never been,
The thrill is gone and when yobs misbehave
In youthful ways that tend towards the strenuous,
Thatcher's New Spirit looks a trifle tenuous.

A young man penetrates Buck House by night
And duns the monarch for a cigarette.
It's her behalf on which we all take fright,
Loath to admit the idea makes us sweat
Of some dark whisper asking for a light . . .
But this chill prospect's easily offset,
For though the endless train strike makes you chafe
It means rail travel's absolutely safe.

The man who shook the Queen down for a fag
Is nabbed and named unsmilingly as Fagan.
Though young, it seems he rates as an old lag.
He's got a dossier on him like Lord Kagan.
He's dropped in several times to chew the rag
And strolled around at leisure like Carl Sagan.
An expert on the palace architecture
Perhaps he wanted her to hear him lecture.

The police, alas, were clueless by comparison.
One of the cops was in bed with a maid.
While as for all that military garrison,
It turns out they do nothing but parade.
You'd think that they might detail the odd Saracen
To park outside her bedroom . . . Feeling frayed,
The Queen perhaps is not best placed to hear
Her personal detective is a queer.

No doubt she sort of sussed but did not mind,
Certain at least the poor klutz wasn't chasing
The tweenies, but now that the clot's resigned
So publicly, it must be less than bracing

For her to know the best men they could find
To guard against the danger that she's facing
From acid, knife, gun, gas, napalm and bomb
Had rings run round them by a peeping Tom.

Foot plumps for ASLEF but as if in spite
The TUC does not and the strike's broken.
Foot's coiffe should go a purer shade of white
Unless his fiery gesture was a token
To make him look a tough nut in a fight
For all those gritty doctrines he has spoken
On that day when they have to be renounced
And Arthur Scargill's strike bid must be trounced.

But Arthur's rhetoric is like his hair.
Though spurious, transparent and bombastic,
It's legal and has some right to be there.
The threat it poses to the state is drastic
But one democracy's equipped to bear.
He's less fanatical than he's fantastic.
That puffball pan's so openly ambitious
Only a stocking mask could make it vicious.

Indeed his nimbus of elated strands
Bespeaks not just the patience of a saint
But holiness. It balances no hands.
The halo Giotto botched with thick gold paint
On Arthur's a UFO that never lands,
A cap of gossamer you might find quaint
But can't deny has something brave about it –
He's sparing us the way he'd look without it.

The real and lasting threat to national sanity
Has no objection to remaining nameless.
Among its vices you could not count vanity.
On that score its participants are blameless.
They aim to wake your sense of shared humanity
By perpetrating outrages so shameless
That you will grant a view must have validity
Which gives rise to such murderous stupidity.

In Knightsbridge a car bomb with up-to-date
Remote controls proves powerful competition
For horsemen wearing plumes and silver plate,
While up in Regent's Park a similar mission
Is carried out with a success as great,
Ensuring, at the moment of ignition,
Musicians who have never hurt a soul
Are shown up in their true repressive role.

For what's a bandsman, when all's said and done,
If not a soldier of a certain sort?
What is a trombone but a type of gun?
What is a bandstand but a kind of fort?
Objectively, the difference is none:
These men were troops no matter what they thought,
And as for sleepy listening civilians –
They symbolize the acquiescent millions

Who now unquestionably come awake
And wonder for a week stretched to nine days
If this is not more than the nerves can take.
The horses' wounds bared to the public gaze
Cause many a grave thoughtful head to shake.
Dumb pain is real but how strange that it weighs
Thus heavily, when humans ask what mattered
So much it left them or their loved ones shattered.

Did Cromwell's ruthlessness bring this to pass,
A woman crawling with a face of blood?
Did the Earl of Essex raise a storm of glass
When he set fire to houses of thatched mud?
A bugle boy for being armed with brass
Was pricked to die. What caused that? The Great Flood?
The grievous debt goes back to the beginning
That makes these men more sinned against than sinning.

The guilty live, the innocent lie dead:
The summer sun shines warmly on them all.
In Biarritz it shines on my bald head.
My scalp accepts the photons as they fall.

No Scargill I, I let my skull turn red,
Building my daughters a thick sand sea wall.
They crouch behind it, clinging to the notion
Somehow their father can control the ocean.

I can't stop waves, or much else, reaching them.
Relieved they're not in Belfast or Beirut
I'm flattered in a way some might condemn
To find their sense of beauty so acute.
Each shell's looked at as if it were a gem,
Held to the ear, then blown on like a flute.
By those too young to know the world is cruel
A cured sea horse is treasured as a jewel.

The London papers bring the usual news –
Inflation's down yet unemployment climbs.
But here the gulf's laid out in greens and blues:
Lapis, fresh lettuce and the juice of limes.
Lulled by the heat, one's body cells refuse
To wait for the return of better times:
They take their holiday though deprivation
Should devastate the luckless British nation.

The spirit's willing but the flesh is weak.
Skin will be free and easy if it can.
Through downturned mouth with deep concern we speak:
The epidermis has its selfish plan
To look less like the thick end of a leek.
The height of its ambition is a tan.
For two weeks while the tide goes up and down
I watch it and react by turning brown.

In Biarritz the sun sets like a peach
That ripens and ignites towards the water.
Waves which were blue like denims when they bleach
Turn silver as a newly minted quarter.
Absorbed by darkness outwards from the beach,
Like lemon ice licked by my younger daughter
White light is ineluctably consumed,
Ripples erased. Desired and therefore doomed.

Something fulfilled this hour, loved or endured –
A line of Auden's that burns in the mind.
By now just like the sea horse I am cured.
Having acquired a dark and brittle rind,
I feel resigned again, if not inured,
To how the real world out there is unkind,
As flying back to it I read Camus
Amazed how he continues to come true.

The innocent, he once wrote, in our age
Must justify themselves. That still sounds right.
The Jews in Paris now take centre stage.
A restaurant is reamed with gelignite.
The elders might express old-fashioned rage
But modern anti-Semites are more polite,
Claiming that Zionism must be fought
Wherever Jews might offer it support.

Thus reason the Jew-baiters of the Left
As once the Right spoke in *Je suis partout.*
The warp's formed by the same thread as the weft:
Woven together, they are what they do.
Between them there's no fundamental cleft,
A fact appreciated by Camus
Whom both sides honoured with their deepest hate –
In my view a most enviable fate.

IX

In Britain the health workers strike for pay
Which surely in all conscience they've got coming.
The harvest's in and farmers stack the hay.
Around the rotting fruit the wasps are humming.
The CBI says Thatcher must give way.
It's all so soothing, not to say benumbing.
England is now and history is elsewhere.
Most of the rough stuff isn't here, it's there.

It's there in Israel where General Sharon
Even by Begin's found intransigent.
In Gdansk the water cannon are turned on
As if cold spit could wash away cement.
Now Arafat with all his options gone
Concedes perhaps it's time his people went.
The PLO might recognize Israel.
The Poles pretend Walesa's not in jail.

But history here at home is the two Krays
Let out of clink to mourn their saintly mother.
The boys for all their rough-and-tumble ways
Both loved her as they never loved another.
People repaired with grafts, pins, splints and stays
Still can't decide which was the nicer brother –
The Kray who'd chat you up before he grabbed you
And held you helpless, or the Kray who stabbed you.

The other big event is Poet Sue,
A scribbling Cambridge undergraduette,
Who as the French once went mad for Minou
Is cried up as the greatest talent yet
By dons who should have better things to do,
You might think, than to stand there getting wet
Drooling about the girl's supreme facility
For sonnets of Shakespearean fertility.

It seems she churns them out like a machine
That manufactures plastic souvenirs,
And on the whole that's roughly what they mean:
They're so banal you can't believe your ears.
They echo everything that's ever been
Created in the last five hundred years.
Sue's poor brain is a boneyard, a Sargasso,
A pulping mill, a collage by Picasso.

The dons who praise her were once Leavisites,
Slow to admire and vicious in dismissal.
What aberration has brought on these flights
Of rapture as they cluster round a thistle

And call the thing a rose and spend their nights
Composing articles that make you whistle,
Since even Leavis's worst panegyrics
For Ronald Bottrall didn't sound like lyrics?

The dons are punished for their dereliction
With dour gibes from the joyless Donald Davie
Who demonstrates at length Sue's vaunted diction
Tastes thin compared with dehydrated gravy,
While as for her alleged powers of depiction . . .
The dons must feel they've been shelled by the navy.
He calls them symptoms of a deep malaise
As Cambridge English falls on evil days.

But dons were ever shaky in their taste.
Davie himself is nuts for Ezra Pound.
It's not on judgement their careers are based.
They tend the fields but they break no new ground.
Old Leavis thought that writers could be 'placed'
Even while they still lived and moved around.
Alas, he was so tone-deaf that his scrutiny
Made spinning poets in their graves plot mutiny.

The reason why the dons find Sue prodigious
Is patent when you see a photograph.
No wonder they forgot to be prestigious:
The girl's so pretty that she makes you laugh.
I trust no don involved will get litigious
For being likened to a lovesick calf –
I understand completely how the urge'll
Emerge to call a virgin a new Virgil.

A summer madness that began in spring
The Sue Affair's explained by a don's life.
His winter schedule is a humdrum thing
And often the same goes for the don's wife.
Though every day the sweet girl students bring
Their essays which he goes through like a knife,
The whole deal's on the intellectual level
And busy hands do no work for the Devil.

But then the crocus drives up to the sun
And Sue puts on a floating cotton dress
And that fine friendship as of priest and nun
Erupts into a secular distress.
Those sonnets that she turns out by the ton
Must mean the girl's a gifted poetess:
Sue's such a doll she'd make Professor Carey
Say that she wrote like Dante Alighieri.

Sue's bubble reputation having popped,
Her teachers must wipe soap out of their eyes,
But one would hate to see those young wings cropped
Merely because her mentors were not wise.
If that compulsive gush of hers is stopped
It ought to be because she's learned to prize
The disciplines that temper and anneal,
Growing slow blooms of strength inside the steel.

There's energy in Sue's headlong slapdash
Which most of our young careful craftsmen lack.
They watch their language and do nothing rash.
Crushed in the boot and wound tight on the rack,
Pressed thin with weights and strung up for the lash,
Each poem is a puzzle that won't crack.
Yielding its meaning drop by anguished drop
Until, drained dry, it dies with a full stop.

One image per two stanzas is the ration,
Though some there are who don't risk even that.
Such level surfaces are hard to fashion.
It takes a kind of built-in thermostat
To ward off sudden puffs of wayward passion
Which might cause pimples in what should be flat,
Protected in all possible directions
Against the threat of critical objections.

Better to write in quite another style
And be accused of sentimental clowning.
Better to court the condescending smile
Of that drear ghost still droning on in Downing.

In Italy for all too short a while
I grapple with the greatest work of Browning.
What chance would it have stood against those wits
Of our day whose chief skill is to pick nits?

But even Browning sweated for more density
Than line could hold which brain could still retain.
Astonished by the man's sustained intensity
I see the packed force of that hardwood grain,
But find his parquetry's compressed immensity
Undone by a pervading sense of strain:
The book runs such tight rings around itself
No wonder it sits heavy on the shelf.

Perhaps there's now no hope of being clear
Unless one's also hopelessly naive;
An air of easiness is bought too dear
If cheap effects are all it can achieve;
But in Ferrara I stand very near
The kind of art in which I can believe –
That generous tribute to a mean employer,
Cossa's great frescoes in the Schifanoia.

Faded to pastel they're still full of light.
Each panel has an effortless proportion.
It's love of life that makes those faces bright.
The skill is consummate without distortion.
Sure of its knowledge like a bird in flight,
Such perfect freedom feels no need of caution,
And so the teeming polychrome quotidian
Enjoys perpetually its just meridian.

But just only as art. Injustice then,
As rank as now, had no redress at all.
Below those stately dames and lolling men
A Jew sprints for his life across the wall,
Insistently reminding you of when,
In recent days still well within recall,
So many innocent were naked runners
Towards the mass graves and the machine-gunners.

X

The past gives solace and rededication
But offers no escape from harsh reality.
Back in the present, all one's information
Suggests the air of gracious informality
The Quattrocento brought to relaxation
Would now seem strained whatever the locality –
There are no independent city states
Equipped to keep the world outside their gates.

From West Beirut into the waiting ships
The PLO pulls out on television.
With gestures of one cashing in his chips
According to some tactical decision
Their leader puckers those unlovely lips,
But only fools would whistle in derision
As his sad captains all get kissed goodbye –
Mere military defeat won't stop *that* guy.

I must say he's no oil painting, Yasser,
Or if he is then it's of something weird.
Nothing would make him look as good as Nasser
But still you'd think he'd try a *proper* beard.
For headgear an entire antimacassar
Arranged so that his features disappeared
Would do more than that tea towel does at present
To make his aspect generally more pleasant.

One day no doubt he will be played on screen
By some young ringer for Alain Delon.
Most people look at odds with what they mean:
We're bound to simplify them when they're gone.
Golda Meir's reported to have been
Transformed by Ingrid Bergman to a swan,
But now, with Bergman dead at sixty-five,
No one in *Casablanca*'s left alive.

It was a clumsy film with a bum script
Yet watching it once more I sit and dream.

The cigarettes they smoke aren't filter-tipped.
Bogie pours whisky in a steady stream.
Small vices. It's by virtue they are gripped.
Of self-indulgence there is not a gleam.
She wavers but he has the strength of ten
As time goes by and Sam plays it again.

Reagan and Thatcher ought to be like that.
Instead they have a frightful falling-out.
The Russian pipeline has inspired the spat,
Or that's what spokesmen *say* it's all about.
In private Maggie's spitting like a cat.
In public, as per usual, she says nowt,
Calling the USA our greatest friend
While thinking its top man the living end.

Scargill and Benn say let's break Tebbit's law.
Jim Callaghan less bluntly says that too.
Israel and Syria might go to war.
The boggled mind wonders what else is new.
In Berne the Polish Embassy's front door
Is opened while some breakfast is pushed through:
The terrorists are hauled out bearing traces
Of the omelette which has blown up in their faces.

But wait a second. Don't you find it odd
So dumb a move comes from pro-liberal Poles?
Are these a self-selected awkward squad
Or has the other side smartly switched roles?
To keep Walesa endlessly in quod
It might help if more tender-hearted souls
Thought *Solidarnosc* meant armed insurrection
Against the Party's warm clasp of affection.

It's possible one's getting paranoid:
Walesa's just too big to disappear.
But murder's been a frequently employed
Political technique in this past year.
To show the Government what to avoid
Sicilian *mafiosi* arouse fear

By gunning down the general sent to face them
Before he even gets a chance to chase them.

Dalla Chiesa's death convinces me –
I think that all in all and on the whole
I won't go righting wrongs in Sicily.
Nor will a few lines praising a brave Pole
Do very much to set his people free.
Perhaps a phantom quest's the one sane goal –
As now the *Sun* claims to have found Lord Lucan
In deepest jungle with tapir and toucan.

The Jungle Fugitive's a Fleet Street thriller
That Martin Bormann starred in last time round.
Embezzler on the lam and missing killer
Swathed in lianas are abruptly found.
One day no doubt they'll bump into Glenn Miller,
So many scribes are covering the ground.
He'll be with Harold Holt and all the rest
Back to the crew of the *Marie Celeste.*

No news is good news and fake news is fun
Or would be if the bad news caused less strain.
To stop us laughing too long at the *Sun*
Another DC10 comes down in Spain.
The Lebanon's Gemayel lived by the gun.
He puts the gun down and is promptly slain,
While in her palace chapel Princess Grace
Too soon lies dead in high-necked silk and lace.

Our big affair was over years ago
And merits no more than this brief report.
I claimed her for my own in *Rear Window*
And from the Odeon walked lost in thought
The long way home exuding love's hot glow.
Believing Rainier was far too short,
I gave her up in fury mixed with grief
The seventh time I saw *To Catch a Thief.*

Flying above Beirut towards Bombay
By night en route to faraway Peking
One's well aware that earlier today
Down there the corpses were still quivering.
The most the Israelis are prepared to say
Is that the Christians had their little fling
Unsupervised, with awkward consequences
For Muslims not equipped with barbed-wire fences.

Thousands of blameless people lying dead,
The State of Israel's credit well-nigh wrecked,
And all of it on Begin's bullet head
Who should have seen his duty to protect
Civilian lives if his invasion led
To the point where each and every local sect
Was tempted to vent pent-up animosity
By staging the odd small-scale mass atrocity.

The least that Begin and Sharon can do
Is step down and donate their brains to science.
What few friends Israel has left urge them to
But neither hero seems moved to compliance.
The Knesset is a Hebrew hullabaloo,
The blunderers are childish in defiance,
But for the nonce I put off shame and pity
Standing entranced in the Forbidden City.

For Mrs Thatcher's visit the Chinese
Have laid on a Grade Three official greeting.
Which doesn't mean the bum's rush or the freeze:
She gets an honour guard at the first meeting.
But not much bunting flutters in the breeze.
Tiananmen Square contains no special seating.
Instead there is a lot of open space
With here and there a mildly curious face.

She's here to pin them down about Hong Kong.
She'd like to have a written guarantee.
The PM's habit is to come on strong.
The Chinese instinct is to wait and see.

Any idea the business won't take long
Ebbs when the welcome turns out so low key.
China in that respect remains immutable –
The people speak Chinese and look inscrutable.

The great Hall of the People is the venue
For a fifteen-course State Banquet every night.
There isn't any need to read the menu:
You take a pinch of everything in sight.
It all tastes at least wonderful and when you
Happen upon a dish that's sheer delight
Just go on eating while they bring you more.
They'll keep that up until you hit the floor.

Shown how by locals in black Beatles suits
We find out what to chew and what to suck.
First having added sauce and onion shoots
We fold the pancake round the Peking Duck.
Maddened by fish lips and sliced lotus roots
The journalists eat like a rugby ruck.
Even our diplomats up there with Her
Tuck in so fast their chopsticks are a blur.

A thousand million ordinary Chinese
Are outside staunchly doing what they're told.
They'd never even dream of meals like these.
It's luxury for them just to grow old.
From dawn to dusk the streets swarm with belled bees.
I hire a bike and join them, feeling bold
And bulking large against the average male
As if I were a wobbly, two-wheeled whale.

Petite they are and easy on the eye,
This quarter of the world's whole population.
The same seems even more true in Shanghai.
Each city stuns you like a whole new nation.
They march together under a red sky
Towards a dream of human transformation.
It's awe-inspiring yet one has to say
One's heart goes out still to the student Wei.

Young Wei it was who, raised as a Red Guard,
Looked back on his achievements with remorse.
With Mao set to cash in his Party card
Deng and the boys announced a change of course.
The student Wei invited ten years hard
Saying they'd got the cart before the horse:
If freedom came first, progress might begin.
He pulled his ten years and five more thrown in.

XI

If only freedom had a sharper taste.
In Hong Kong kneeling by my father's grave
It's not of his life I regret the waste
But my life he kept safe by being brave.
Even in slavery he was not disgraced,
But self-reproach goes through me like a wave
For all the precious daylight I let spill
While he lies tightly locked in that steep hill.

As Thatcher's VC10 with me aboard
Spears up and doubles westward from Kai Tak
At 30,000 feet I still feel floored
By China and make large plans to go back.
It wasn't Communism I adored:
It was the beauty too refined to crack
From history's hammer blows, and yet possessed
In common, everywhere made manifest.

I never knew the sky was full of dust
Above Peking and turned plum at sunset
While all the palace roofs acquired a crust
Of crumbling honeycomb. If I forget
The details or confuse them as one must,
That first sigh of assent is with me yet.
In China though the mind recoils offended
One's visual range can't help but be extended.

With due allowances, the same's applied
To local artists since the Shang at least.
No bronze bell has been cast or silk bolt dyed
If not with reference to the visual feast
Spread out what still must seem the whole world wide
Each day that dawns where else but in the East?
A boundlessness which suffers no real border
Except the outline of an ideal order.

Sung pictures fix my dreams of public art:
Intensely subtle, spaciously compact,
Produced by an elite not set apart,
The theory left implicit in the fact,
A measured naturalness felt from the heart,
The intellect controlled by natural tact –
Schooled to the limit yet prepared to meet
Halfway the average cyclist in the street.

The cyclist, one need hardly add, sees few
Fine paintings from one year's end to the next,
But still the small extent to which his view
Of local architecture has been vexed
By modern public buildings must be due
To precepts found in no official text,
And least of all in Mao's Little Red Book –
Which you can't buy however hard you look.

Yes, Mao has been reduced from god to man.
He's back to being ordinary flesh.
His mausoleum's small extractor fan
Must now work overtime to keep him fresh.
The Party's cranking out a whole new plan
In which, they say, the word and deed will mesh.
Good luck to them and let's hope Wei gets sprung
In time to share the wealth while he's still young.

We've flown so far that distances deceive
But back in the real world we left behind
The demonstrators march through Tel Aviv.
Sharon and Begin still have not resigned,

But ask their best young people to believe
They never had a massacre in mind.
It must be true since who'd be such a klutz?
Which leaves you thinking they must both be nuts.

There's uproar in the Bundesrepublik
As Schmidt's brought down. Some say he'll get back in
Stronger than ever, others he's so weak
There's just no chance that he can save his skin.
These latter prove correct. Schmidt's up the creek
Without a paddle and Herr Kohl must win.
All those refreshed by Schmidt's astringent attitude
Must now adapt to Kohl's gift for the platitude.

Though Kohl's arrival means there's one bore more
The net effect seems no worse than narcosis.
We know from sub-Orwellian folklore
That bombast by a process of osmosis
Corrupts the social fabric to the core,
That rhetoric is verbal halitosis –
And yet one still tends to be more afraid
Of forthright men who call a spade a spade.

In Rome some group propounding the belief
That baiting Jews is simply common sense
Creates the optimum amount of grief
By firing shots at minimal expense
Into a crowd of worshippers. Though brief
The sense of satisfaction is intense:
Just one dead child can seem like a whole lot
When that's the only pogrom that you've got.

You know just where you are with men like these.
They say they want to kill you and they mean it.
In Ireland when they nail you through the knees
You know they've got a point because you've seen it.
Be grateful there are no more mysteries:
Thugs hold the slate and you must help them clean it.
You wanted honest politics? They're here.
Answer the door. What have you got to fear?

In Poland where all terror's state controlled
The time for Solidarity has come
To be outlawed. Leaders left in the cold
Until their lips turned purple and tongues numb
In dribs and drabs are let loose to grow old
As proof it's wiser to be deaf and dumb
When there's few friends outside to be inspired
And room for them inside if so desired.

But though the days are quicker to grow dark
In Europe now the year starts bowing out,
The flow of dreadful news lifts up an ark
Of hope as all good men combine to shout
Hosannahs for Prince Andrew and Koo Stark,
Who when the chips are down are not in doubt
That what needs doing when the world looks bleak
Is best done on the island of Mustique.

Too bad that jealous Fleet Street crabs the act.
Andrew deserves a break with his show-stopper,
In view of all the dreary weeks he hacked
Around the Falklands with his lonely chopper.
Nevertheless you have to face the fact
Young Koo's the next thing to a teenybopper:
Highly unsuitable and, if adorable
From certain angles, all the more deplorable.

Page Three pin-ups and skin-flick clips of Koo
Are dug out so the Palace might take note
That Koo viewed in the long term just won't do
Though in the short term she would stun a stoat.
We're told the Queen has carpeted Andrew
And warned him not to act the giddy goat.
How do the papers get this information?
Let's hope not by nocturnal infiltration.

Gdansk erupts but martial law's imposed
To boost the standard military rule.
The Lenin Shipyard wound is not quite closed
But treatment nowadays is prompt if cruel.

The Zomos leave the area well hosed
With noxious matter flushed down the cesspool.
When Jaruzelski reads the fever chart
He'll see the outbreak stymied at the start.

At home the NUR's lost Sidney Weighell.
The SDP has lost points in the polls.
For parties needing TV time I feel
It's mad to have a Conference that rolls
Instead of staying put, while the appeal
Of packing up each night as for the hols
Is hard to see, unless they're taking pains
To prove that Shirley Williams can catch trains.

More serious than polls for the Alliance,
Roy's Statutory Incomes Policy
Is greeted with a vote of non-compliance,
Thus demonstrating that the SDP
Is not just for a gang of famous giants
But ordinary folk like you and me –
Stout thinking, yet the move, if not divisive,
Can't help at this stage seeming indecisive.

But John De Lorean shows more than strain
In several parts of that uplifted face.
The handcuffs induce shame on top of pain
As in Los Angeles he falls from grace.
Busted with many kilos of cocaine
Packed neatly in a custom pigskin case,
He's proved his gull-winged dream car always flew
On snowy puffs of powder from Peru.

And there but for the grace of God go I
Who also in an excess of belief
Am swept up in wild schemes that I swear by
And feel the impact when they come to grief.
But then the raucous critical outcry
Condemns one as more mountebank than thief,
Unless one deals with state funds like De Lorean
And fiddles them like Sallust the historian.

The artist when he claims the Right to Fail
Just means the risk he takes is a sure bet.
Success occurs on an eternal scale.
The lack of it we instantly forget.
The man of action's not free to avail
Himself of such a useful safety net:
He bites the sawdust with the floodlights shining.
The crowd stays put to watch the vultures dining.

XII

A fact which Arthur Scargill demonstrates
By calling on his membership to strike.
Most of the men down mines are Arthur's mates –
He fights on their behalf and that they like,
However much his bumptious manner grates –
But now they tell him to get on his bike.
From lower chin to fairy-floss beret
His visage holds more egg than a soufflé.

You'd almost think 'poor Arthur' were it not
That Solidarity's new riots show
How little chance a free trade union's got
Once fear is planted and has time to grow.
There's no need nowadays to fire a shot.
Just make them run. They've got nowhere to go.
The hoses gush, the truncheons rise and fall
And where a thousand marched, a hundred crawl.

The movement is just two years old today
And looks already paralysed with age.
That fine collective courage drains away
Into a helpless, inward-turning rage.
The price of protest gets too high to pay.
You shake the bars but cannot shift the cage.
Only the young can be brave as they wish
When one-time physicists are selling fish.

Atomic bombs are our first-string defence
Against all this. A reassuring sign
Is that they're backed up by Intelligence:
From GCHQ any foe's phone line
In two ticks can be tapped at his expense.
A man employed there says it works just fine,
And if he sounds a trifle well rehearsed
It's just because he told the Russians first.

One secret, though, the Russians couldn't keep
A moment longer even if they tried.
Brezhnev might well be more than just asleep.
It's reasonably certain he has died.
The time has come for crocodiles to weep
And stir the bucket of formaldehyde.
The last spark has winked out in that great brain
Which once did Stalin's work in the Ukraine.

Andropov of the KGB emerges
Inevitably as the next big cheese.
In Hungary he supervised the purges
Which taught them just how hard the Bear can squeeze.
But now it seems he has artistic urges
And intellectual proclivities.
At speaking English he is Leslie Howard:
At playing the piano, Noel Coward.

There's consolation in a fairy tale,
But none when Lech Walesa is released –
Surely the final proof that he must fail.
In back rooms as a species of lay priest
He might say Mass but only in a pale
Reflection of that sacrificial feast
When Poland at the hour of dedication
Tasted what life is like in a free nation.

In Congress Reagan loses the MX
Because they don't think much of the Dense Pack –
A grand scheme calculated to perplex
Red rockets as they swoop to the attack.

Them critters will collide and break their necks.
Some will run wild and others will head back
To blow the roof off the Politburo.
Remember John Wayne and the Alamo!

But there will be, should our blue planet burn,
At least some shred of reason for the fire;
There's just no guarantee we'd ever learn,
Try as we might, to live behind barbed wire;
So threat and counter-threat, though they might turn
The stomach, are not terminally dire –
Although we say it sitting in a crater
The aim was to talk first instead of later.

Someone thinks otherwise in Ballykelly.
A pub explodes and falls on those inside.
The whole platoon of soldiers blown to jelly
Must constitute a cause for secret pride.
Those girls who should have been home watching telly
You'd have to say committed suicide,
An act which no true Christian can condone.
So ends the newsflash from the battle zone.

Ken Livingstone has failed to uninvite
The IRA to meet the GLC.
The Fleet Street hacks with ill-concealed delight
Pour hot lead on his inhumanity.
I like his gall but question his eyesight.
When looking at his newts what does he see?
You'd think that his pop eyes could count their eggs.
No doubt he'd spot it if *they* lost their legs.

In Florida the last month of the year
Is balmier than England was in June.
There's wild hogs in the boondocks around here
And manatees asleep in the lagoon.
Launch Complex 39's the stack of gear
That fired the first Apollo at the Moon.
Beside Pad A the storks pose poised to scuttle
At any sign of life from the Space Shuttle,

Which stands on end all set to hit the trail
Out of this charnel house that we inhabit.
It's an ejector seat on a world scale.
Given just half a chance who wouldn't grab it?
Sit still for the volcano up your tail
And you'd be off and running like a rabbit –
Till upside down, a baby before birth,
Floating in silence you would see the Earth.

Earth shows no signs of us viewed from up there
Except the Wall of China, so no wonder
It looks a vision in its veils of air,
The white opacities we hear as thunder
Braided with azure into maidenhair –
It's those conditions we are living under.
That stately clockwork of soft wheels and springs
Keeps time whatever mess we make of things.

Back in the London frost I pile up drifts
Of crumpled A4 as I type my piece.
Some halfwit has been spitting in the lifts.
The thieves patrol more often than the police.
I head for Cambridge with the children's gifts,
Walk down a street made loud by sizzling geese
And am appropriately stunned to see
The work continues on our Christmas tree.

An angel where there used to be a star.
Twin tinsel strings like stage-struck DNA.
The leaves peel off the Advent calendar
Uncovering one chocolate every day.
The decorators may have gone too far
In hanging Santa Claus from his own sleigh.
Behold two members of the privileged class –
The young, who think that time will never pass.

Too soon to tell them, even if I knew,
The secret of believing life is good
When all that happened was the scythe spared you
While better men were cut down where they stood.

My fortunes thrived in 1982.
I'd have it on my conscience if I could,
But next year will be time to make amends
For feeling happy as the old year ends.

SONG LYRICS

Prefatory Note

This selection from the song lyrics I have written for the music of Pete Atkin adds up to less than half of the total in existence. I have left out all the love songs. (There was a time when that sentence would have started me writing another one.) Many of them I am quite proud of and I hope there is none without its turn of phrase. But they are all written within the courtly love tradition; and are thus mainly more about the loss of love than its acquisition; and so, without the music to help them sound universal, they give the exact effect of a single, lonely man crying repeatedly into his beer.

Other strong candidates for exclusion were those lyrics, mainly from early on, which needed too much help to get started from phrases unwittingly lent by Ronsard, Nerval, Laforgue, Apollinaire, Leopardi, Rilke, W. B. Yeats or T. S. Eliot. Some of the lyrics I have included do indeed contain literary allusions, but the allusions are not the driving force. When listened to, such anacreontic borrowings can add to the texture without insisting on separate notice. But on the page, if they come too thick and fast, they can look like a misplaced claim to erudition. In the nineteenth century, Thomas Moore, for the publication of his collected lyrics along with his poems, would unapologetically gloss his Latin and Greek borrowings with learned footnotes, to a total length that often exceeded that of the lyric itself. Still feeling obliged to prove his kinship with learned colleagues, he failed to realize that when his lyrics were sung in the salons, they silenced not only the audience but the competition. With the living laurels already his, he went on striving for the bronze simulacrum, never publishing even the slightest lyric about a shy damsel of Dublin without appending some supererogatory rigmarole about an intransigent priestess on the island of Hypnos. Today the practice would look absurd, not because the lyrical tradition is less robust but because it is much more so. If Dorothy Fields could draw a perfect lyric from what she heard on the sidewalk or in the subway, we can expect no points for flagging the help we got from Dante.

As for the lyrics that have been included, the first criterion was that they should have enough poetic content to be of interest when read. But they would be true poems only if they could altogether do without their common organizing principle, which was music.

Deprived of that, they are something else. I hope they are not something less, but some readers might decide they can be safely skipped. Other readers, however, might be encouraged to seek them out in recorded form. If that happened, I could give myself credit for a cunning plan.

The Master of the Revels

Allow me to present myself, my ladies
And gentlemen of this exalted age
Before my creatures take the stage
For I am the Master of the Revels
In what appertains to mirth I am a sage

I work myself to death for each production
And though the world's great wits are all on file
I have not been known to smile
For I am the Master of the Revels
And mastery demands a certain style

In my office hang the blueprints
Of the first exploding handshake
And the charted trajectories of custard pies
For Harlequin ten different kinds of heartbreak
For Columbine the colour of her eyes

Some other windows darken in the evening
And never before morning show a light
But for me there is no night
For I am the Master of the Revels
The caller-up and caster-in of devils
And I am here for your instruction and delight

The Ice-cream Man

This afternoon the ice-cream man
Has driven his magnetic van
From Angkor Wat or Isfahan
To park down by the meadows

The captain of a pirate ship
He struggles hard to keep his grip
With cannonades of strawberry whip
Delivered through the windows

A battered Bedford Dormobile
Done over pink for eye appeal
With rainbow discs on every wheel
It makes a magic wagon

A mass of metal glorified
Sesame thrown open wide
And this amazing man inside
Fantastic as a dragon

It must be standing on tiptoe
And reaching up to trade your dough
For scoops of technicolor snow
That makes the man look royal

To me he looks a normal bloke
With a second line in lukewarm Coke
Busting for a decent smoke
To break the round of toil

I guess I've got a jaundiced eye
The children never spot the lie
They're queueing up and reaching high
For something that tastes lovely

Neapolitan wafers make the day
The king is in his castle gay
And they're behind him all the way
Below me they're above me

Who'd guess from how they make a meal
With darting tongue and teeth of steel
From a mess of frigid cochineal
That they were born to sorrow

Gone to dust the age of kings
Lost the taste for simple things
If only time would give me wings
I'd double back tomorrow

Stranger in Town

I never will remember how that stranger came to town
He walked in without a swagger, got a job and settled down
The place would have seemed the same without him
And now I can't recall a thing about him

He didn't wear a poncho or a gun with a filed sight
And he wasn't passing through like a freight train in the night
He rarely wore a stetson with a shadowy big brim
And I still can't be sure if he was him

From Kansas to Wyoming, from Contention to Cheyenne
His name meant less than nothing and it didn't scare a man
So folks didn't worship him or fear him
And I can't remember ever going near him

He didn't tote a shotgun with the barrels both sawn off
So people didn't hit the deck or dive behind a trough
He walked the street in silence, ignored on every side
And it's doubtful if he could even ride

I never could remember how that stranger met his death
He was absolutely senile and with his dying breath
He forgot to ask his womenfolk to kiss him
And afterwards they didn't even miss him

Nothing Left to Say

The breakers from the sea that kept me sane
Were clean and lucid all along the line
Like shavings tumbled upward from the plane
That leave with ease the surface of the pine
When the carpenter is planing with the grain
It's nothing
Nothing but a dream of mine

    And I have come to nothing in a way
    That leaves me with nothing left to say

Half a lifetime bending with the breeze
To buy the stuff I don't know how to use
A deck of credit cards, a bunch of keys
A station I achieved but didn't choose
The screws are on and no one beats the squeeze
It's nothing
Nothing I can't bear to lose

    And I have come to nothing in a way
    That leaves me with nothing left to say

The sea I dreamed of closes like a vice
Parading waves are frozen into place
Their veils of vapour scattering like rice
And far below, the ultimate disgrace
A mermaid crushed to death inside the ice
It's nothing
Nothing but a frightened face

    And I have come to nothing in a way
    That leaves me with nothing left to say

National Steel

Shining in the window a guitar that wasn't wood
Was looking like a silver coin from when they still were good
The man who kept the music shop was pleased to let me play
Although the price was twenty times what I could ever pay

   Pick it up and feel the weight and weigh the feel
   That thing is an authentic National Steel

A lacy grille across the front and etchings on the back
But the welding sealed a box not even Bukka White could crack
I tuned it to an open chord, picked up the nickel slide
And bottlenecked a blues that sounded cold yet seemed to glide

   The National Steel weaves a singing shroud
   Just as sure as men in winter breathe a cloud

Scrapper Blackwell, Blind Boy Fuller and Blind Blake
Son House or any name you care to take
And from many a sad railroad, mine or mill
Lonnie Johnson's bitter tears are in there still

   Be certain, said the man, of who you are
   There are dead men still alive in that guitar

Back there the next morning half demented by desire
For that storybook assemblage of heavy plate and wire
I sold half the things I valued but I'll never count the cost
While I can pick a note like broken bracken in the frost

   And I hear those fabled names becoming real
   Every time I feel the weight or weigh the feel
   Of the vanished years inside my National Steel

I See the Joker

Mornings now I breakfast in the tower
Then travel thirty floors to the garage
My sons are with me even underground
With nothing but our gun-cars all around
From anything but nuclear attack
That place is safe, but when I cut the pack I see the Joker
I cut the pack and see the Joker

The forecourt is crawling with our boys
A heavy weapon rides in every car
My Cadillac's a safe-deposit box
With plastic armour in the top and sides
Solid like a strongroom in Fort Knox
And all along the parkway into town
We're covered for a mile front and back
By Family cars, but when I cut the pack I see the Joker
I cut the pack and see the Joker

Who is this guy and why does he want me?
This city has been ours since Christ knows when
At first from booze and girls and junk, and then
Legitimate, from rents and industry
The Chief of Police is ours to buy and sell
The DA and the Mayor are ours as well
There's no one left to fight, the enemy
Are dead and gone, or just some juicehead black
Loose with a knife, but when I cut the pack I see the Joker
I cut the pack and see the Joker

The cops are checking each incoming flight
For solo hitmen with an urge to die
No one gets in here by day or night
Without I don't know who they are and why
I'm in the clear, at barely fifty-five
One of the most respected men alive
Some blubber here and there, but nothing slack

I'm right on top, but when I cut the pack I see the Joker
I cut the pack and see the Joker

We do the journey different every day
Today we hit the garment district first
Then double back and take the boulevard
And as we drive I don't know which is worst
To know he'll come but not to know the way
To know he'll make a play but not know how
Is he somewhere out there setting up the gun?
Is this headache from his crosshairs on my brow?
There's no way, not a crevice, not a crack
That he can reach me, but when I cut the pack I see the Joker
I cut the pack and see the Joker

Sessionman's Blues

I've got the sessionman's blues
I played on three albums today
I paid a sessionman's dues
I played what they told me to play
Then I climbed in my Rover three-litre and motored away

 I've got the sessionman's blues
 The squattin' in a booth alone blues

I've got the sessionman's blues
But I get the dots right from the start
I drink a sessionman's booze
But my tenor blows what's on the chart
A single run through and I've got the whole solo by heart

 I've got the sessionman's blues
 The squattin' in a booth alone
 Isolated microphone blues

I've got the sessionman's blues
I'm booked up a lifetime ahead
I get a sessionman's news
The voice on the blower just said
They want me to work on the afternoon after I'm dead

 I've got the sessionman's blues
 The squattin' in a booth alone
 Isolated microphone
 Doublin' on baritone blues

My Egoist

The garden was in bloom, my egoist
The light was right, the show was very brave
You simply had to shy your hat away and rave
Because the colours looked so gay

The garden was your home, my egoist
You grew blasé, you asked 'What else is new?'
Or perhaps it crushed your spirit, it was all for you
And the surroundings were too plush

The garden felt your loss, my egoist
And what it gained were others not your kind
At first the heavy-handed came and finally the blind
Until nothing looked the same

The garden is alone, my egoist
They've all flown on, the butterflies of day
And nothing now takes flight above this sad display
Except the butterflies of night

Song for Rita

A tribute to Kris Kristofferson

The way my arms around you touch the centre of my being
As I step inside the marshland of your mind
Makes me weak inside my senses like a dog hit by a diesel
And more alone than Milton goin' blind

And I know I need to lose you if I ever want to find you
'Cause the poet's way is finished from the start
And I feel a palpitation kinda flutter in my forehead
As I think the problem over in my heart

    Yes I guess I'll always never know the question to your answer
    If I can't be doin' wrong by feelin' right
    But I'm really lookin' forward to how you'll be lookin' backward
    When I'm walkin' with you sideways through the night

I can keep this kind of writin' goin' more or less forever
But I can't undo destruction when it's gone
I can only think of you and what you cost me in hotel bills
As I settle down to dream of movin' on

If I've never longed to love you less than now you'll know the reason
Is because my whole desire is to sing
And everything I'm sayin' is the mirror of your beauty
As it hovers like a vulture on the wing

    Yes I guess I'll always never know the question to your answer
    If I can't be doin' wrong by feelin' right
    But I'm really lookin' forward to how you'll be lookin' backward
    When I'm walkin' with you sideways through the night

Senior Citizens

You've seen the way they get around
With nothing beyond burdens left to lose
The drying spine that bends them near the ground
The way their ankles fold over their shoes
They've had their day and half of the day after
And all the shares they ever held in laughter
Are now just so many old engravings
Their sands have run out long before their savings
And the fun ran out so long before the sands
They've lost touch with the touch of other hands
That once came to caress and then to help
A single tumble means a broken hip
The hair grows thinner on the scalp
And thicker on the upper lip
And who is there to care, or left to please?

It's so easy when we're young
For me to wield a silver tongue
And cleverly place you among
The girls the boys have always sung

It's so simple when it's you
For me to coax from my guitar
The usual on how fine you are
Like this calm night, like that bright star

And the rest would follow on
The rest would follow on

And there'll be time to try it all
I'm sure the thrill will never pall
The sand will take so long to fall
The neck so slim, the glass so tall

Shadow and the Widower

As we left each other on our final night
And I walked away with all the love remaining
A classic whisper near the station wall
I could just hear without straining
Asked if I was scared to realize this was all
Disappointed there was only this much in it
The perfume and suppliance of a minute?
It was him – the Shadow and the Widower

There's that all right, I said, and so much more
An hour of life inside a world of dying
A wider limit set to one's regard
The kinder forms of lying
And beyond all that the privilege of a memory scarred
In prettier ways than most, perhaps than any
Such a fate must seem desirable to many
Even you, the Shadow and the Widower

The classic laughter echoed near the wall
A strip torn from a three-sheet stirred and fluttered
The whisper said, Well don't that just beat all
What this oracle hath uttered?
A straight-up scalp-collector I could understand
All those lineaments of gratified desire
But he's handing me that old refining fire
This to me, the Shadow and the Widower

The whisper moved with me into the light
Where the access tunnel ran beneath the tracks
The wind searched for a way back to the night
But no romance, no lonely alto sax
Just litter and the notes left for the blacks
The graffiti stopped your pulse like heart attacks

To perdition with that rarefied regret
Those half-remembered ladies swathed in yearning

Said the whisper just an inch behind my head
The world is burning
And the tales of love fit for the guiltless dead
Will have little in them of the airs and graces
With which your tender soul goes through its paces
Commit that to your fragrant memory
And while you're doing that, remember me
The Shadow and the Widower

Payday Evening

Of late I try to kill my payday evenings
In many an unrecommended spot
Curiosity accounting for a little
Loneliness accounting for a lot

The girls who pull the handles force their laughter
The casual conversation's not the best
Indifference accounting for a little
Unhappiness accounting for the rest

And the gardens of the heyday in Versailles
And Pompadour's theatre in the stairs
Should be created in my magic eye
From a jukebox and a stack of canvas chairs

But somehow we have failed to come through
The styles are gone to seed, no more parades
There seems to be no talk of me and you
No breath of scandal in these sad arcades

Concerning us there are no fables
No brilliant poems airily discarded
Just liquid circles on Formica tables
A silence perhaps too closely guarded

Outside a junkie tries to sell his girl
Her face has just begun to come apart
Look hard and you can see the edges curl
Speed has got her beaten at the start

And what care these two for a broken heart?

The lady's calling Time and she is right
My time has come to find a better way

A surer way to navigate at night
The poetic age has had its day

In midnight voices softer than a dove's
We shall talk superbly of our lost loves

Screen-freak

You've got to help me, doc, I see things in the night
The tatters of my brain are bleached with flashing light
Just the way Orion's sword is pumping stars in flight
My mind's eye's skies are glittering and white

The Lady in the Dark has shot the Lady from Shanghai
The Thin Man and the Quiet Man are comin' through the rye
At Red Line Seven Thousand there's No Highway in the sky
The villains are the deepest but they plumb refuse to die

    Dance, Ginger, dance
    The caftan of the caliph turns to powder at your glance

The Ambersons have spiked the punch and livened up the ball
Cagney's getting big and Sidney Greenstreet's getting small
The Creature from the Black Lagoon left puddles in the hall
And Wee Willie Winkie is the most evil of them all

Strangers on a Wagon Train have crashed the China Gate
The Portrait of Jennie has decided not to wait
The Flying Leathernecks arrived a half a reel too late
The Broadcast wasn't big enough and Ziegfeld wasn't great

    Dance, Ginger, dance
    The caftan of the caliph turns to powder at your glance
    This one for Funny Face and Fancy Pants

The love of Martha Ivers caused the death of Jesse James
Kitty Foyle guessed it though she didn't link their names
I've seen the plywood cities meet their doom because of dames
Atlantis down in bubbles and Atlanta up in flames

And I've seen the Maltese Falcon falling moulting to the street
He was caught by Queen Christina who was Following the Fleet
And Scarface found the Sleep was even Bigger than the Heat

When he hit the Yellow Brick Road to where the Grapes of Wrath
  are sweet

Dance, Ginger, dance
The caftan of the caliph turns to powder at your glance
This one for Funny Face and Fancy Pants
A buck and wing might fix the Broken Lance
And break my trance

The Double Agent

Your manifest perfections never cease
To drive the day-long terrors out of mind
They are the lights the darkness hides behind
Allowing satisfaction its increase
Beyond the petty boundaries designed
To keep us well aware the world's unkind
And still your eyes proclaim a reign of peace

A ruined man falls sideways far away
And too far gone to see my lady's hair
Supposing he was here or she was there
My lover's mouth has not a word to say
To stanch the flow or slow him on his way
It sends a smile to me across the air
And still I feel that fortune smiles today

Between the breaking of your morning bread
And the final pretty speeches of the night
A million destinies drop out of sight
A million people get it in the head
You join the silks and perfumes of your bed
Like a long delightful insult to the dead
And still your breast is where I'd lay my head

Forgive, forget the rest of what I said
And still your breast is where I'd lay my head

A King at Nightfall

The ring hangs on a string inside your shirt
You wedge the stable door
You eat your beans and bunk down in the straw
A king at nightfall

You're going to have to learn to live with this
As you work or beg your way towards the border
And shade your face to miss
The multiplying eyes of the new order

You spun the crown away into a ditch
And saw the water close
The army that you fed now feeds the crows
A king at nightfall

You're going to have to watch your manners now
And never let your face show what you're missing
Don't wait for them to bow
Stick out your hand for shaking, not for kissing

Tomorrow's men who trace you from the field
Will be in it for the bread
There'll be a price on your anointed head
A king at nightfall

You're going to have to learn how quick to run
And that means slowly, watching all the angles
Don't try to use that gun
Stay very loose and cool and out of tangles

You reach to brush your collar free of straw
And then you feel the string
There's light enough for one look at the ring
And it's lovely but it doesn't mean a thing
A king at nightfall
A king at nightfall

Apparition in Las Vegas

When the King of Rock and Roll sang in the desert
He didn't seem to age like other men
To Vegas came the ladies with pink rinses
Agog to see the dreamboat sail again

To Vegas came the shipwrecked and the broken
Their long regrets, their searing midnight rages
Their disappointment seldom left unspoken
In marriages that turned to rows of cages
He wrote and bound the book of which their early aspirations
    were the pages

When the King of Rock and Roll sang in the desert
With a ring of confidence around his smile
He sparkled like the frosting on a drumkit
He was supple as the serpent of the Nile

To Vegas came the ladies with pink rinses
With all their ills and all their soured karma
With all their pills and all their tics and winces
To feel again the liberating drama
Of a shining silver buckskin suit against a solid purple cyclorama

When the King of Rock and Roll sang in the desert
He broke no hearts that hadn't burst before
To Vegas came the ladies with pink rinses
It was they and never he that knew the score
And knowing that they only loved him more

To Vegas came the debris of an era
For the promise that no longer could deceive them
Their eyes grew misty as their sight grew clearer
With a drum roll the past began to leave them
And it all drew further from them as the spotlight caught the
    King and brought him nearer

Be Careful When They Offer You the Moon

Be careful when they offer you the moon
It gives a cold light
It was only ever made to light the night
You can freeze your fingers handling the moon

Be careful when they offer you the moon
It's built for dead souls
It's a colourless and dusty ball of holes
You can break an ankle dancing on the moon

When you take the moon you kiss the world goodbye
For a chance to lord it over loneliness
And a quarter-million miles down the sky
They'll watch you shining more but weighing less

So be careful when they offer you the moon
It's only dream stuff
It's a Tin Pan Alley prop held up by bluff
And nobody breathes easy on the moon
Nobody breathes easy on the moon
Count to ten when they offer you the moon

Touch Has a Memory

Touch has a memory
Better than the other senses
Hearing and sight fight free
Touching has no defences
Textures come back to you real as can be
Touch has a memory

Fine eyes are wide at night
Eyelashes show that nicely
Seeing forgets the sight
Touch recollects precisely
Eyelids are modest yet blink at a kiss
Touching takes note of this

When in a later day
Little of the vision lingers
Memory slips away
Every way but through the fingers
Textures come back to you real as can be
Making you feel
Time doesn't heal
And touch has a memory

Frangipani Was Her Flower

Frangipani was her flower
And amethyst her birthday stone
The fairest blossom of the bower
She wasn't born to be alone
And now she was terribly alone

A Ford Cortina was the car
Eleven thirty-five the hour
The squeak of gravel in the drive
Left the damsel in the tower
Pondering her vanished power

Always, everything had gone so well
Her dolls had been the best
She was better than the rest
Always, everything had gone so well
The world at her behest
Had fed her from the breast

Always, everything had gone so well
She was married all in white
To a lad serenely trite
Always, everything had gone so well
And on her wedding night
Things had more or less gone right

By fairest fortune she was kissed
Frangipani was her bloom
A silver spoon was in her fist
Upon emerging from the womb
Tonight she wrecked the room

The Rider to the World's End

From a phrase by Lex Banning

You simply mustn't blame yourself – the days were perfect
And so were exactly what I was born to spoil
For I am the Rider to the World's End
Bound across the cinder causeway
From the furnace to the quarry
Through the fields of oil

And I left you with the sign of the Rider to the World's End
It was not the mark of Zorro
Written sharply on your forehead with a blade
Just a way of not turning up tomorrow
And of phone calls never made

My time with you seemed ready-made to last for always
And so was predestined to be over in a flash
For I am the Rider to the World's End
Bound across the fields of oil
Through the broken-bottle forest
To the plains of ash

And I left you with the sign of the Rider to the World's End
It was not the ace of diamonds
Or the death's head of the Phantom on your jaw
Just a suddenly relaxing set of knuckles
Never rapped against a door

You were more thoughtful for and fond of me than I was
And so were precisely what I can never trust
For I am the Rider to the World's End
Bound across the plains of ashes
To the molten metal valleys
In the hills of dust

No Dice

I tried hard to be useful, but no dice
With no spit left I couldn't soften leather
With these old hands I couldn't even sew
So yesterday they left me on the ice
I could barely lift my head to watch them go
The sky was white, my eyes grew full of snow
And whatever reached me first, bears or the weather
I just don't know
Yesterday was oh so long ago – so very long ago

I saw across our path through the lagoon
Thick shrubberies of hail collide and quarrel
Sudden trees of shellburst hump and blow
Our LVT turned through the reef too soon
The front went down, we all got set to go
But the whole routine was just too friggin' slow
What kind of splinters hit me, steel or coral
I just don't know
Yesterday was oh so long ago – so very long ago

We hit the secret trails towards thin air
Aware we'd never live to tell the story
And at the last deep lake before the snow
We rigged the slings, chipped out the water-stair
Swung out the holy gold and let it go
It sank so far it didn't even glow
And if the priests died too to share our glory
I just don't know
Yesterday was oh so long ago – so very long ago

Yesterday we finished with the ditch
We stacked our spades and knelt in groups of seven
Our hands were wired by an NCO
With a fluent-from-long-practice loop and hitch
No dice – there was nothing left to throw
A bump against your neck and down you go

And if I kept my peace or cried to heaven
I just don't know
Yesterday was oh so long ago – so very long ago

Yesterday from midnight until dawn
I lay remembering my lost endeavour
The love song that would capture how things flow
The one song that refuses to be born
For I have tried a thousand times or so
To link the ways men die with how they grow
But no dice, and if I'll do it ever
I just don't know
Yesterday was oh so long ago

Driving through Mythical America

Four students in the usual light of day
Set out to speak their minds about the war
Unaware that Eddie Pru was on the way
Things had to snap before they knew the score

They were driving through mythical America

    A Rooney–Garland show was in the barn
    Fields was at the Pussycat Cafe
    No one had even heard of Herman Kahn
    And Jersey Joe was eager for the fray

Four students had to take it in their stride
And couldn't feel the road beneath the wheels
Of the car they didn't know they rode inside
Across the set and through the cardboard hills

They were driving through mythical America

    They sold their Studebaker Golden Hawk
    And bought a Nash Ambassador Saloon
    Bogart said 'Even the dead can talk'
    And suddenly the coats were all raccoon

Four students never knew that this was it
There isn't much a target needs to know
Already Babyface had made the hit
And Rosebud was upended in the snow

They were driving through mythical America

    Gatsby floated broken in the pool
    The Kansas City Seven found a groove
    Barrymore and Lombard played the fool
    And Cheetah slowly taught John Wayne to move

Four students watched the soldiers load and aim
And never tumbled they were on the spot
Moose Molloy pulled ten years on a frame
The dough was phoney and the car was hot

They were driving through mythical America

Henry Ford paid seven bucks a day
Rockwell did the covers on the Post
FDR set up the TVA
And the stars rode silver trains from coast to coast

Four students blinked at ordinary skies
But the sunlight came from thousands of motels
A highway through the night was in their eyes
And waiting at the roadblock Orson Welles

They were driving through mythical America

Four students never guessed that they were through
Their history had them covered like a gun
It hit them like a bolt out of the blue
Too quick to grasp and far too late to run

They crashed and died together in the sun

They were driving through mythical America

Thief in the Night

A guitar is a thief in the night
That robs you of sleep through the wall
A guitar is a thin box of light
Throwing reflections that rise and fall
It reminds you of Memphis or maybe Majorca
Big Bill Broonzy or Garcia Lorca
A truck going north or a cab to the Festival Hall

And the man who plays the guitar for life
Tests his thumbs on a slender knife
Forever caresses a frigid wife
His fingers travel on strings and frets
Like a gambler's moving to cover bets
Remembering what his brain forgets
While his brain remembers the fears and debts

Long fingernails that tap a brittle rhythm on a glass
Around his neck a ribbon with a little silver hook
Like some military order second class
You can read him like an open book
From the hands that spend their lives creating tension
From the wrists that have a lean and hungry
Eyes that have a mean and angry look

A guitar is a thief in the night
That robs you of sleep through the wall
A guitar is a thin box of light
Throwing reflections that rise and fall
A guitar reminds you of death and taxes
Charlie Christian outplaying the saxes
The beginners' call and the very last call of all

Practical Man

Last night I drank with a practical man
Who seemed to think he knew me well
He had no debts and he had no troubles
All night long he kept setting up doubles
And he asked me 'What have you got to sell?'

'I'll see you right' said the practical man
'A boy like you should be living high
All you do is get up and be funny
And I'll turn the laughs into folding money
Can you name me anything that can't buy?'

'So you deal in dreams' said the practical man
'So does that mean you should be so coy?
I fixed one chap a show on telly
Who limped like Byron and talked like Shelley
Through a ten-part epic on the fall of Troy'

'I'll tell you what' said the practical man
As he tapped the ash from a purple fag
'Let's head uptown for a meal somewhere
You can sing me something while we're driving there
There's a grand piano in the back of my Jag'

So I sang my song to the practical man
It sounded bad but she couldn't hear
And the silent lights of town went streaming
As if the car was a turtle dreaming
The night was sad and she was nowhere near

'It's a great idea' said the practical man
As they brought in waiters on flaming swords
'You love this chick and it's really magic
But she won't play ball – that's kind of tragic
Now how do we get this concept on the boards?'

'I see it like this' said the practical man
As he chose a trout from the restaurant pool
'We change it round so she's going frantic
To win the love of the last romantic
And you're the one, her wild creative fool'

So I thought it all over as the practical man
Watched them slaughter the fatted calf
I saw again her regretful smile
Sweet to look at though it meant denial
It was bound to hurt but I had to laugh

And that's when I told the practical man
As he drank champagne from the Holy Grail
There are some ideas you can't play round with
Can't let go of and you can't give ground with
'Cause when you die they're what you're found with
There are just some songs that are not for sale

Cottonmouth

Cottonmouth had such a way of saying things
Phrases used to fly like they were wearing wings
Never had to weigh a word
Said the first thing that occurred
And round your head the stuff he said went running rings

Cottonmouth, what a brain
Absolutely insane

Cottonmouth would tell the girls he sighed for them
He talked of all the lonely nights he cried for them
Afterwards they told their men
I just saw Cottonmouth again
That guy's a scream, and never guessed he died for them
Cottonmouth, what a brain
Absolutely insane

Cottonmouth packed up one day and did a fade
Turned edgeways on and vanished like a razor blade
Considering how people here
Are downright simple and sincere
It could have been the smartest move he ever made

Beware of the Beautiful Stranger

On the midsummer fairground alive with the sound
And the lights of the Wurlitzer merry-go-round
The midway was crowded and I was the man
Who coughed up a quid in the dark caravan
To the gypsy who warned him of danger
'Beware of the beautiful stranger'

'You got that for nothing' I said with a sigh
As the queen's head went up to her critical eye
'The lady in question is known to me now
And I'd like to beware but the problem is how
Do you think I was born in a manger?
I'm in love with the beautiful stranger'

The gypsy (called Lee as all soothsayers are)
Bent low to her globular fragment of star
'This woman will utterly screw up your life
She will tempt you from home, from your children and wife
She's a devil and nothing will change her
Get away from the beautiful stranger'

'That ball needs a re-gun' I said, shelling out
'The future you see there has all come about
Does it show you the girl as she happens to be
A Venus made flesh in a shell full of sea?
Does it show you the shape of my danger?
Can you show me the beautiful stranger?'

'I don't run a cinema here, little man
But lean over close and tune in if you can
You breathe on the glass, give a rub with your sleeve
Slip me your wallet, sit tight and believe
And the powers-that-be will arrange a
Pre-release of the beautiful stranger'

In the heart of the glass I saw galaxies born
The eye of the storm and the light of the dawn
And then with a click came a form and a face
That stunned me not only through candour and grace
But because she was really a stranger
A total and beautiful stranger

'Hello there' she said with her hand to her brow
'I'm the one you'll meet after the one you know now
There's no room inside here to show you us all
But behind me the queue stretches right down the hall
For the damned there is always a stranger
There is always a beautiful stranger'

'That's your lot' said Miss Lee as she turned on the light
'These earrings are hell and I'm through for the night
If they'd put up a booster not far from this pitch
I could screen you your life to the very last twitch
But I can't even get the Lone Ranger
One last word from the beautiful stranger'

'You live in a dream and the dream is a cage'
Said the girl 'And the bars nestle closer with age
Your shadow burned white by invisible fire
You will learn how it rankles to die of desire
As you long for the beautiful stranger'
Said the vanishing beautiful stranger

'Here's a wallet for you and five nicker for me'
Said the gypsy 'And also here's something for free
Watch your step on my foldaway stairs getting down
And go slow on the flyover back into town
There's a slight but considerable danger
Give my love to the beautiful stranger'

Have You Got a Biro I Can Borrow?

Have you got a biro I can borrow?
I'd like to write your name
On the palm of my hand, on the walls of the hall
The roof of the house, right across the land
So when the sun comes up tomorrow
It'll look to this side of the hard-bitten planet
Like a big yellow button with your name written on it

Have you got a biro I can borrow?
I'd like to write some lines
In praise of your knee, and the back of your neck
And the double-decker bus that brings you to me
So when the sun comes up tomorrow
It'll shine on a world made richer by a sonnet
And a half-dozen epics as long as the Aeneid

Oh give me a pen and some paper
Give me a chisel or a camera
A piano and a box of rubber bands
I need room for choreography
And a darkroom for photography
Tie the brush into my hands

Have you got a biro I can borrow?
I'd like to write your name
From the belt of Orion to the share of the Plough
The snout of the Bear to the belly of the Lion
So when the sun goes down tomorrow
There'll never be a minute
Not a moment of the night that hasn't got you in it

Laughing Boy

In all the rooms I've hung my hat, in all the towns I've been
It stuns me I'm not dead already from the shambles that I've seen
I've seen a girl hold back her hair to light a cigarette
And things like that a man like me can't easily forget

I've got the only cure for life, and the cure for life is joy
I'm a crying man that everyone calls Laughing Boy

A kid once asked me in late September for a shilling for the guy
And I looked that little operator in her wheeling-dealing eye
And I tossed a bob with deep respect in her old man's trilby hat
It seems to me that a man like me could die of things like that

I've got the only cure for life, and the cure for life is joy
I'm a crying man that everyone calls Laughing Boy

I've seen landladies who lost their lovers at the time of Rupert
    Brooke
And they pressed the flowers from Sunday rambles and then forgot
    which book
And I paid the rent thinking 'Anyway, buddy, at least you won't
    get wet'
And I tried the bed and lay there thinking 'They haven't got
    you yet'

I've got the only cure for life, and the cure for life is joy
I'm a crying man that everyone calls Laughing Boy

I've read the labels on a hundred bottles for eyes and lips and hair
And I've seen girls breathe on their fingernails and wiggle them in
    the air
And I've often wondered who the hell remembers as far back as
    last night
It seems to me that a man like me is the only one who might

I've got the only cure for life, and the cure for life is joy
I'm a crying man that everyone calls Laughing Boy

Sunlight Gate

The heroes ride out through the Sunlight Gate
And out of the sunset return
I have no idea how they spend their day
With a selfless act, or a grandstand play
But high behind them the sky will burn
In the glittering hour of return

The heroes ride out in unbroken ranks
But with gaps in their number come back
I have no idea how they lose their men
To some new threat, or the same again
But they talk a long while near the weapon stack
In the clattering hour they come back

The heroes return through the Sunset Gate
But their faces are never the same
I have no idea why their eyes go cold
And the young among them already look old
But high behind them the sky's aflame
In the flickering hour of their fame

The Faded Mansion on the Hill

When you see what can't be helped go by
With bloody murder in its eye
And the mouth of a man put on the rack
The voice of a man about to crack

When you see the litter of their lives
The stupid children, bitter wives
Your self-esteem in disarray
You do your best to climb away
From the streaming traffic of decay

Believing if you will that all these sick hate days
Are just a kind of trick fate plays
But still behind your shaded eyes
That mind-constricting thick weight stays

When on the outskirts of the town
Comes bumping cavernously down
Out of the brick gateways
From the faded mansion on the hill
The out-of-date black Cadillac
With the old man crumpled in the back
That time has not yet found the time to kill

Between the headlands to the sea the fleeing yachts of summer go
White as a sheet and faster than the driven snow
Like dolphins riding high and giant seabirds flying low

And square across the wind the cats and wingsails pull ahead
Living their day as if it almost could be said
The cemetery of home could somehow soon be left for dead

But the graveyard of tall ships is really here
Where the grass breaks up the driveway more each year
And here is all these people have
And everything they can't retrieve

The beach the poor men never reach
The shore the rich men never leave

Between the headlands from the sea the homing yachts of
    summer fill
The night with shouts and falling sails and then are still
The avenues wind up into the darkness of the hill
Where time tonight might find the time to kill

Thirty-year Man

Nobody here yet
From the spotlight that will ring her not a glimmer
Not a finger on its squeaky dimmer
I play piano in a jazz quartet
That works here late with a young girl singer

   And along from the darkened and empty tables
   By the covered-up drums and the microphone cables
   At the end of the room the piano glistens
   Like the rail at the end of the nave

   Thirty years in the racket
   A brindled crew cut and a silk-lined jacket
   And it isn't my hands that fill this place
   It's a kid's voice still reaching into space
   It's her they're driving down to hear
   And it's my bent-over back she's standing near

Nobody talks yet
From the glasses that will touch soon not a tinkle
Not a paper napkin shows a wrinkle
I play piano in a jazz quartet
That backs a winner while the big notes crinkle

   And along from the darkened and empty tables
   By the covered-up drums and the microphone cables
   At the end of the room the piano glistens
   Like the rail at the end of the nave
   And I play a few things while no one listens

   Thirty years in the racket
   A brindled crew cut and a silk-lined jacket
   And it isn't my name that brings them in
   It's a little girl just starting to begin
   It's her they're piling in to see
   And I'd kill that kid if she wasn't killing me

Nobody moves yet
From the tables near the bandstand not a rustle
Not a loudmouth even moves a muscle
I play piano in a jazz quartet
That backs a giver while the takers hustle

And along from the darkened and empty tables
By the covered-up drums and the microphone cables
At the end of the room the piano glistens
Like bones at the end of a cave
And I play a few things while no one listens
For an hour alone spells freedom to the slave

Carnations on the Roof

He worked setting tools for a multi-purpose punch
In a shop that made holes in steel plates
He could hear himself think through a fifty-minute lunch
Of the kids, gas and stoppages, the upkeep and the rates
While he talked about Everton and Chelsea with his mates

With gauge and micrometer, with level and with rule
While chuck and punch were pulsing like a drum
He checked the finished product like a master after school
The slugs looked like money and the cutting-oil like scum
And to talk with a machinist he made signals like the dumb

> Though he had no great gifts of personality or mind
> He was generally respected, and the proof
> Was a line of hired Humbers tagging quietly behind
> A fat Austin Princess with carnations on the roof

Forty years of metal tend to get into your skin
The surest coin you take home from your wage
The green cleaning jelly only goes to rub it in
And that glitter in the wrinkle of your knuckle shows your age
Began when the dignity of work was still the rage

He was used and discarded in a game he didn't own
But when the moment of destruction came
He showed that a working man is more than flesh and bone
The hands on his chest flared more brightly than his name
For a technicolor second as he rolled into the flame

> Though he had no great gifts of personality or mind
> He was generally respected, and the proof
> Was a line of hired Humbers tagging quietly behind
> A fat Austin Princess with carnations on the roof

The Hypertension Kid

Last night I met the Hypertension Kid
Grimly chasing shorts with halves of bitter
In a Mayfair club they call the Early Quitter
He met my eyes and hit me for a quid

'I spend fortunes in this rat-trap' said the Kid
'But the plush and flock soak up the brain's kerfuffle
And I like to see a servile barman shuffle
If sympathy's your need let's hear your bid'

'It's my lousy memory' I told the Kid
'What other men forget I still remember
The flies are still alive inside the amber
It's a garbage can with rubbish for a lid'

'Your metaphors are murder' said the Kid
'I know the mood – give in to it a little
The man who shatters is the man who's brittle
Lay off the brakes and steer into the skid'

'Strained virtue warps the soul' announced the Kid
'Those forced attempts at cleanliness that linger
Like soap between your wedding ring and finger
They're residues of which you're better rid

'For evil' said the Hypertension Kid
'Is better contemplated in the deeds of others
Mass murderers and men who knife their mothers
Be glad that what you've done is all you did

'With me the problem's women' said the Kid
'Befuddled, fondled under separate covers
One and all they've gone to other lovers
As I powered down to zero from the grid

'But I love the little darlings' sighed the Kid
'The slide from grace is really more like gliding
And I've found the trick is not to stop the sliding
But to find a graceful way of staying slid

'As for the dreadful memories' said the Kid
'The waste and poison in the spirit's river
Relax your hands and let the bastards quiver
They tremble more the more you keep it hid'

We turned to leave the bar, me and the Kid
I with lightened head and lessened terror
Toward the street, and he into the mirror
My second self, the Hypertension Kid

Perfect Moments

Perfect moments have a clean design
Scoring edges that arrest the flow
Skis cut diamonds in the plump of snow
Times my life feels like a friend of mine

Perfect moments wear a single face
Variations on each other's theme
Renoir's mistresses in peach and cream
Rembrandt's mother in a ruff of lace

Perfect moments bear a single name
They're placed together though they never meet
Charlie Chaplin policing Easy Street
Charlie Parker playing 'My Old Flame'

Perfect moments should redeem the day
Their teeming richness ought to be enough
To take the sting out of the other stuff
A perfect bitch it doesn't work that way

The Road of Silk

And still his dreaming eyes are full of sails
The tree house leaves the peach tree like a bird
In time the swelling bark takes in the nails
Of those adventures nothing more is heard
Easy
Let him sleep now
Not a word

He's losing what he hardly knew was there
The lead dragoons pack up and quit the tray
The early snowfalls lift into the air
The Road of Silk rolls backward from Cathay
Easy
Let him sleep now
Come away

His fondest memories have left their mark
For just so long as lipstick on a glass
The highway scatters jewellery through the dark
The circus leaves a circle on the grass
Easy
Let him sleep now
Let it pass

The Hollow and the Fluted Night

This kind of ocean fails to reach the coast
A special famine rages at the feast
The one loved most is always present least

You are the loved one, very nearly here
Who did not feel so far away before
But now I fear our separation more

The hollow and the fluted night that weaves
The cloth combining loves divides their lives
Black velvet hills between the silver knives

The sunlight on the window sill kowtows
And opens up the sky to further skies
For all the thousand miles to your eyes

The realization daunts the both of us
And so we draw a deep breath through a kiss
When was it ever otherwise than thus?
And what goodbyes are more alone than this?

Secret Drinker

Perching high like an old-time man of law
He travels on a bar stool to enchanted lands
And as the world before him swims and glows
The secret drinker's only sure that he is real
By the feel of his elbows and the steadily increasing
Weight of his forehead in his hands

    And behind the bar
    Like turreted and battlemented towns of long ago
    The lines of coloured bottles swim and glow
    Brilliantly as at the day of wrath
    Or the year of the comet
    But the secret drinker is far from it
    Away from it all

He can ease the present back into the past
Staring at the pastels and the prisms on the shelf
With the magic words that make the evening last
The same again and have one for yourself

    He's a connoisseur
    He can space it out with chasers, he can let it burn
    It's a trick it takes a little while to learn
    You might see the youngsters of today sniff a cork and
        they vomit
    But the secret drinker is far from it
    Away from it all

He can make the looming future lose its sting
Staving off the pressure is a bargain at the price
Of the magic words that make the angels sing
The same again, go easy on the ice

Perching high like an old-time man of law
He travels on a bar stool to enchanted lands
And as the world before him swims and glows

The secret drinker's only sure that he is real
By the feel of his elbows and the steadily increasing
Weight of his forehead in his hands that should be ceasing
To tremble by now and beginning to resemble
The hands of a man he used to know

Search and Destroy

I'm glad to say we're mopping up up here
I'm sending you today's report in clear
Security's no problem now at all
You just pick up the phone and make a call

    We should have done all this back at the beginning
    And never let the clowns think they were winning

We took a month to crack their second man
But when he talked the strudel hit the fan
He named eleven leaders who we shot
And then the top guy's girl who we've still got
The chick was tough and held out for a week
But spilled a bibful when we made her speak
We picked his mother up and worked on her
He came in on his own and there you were

    We should have nailed the first ones when we found them
    Before all the mystique built up around them

We never gave the local heat a chance
To get him on their own and make him dance
We did him in upcountry, bombed the cave
And made the whole damn mountainside his grave
The faithful talk some wishful-thinking cock
About a spook who rolls away the rock
At which point golden boy walks out alive
We're bumping them all off as they arrive

    And that winds up this dreary exhibition
    A total waste of time and ammunition

Tenderfoot

Beyond the border town they call Contrition
The badlands are just boulders and mesquite
A school of Spanish friars built the mission
But left because they couldn't take the heat
And further on the road to Absolution
The mesas turn to mountains capped with snow
And the way becomes a form of execution
That only hardened travellers can go

    You can tell the horseman grieves for how he sinned
    He rides a killing trail
    Reminded of his hard heart by the hail
    And of his folly by the chilling wind

By day the canyon ramparts blaze their strata
Like purple battlements he shall not pass
The sunlight sears the horseman like a martyr
The glacier's a magnifying glass
And by night the clouds black out the constellations
While veils of icicles lock up his eyes
He moves by echo through the cold formations
Walls of drift and ice-fall fall and rise

    You can tell the horseman grieves for how he sinned
    He rides a killing trail
    Reminded of his hard heart by the hail
    And of his folly by the chilling wind

He knows he made pretense of love too often
His deadly carelessness went on for years
At dawn the shields on his eyes will soften
And all of his regrets will be in tears
But far too late to go back and be gentle
Or say how clearly now it comes to mind
His pride at never being sentimental
Was just a clever way to be unkind

You can tell the horseman grieves for how he sinned
He rides a killing trail
Reminded of his hard heart by the hail
And of his folly by the chilling wind

Around him lie the stunning and the drastic
Where nothing but the utmost can be felt
The temperatures will always be fantastic
Noon will never cool nor midnight melt
A fitting climate for one so unfeeling
Who once was so indifferent to distress
He's goaded onward with his senses reeling
Without the prospect of forgetfulness

You can tell the horseman grieves for how he sinned
He rides a killing trail
Reminded of his hard heart by the hail
And of his folly by the chilling wind

The golden handshake and the lightning kisses
Were all his for the asking in the past
But the subtlety and softness that he misses
For them the horseman always moved too fast
And now at last to contemplate his error
Facing the dimensions of his loss
He journeys where the sky meets the Sierra
That every man alive must one day cross

You can tell the horseman grieves for how he sinned
He rides a killing trail
Reminded of his hard heart by the hail
And of his folly by the chilling wind

Care-charmer Sleep

I've come to think
Of what you are and everything you seem
As mine to keep
I am the sleep of which you are the dream

A state of mind
Where seeing you and thinking are the same
But there's a catch
I strike a match to set the glass aflame

And pale purple on a clear liqueur
That ring of light is all we ever were

So slight a thing
In no one's mind should ever reign supreme
I'm in deep
I am the sleep of which you are the dream

Canoe

The perfect moon was huge above the sea
The surf was easy even on the reef
We were the lucky three
Who slid in our canoe
Through the flowers on the water
And tried to read the signals in the sky

We travelled with our necklaces of shell
The moon was waning through the nights and days
And how we dreamed of home!
We couldn't find the island
Where you trade the shells for feathers
We fainted in the sun's reflected blaze

With cracking lips I turned to tell my friends
The time had come for all of us to die
'She's out a whole degree'
I told them as I floated
Checking navigation read-outs
'Re-enter at this angle and we'll fry'

The go for override came up from Earth
We took control and flew her with our hands
And how we dreamed of home!
We saw the south Pacific
As we fought to get her zeroed
Before the heat shield started hitting air

We came home in a roaring purple flame
And gave the mission back to the machines
We were the lucky three
The parachutes deployed
We were rocking like a cradle
As we drifted down in silence to the sea

I Feel Like Midnight

I feel like midnight
And whether a new day
Will ever dawn
Is just a guess

I see by starlight
The long road from the day
That I was born
To this address

And I look at where you slept
And I taste the tears you wept
And you're here again except
I feel like midnight

I feel like midnight
And you are here again
To mock me with a smile
Each time I say

I feel like midnight
And the only chance I had
To rest a while
I threw away

Give me a break
Give me the break of day –
I feel like midnight

Ready for the Road

A belt with a bull's head for a buckle
High boots that satisfy the western code
A signet ring the size of Samson's knuckle
And I'm gettin' ready for the road

I'm gettin' ready, I'll soon be good an' ready
Yes I'm gettin' ready for the road
I'm gettin' ready, yes I'll soon be good an' ready
For the road

Blue jeans that clutch me tighter than a pipe wrench
Two guns it took a forklift truck to load
I feel like I'm standin' in a slit trench
But I'm gettin' ready for the road

For the road is the home of a troubadour
And a troubadour is what I am
And I travel the trail of a troubadour
From the Empire Pool to Birmingham

But my heart belongs to Tulsa and to Tucson
For me the Alamo is à la mode
And just as soon as my horse can get its shoes on
I'll be ready for the road

I'm gettin' ready, I'll soon be good an' ready
Yes I'm gettin' ready for the road
I'm gettin' ready, yes I'll soon be good an' ready
For the road

Commercial Traveller

Home early from a meeting of the reps
He leaves the cream-bath samples in the car
A pull-along gorilla guards the steps
Confusion leads to where the children are
At the sandpit
In the garden

He wades into the kitchen through the toys
His wife leans to kiss him with a smile
And neither knows how much distance led to this
How long the while
Since on the sand spit
In the morning
The hero
Lay asleep
Until
The nymph adored him

The early dawn was baby-lotion pink
And softer than the suds of Infacare
She laved him of his brine and saw him blink
He woke to see the sunburst in her hair
And be her captive
Always

He hails the children playing in the sand
Solves the padlock on the garden shed
A giant bow should be waiting for his hand
But there instead
Lie all the implements
Of duty
For centuries
Employed
By the prisoner
On his island

He plants the hose and sets the nozzle fine
Embellishing his roses with the spray
And rainbows of a sea as dark as wine
On which he will never sail away
He will never sail away
He will never sail away

Urban Guerrilla

Automatic weapons rake the roof
Powdered concrete hangs around like spray
He huddles underneath the parapet
And knows there is no way –
This is as far as he will get

The hostages and all his friends are dead
His turn is coming soon
What was it that motherfucker said?
Better chance of conquering the moon
He holds his ringing head

    The happy endings never came
    The terrors were seldom just a dream
    Bambi was finished by the flame
    You still could hear him scream

    Snow White was rubbed out by the witch
    Mary Poppins never made the scene
    Mother Goose was just another bitch
    Full of bullshit like the Fairy Queen

The gas grenades are telling him to run
He does and something stops him like a wall
It puts him back where he has always been
His nightmares laugh to see him fall

I told you they were gonna bust your ass
Says Tom Thumb inside an upturned glass

The Eye of the Universe

I have been where time runs into time
And so partaken of the vanished glamour
Have seen Atlantis and the perfect crime
Felt eloquence replace my mental stammer
Seen every evil brought beneath the hammer
In this mood all that Faust desired is mine

I am the eye with which the universe beholds itself
And knows itself divine

I have been to see my death prepare
Inside a Packard, somnolently cruising
The sure-fire way of giving me the air
And totting up exactly what I'm losing
Found such an end not too far from my choosing
I have settled up with Charon at the Styx

I am the eye with which the universe beholds itself
And knows itself a fix

I've crossed an atlas with the Golden Horde
Seen all the Seven Cities of Cibola
Olympus was a geriatric ward
The Promised Land is just the old payola
It's all the same shellac, the same Victrola
Eternity should have more in the bag

I am the eye with which the universe beholds itself
And knows itself a drag

I have been where age runs into age
Have seen the children burned, the slaves in halters
The cutting edge is wearing off my rage
I leave them their strange gods, their reeking altars
And the way the reign of terror never falters
They were fighting for the right to count the slain

I am the eye with which the universe beholds itself
And knows itself insane

I have seen the gentle meet the savage day
In the sunlight on the spandrels of the towers
And in the moonlight very far away
The honeymoon canoe glide through the flowers
And the party left behind go on for hours
For a while things were as peaceful as they seemed

I am the eye with which the universe beholds itself
And knows itself redeemed

My Brother's Keeper

My brother lives in fear
Of the hidden cries he seems to hear
Somewhere ahead the King of Hell
Somewhere below a kitten in a well

Am I my brother's keeper?
Am I my brother's keeper?

My brother lives a lie
When his laughter splits the summer sky
Somewhere inside he skips a breath
Somewhere in there he dies the little death

Am I my brother's keeper?
Am I my brother's keeper?

Every second morning now for years
My brother has put on my brawn and brain
To wander through the universe in pain
And my happiness of yesterday
Is walked and scorned away
Before he returns to me in tears

My brother lives a life
In the narrow shadow of the knife
Somewhere behind a hill of skulls
Somewhere below a beach of dying gulls

Am I my brother's keeper?
Am I my brother's keeper?

History and Geography

The history and geography of feeling less than wonderful are
    known to me
The dates of broken bubbles and the whereabouts of every lost
    belief
And from the point of tears I see how far away across the sea
    of troubles
The pinnacles of happiness are halfway hidden in the clouds
    of grief

My common sense can tell me all it likes to count myself among
    the lucky
For pity's sake to draw a breath and take a look around me and
    compare
But all I seem to see and hear is something I'm unable to
    remember
The flowing speech that stuttered out, the pretty song that faded
    on the air

When the jet returns me half awake and half asleep to what I call
    my homeland
I look down into the midnight city through the empty inkwell
    of the sky
And in that kit of instruments laid out across a velvet-covered
    table
I know that nothing lives which doesn't hold its place more
    worthily than I

Without a home, without a name, a girl of whom to say this is
    my sister
For I am all the daughters of my father's house and all the
    brothers too
I comb the rubble of a shattered world to find the bright face
    of an angel
And say again and say again that I have written this – this is
    for you

The history and geography of feeling less than wonderful are
   known to me
When sunsets are unlovely and the dawns are coldly calculated
   light
And from the heights of arrogance across the steps that later
   I regretted
I see those angel faces flame their last and flicker out into the
   night

Femme Fatale

It isn't fear I feel, or lack of nerve
Call it just a sensible reserve
When faced with the intoxicating verve
Of anyone who dazzles me like you
The children turning flint-wheels in the mines looked pretty too
And sparks were shaken out like golden rain
And oh so very lovely were the loneliness and pain

It's not because I'm burning out or old
I hesitate to snuggle in the fold
Of body heat that really beats the cold
Though Icarus flew near the sun and fell
The chandeliers above the weeping fields looked warm as well
And flares would crumple down like fairy lights
And oh so very lovely were the long and fearful nights

It's all because you are too much for me
Too good to last, too beautiful to be
That you are doomed to be a casualty
Of the night fight on my deeps of memory
A galleon with fire below falls glowing through the sea
And every mast shall tremble like a tree
And oh so very lovely shine the blast that breaks them free

A Hill of Little Shoes

I live in the shadow of a hill
A hill of little shoes
I love but I shiver with a chill
A chill I never lose
I live, I love, but where are they?
Where are their lives, their loves? All blown away
And every little shoe is a foot that never grew
Another day

If you could find a pair and put them on the floor
Make a mark in the air like the marks beside your door
When you were growing
You'd see how tall they were

And the buckles and the laces they could do up on their own
Or almost could
With their tongue-tips barely showing
Tell you how small they were

And then you'd think of little faces looking fearfully alone
And how they stood
In their bare feet being tall for the last time
Just to be good
And that was all they were

They were like you in the same year but you grew up
They were barely even here before they suddenly weren't there
And while you got dressed for bed they did the same but they
    were led
Into another room instead
And they were all blown away into thin air

I live in the shadow of a hill
A hill of little shoes
I love but I shiver with a chill
A chill I never lose
And I caught that cold when I was chosen to grow old
In the shadow of a hill of little shoes

Dancing Master

As the world goes past me
I have enough to last me
As long as you come to call
And hang your coat and hat on the hook in the hall

This is the step we'll learn tonight
Turn on a dime and stay upright
Come back slowly in your own time
I'll wait for you

As the world goes past me
I have enough to last me
As long as we dance like this
And what a man's never had he will never miss

This is the way the step looks best
Keep it neat as you come to rest
And if my heart seems to skip a beat
Just wait for me

Just wait for me the way I wait for you
For all the endless hours in a week
This is the silent language lovers speak
When they mean nothing except what's true

Just wait for me the way I wait for you
To change your shoes before we say goodbye
This is the world where I will never die
Or lie awake for what I'm going through

As the world goes past me
I have enough to last me
As long as we dance like that
There's a hook in the hall and it's waiting for your coat and hat

I Have to Learn to Live Alone Again

I have to learn
To live alone again
I used to burn
To live alone again
But this is now
And that was then
And now I have to live alone again

Did you paint your bedroom gold the way you planned?
Is the same love song open on the music stand?
Not knowing things like that is part of missing you
As much as never touching you or kissing you

I cross the silver bridge and see your balcony
The vines have filled the trellis with a filigree
I had such plans to see the way your garden grew
But missing out on that is part of missing you
As much as never touching you or kissing you

I have to learn
To live alone again
I used to burn
To live alone again
But now I do
I wonder when
I'll ever learn
To live alone
Again

Winter Spring

This is the way that winter says goodbye to spring
By whispering we will not meet this year
This year I will not see you flower or hear you sing

The time is over now you could look back to me
And see the way the crocus cupped the snow
Part of the picture in your show of pageantry

The grass would not have been as green without the frost
The night prepares the splendour of the day
My hands were cold and now they're cold as cold can be
I fold them to my chest and turn away

This is the way that winter says goodbye to spring
By whispering we will not meet this year
This year I will not see you flower or hear you sing
Or taste the brilliance that you bring
To everything.

PEREGRINE PRYKKE'S
PILGRIMAGE THROUGH THE
LONDON LITERARY WORLD

A Tragic Poem in Rhyming Couplets

To Prue

It is the wound inflicted upon our self-love, not the stain upon the character of the thoughtless offender, that calls for condign punishment. Crimes, vices may go unchecked, or unnoticed: but it is the laughing at our weaknesses, or thwarting of our humours, that is never to be forgotten. It is not the errors of others, but our own miscalculations, on which we wreak our lasting vengeance. It is ourselves that we cannot forgive.

– Hazlitt, *On Will-Making*

A Guide to the Characters of the London Literary World

PEREGRINE PRYKKE, a critic: author of *Loose Laurels*
MRS PRYKKE, his Mother
GRAHAM GROTT, a schoolteacher
F. R. LOOSELEAF, a prophet at Downing, Cambridge
CYNTHIA DEVINE, an *ingénue* at Girton, Cambridge
DOC STEIN, a polymath at Churchill, Cambridge
IAN HAMMERHEAD, poet, critic and editor
L. L. EL AL, poet, critic and mountaineer
SEAMUS FEAMUS, an Irish poet
MARVIN GRABB, a television personality
JELLY-ROLL BELLY, journalist, jazz singer and television
    personality
DOUGLAS DUNGE, a Scots poet
TED THEWS, an animistic icon
HUGO HARSFRIED, a minimalist poet
KLAUS MAULER, editor of the *Listener*
JEFF NUTTCASE and BOB JOBBING, two poets of the people
TERRY TOWELLING, literary editor of the *Observer*
MICHAEL KOITUS, an operator at the ICA
BRIAN GOUGH and HENRI PATTEN, a pantomime horse from
    Liverpool
MITCH L. ADRIAN, a revolutionary poet
CREEPING GEORGE MCDEATH, poet and impresario
ANNA PEST, poet, model and vamp
THE MARCHIONESS OF PROPERLITTLE-RAYVER, a noble
    patroness of the Arts
BOB LULL, an American poet
JOHN BRAINWAVE, a Northern novelist
WEE GEORGIE WIDE, chairman of Tightenbelt and
    Buckledown, publishers
EDWARD PYGGE, a mysterious satirist
BIG JOHN GROSS, editor and man of letters
WALTER WAITER, poet and gentleman
GAVIN SUET and ALAN BROWNJUG, friends to Waiter

Colin Fluck, poet and aesthetician
Richard Bierstein, ale correspondent of the *Guardian*
John Fop and James Flint, two formalist poets
Derwent Meek, assistant editor to Mauler
Professor 'Chris' Rix, a super-Don: author of *Yeats and Humiliation*
Charles Ozbuns, chairman of the State Arts Hand-out Panel
Greer Garstleigh and Kate Millbomb, two feminists
Rock Horrorball, an experimental poet
Pauline and Poogy Scheissenhaus, two sculptors
Haiku Yamashita, an insane Japanese conceptual artist
The Peking People's Puppeteers' Platoon, a dance troupe
The Rubber Freaks For Cuba, another dance troupe
Kingsley Kong and Norman Moonbase, two grand old SF buffs of the Right
Tony Godspell, a whizz-kid editor
Bernard Beaver, a music-loving journalist
Wildwind Wagtail, a zany
Tony Time, a sequential novelist
Philip Lawks, a provincial poet
Lord Teddybear, the Poet Laureate
Mag Scrabble, novelist and broadcaster
Stephen Spindle, a venerable literary figure
Frankie Mode, Ubiquitous Professor of English Literature
Clara Tomahawk, literary editor of different magazines
N. T. Thweet, literary editor of the same magazines at different times
Philip Phrog, producer of *Kritiks' Kworum*
Lady Freesia Fruitcake, a biographer
Margerina Latchkey, a broadcaster
Bron Wan, a permanent adolescent
Kid Kong, son to Kingsley: a boy novelist
Harold Half-Pint, an elliptical playwright
Chief Clerk, an aesthete
Huge Welshman, BBC: Director-General
Stanley Storkins, a Northern playwright
Felicity Fark, an innocent young actress

LORD FRUITCAKE, a humble Peer
LORD FATMAN, a sage
LORD BUTCHFIELD, photographer and motorcyclist
LORD POLAROID, a tragedian

AND MANY MORE

Book One

Because so many ask what he was *like*,
I sing the life and death of Master Prykke,
Whose first name, Peregrine, he shrank to Perry –
His lone and doomed endeavour to be merry.
A worthy youth, whose reasonable gravity
Was so sincere it bordered on depravity –
The kind of finely balanced moral fervour
That fills the Leader Page of the *Observer* –
Although I should at this point quickly add
I find that paper's Arts Page not half bad,
Perhaps because, week in, week out, I'm in it,
And so are (they'll be on stage in a minute)
My co-narrators of this gory story,
Which will, to *Perry Prykke*'s undying glory,
Retrace the apices and plumb the abysses
Of his anabasis and – well, catabasis.
We won't go through (it's all been done before)
The business of how, winding up the War,
The Middle Class – as ever, keen to strive –
Renewed itself in 1945
(Much pleased at having seen off sinful *Jerry*)
By siring many sons, including *Perry*:
A product of the Population Bulge
Whose Fame was foredoomed fiercely to effulge,
But who at first lay listless in his swaddling,
Indifferent to the whole idea of coddling.
It was a solemn babe, with earnest eyes:
The kind that rarely smiles yet never cries.
A shy one, even shame-faced, at the breast,
It gave, for every nappy that it messed,
A long and heartfelt semaphored apology
Betokening an insecure psychology.
Ex-Colonel *Prykke*, with what his loins had wrought
Well pleased (he was not one for abstract thought)
Went dourly back to daily setting forth
From *Audley End* in the commuter's North

387

To keep the same old ledgers in the *City*.
No room for passion there, still less for pity:
Let's give him our ungrudging admiration
And focus on his Offspring's education.
But then, let's not. That territory too
Is too well ploughed by now to plough anew.
Suffice to say young *Perry*'s brain was graded
And deemed an organ fit to be State-aided
(With due allowance for his Father's earnings),
Solidifying thus his Mother's yearnings:
She dreamed of great deeds in a high arena
And saw them promised in her child's demeanour.
By Mum spurred on, and swotting might and main,
Young *Perry* climbed the greasy inclined plane
Towards the next best thing to private schooling
(And near enough to set his Mother drooling) –
An Indirect Grant Semi-Public Grammar
Fee-paying Approved Labour-Camp *cum* Crammer
Yclept *Queen Anne's Academy, King's Lynn.*
He sat the entrance paper, and got in.
We'll set aside his first years at the School.
He proved, by diligence, he was no fool,
Or anyway he showed he was no sluggard.
In fact he slaved away till he was buggered
(Though for the place's sake I'm pleased to say
He was not buggered as he slaved away)
And brought back books of different shapes and sizes
The Beaks had dished out liberally as prizes
To mark his special aptitude for Writing,
At which they thought him far the most exciting
(As well as well-turned-out and soundly grounded)
High-flyer since the day Queen Anne's was founded.
Such praise was hollow – there had been few others –
But stuff like that goes down a treat with Mothers,
And at each calf-bound presentation tome
Our *Perry*'s *Mum* lowed like a cow come home
To give its milk into a friendly pail.
Age well could wither her, and custom stale
Her light-years-less-than-infinite variety,
But nothing short of death could shake her Piety.

To graze green pastures with a Higher Breed
By proxy through her Son was all her creed,
Since no belief or dream in all Creation
Could match her faith in Transubstantiation.
But there. My tale's five minutes under foot
(Or *on* foot? Under way? Which do I put?)
And here I'm standing, still the sole voice telling it.
If this keeps up I'll soon be hoarsely yelling it –
High time that I wheeled on another witness
Beyond reproach on grounds of mental fitness
Whose views are more dispassionate than not:
It's *Perry*'s English master, GRAHAM GROTT –
A solid, stolid *Cantabridge* MA
Who prays to *Downing College* twice a day.
Though one of F. R. LOOSELEAF's also-rans
Grott featured as a Young Turk at *Queen Anne*'s –
The first man to detect our lad's potential
And grasp that careful coaching was essential.
'One can't',
        Grott now recalls,
                      'hope, in the course
Of things, to find the Full Creative Force
Of Felt Thought in the as-yet unformed speech
Of those one is condemn— er, proud to teach
At Institutes of Learning such as ours.
Yet now and then a boy of special powers
Reveals himself as eager to be taught:
A boy in whom the Felt Creative Thought,
The Force of Thought, of Life Felt to the Full . . .'
I ought to warn you that this kind of bull
Was taken down *verbatim* as dictation
By generation after generation
Of listeners to *F. R. Looseleaf*'s preachings,
Who rated them above the Talmud's teachings
As distillations of the True and Serious.
By chanting them, the dull became delirious,
Attaining just as ice cold an hysteria
As anything that goes on in *Siberia*,
Then fell back in a self-obsessed *Satori* –
But more of that anon. On with the story.

By now *Grott*'s run the gamut of abstraction
And might say something pertinent to the action.
'Though not yet free of juvenile frivolities,
His class-work had those Life-Enhancing Qualities –
Felt, Life-Affirming, Reverent of Reality,
Without, I needn't add, Sentimentality –
Which show that one is *For* Life, not Against it . . .'
This man's a total idiot, you've sensed it:
For who except a *kamikaze* pilot
(i.e. one trained from childhood to revile it)
Can look on life in any other way?
'And so I called him to my room one day
To offer – Come in! – an attentive ear
Should he have doubts concerning his Career.'
'Gosh, Sir, I'm sorry in my thing on *Pope*
I got Metathesis mixed up with Trope,'
Whined *Perry*,

         'Unforgivable, I know . . .'
'No, no, *Prykke*,'

       countered *Grott*,

              'don't tremble so.
I called you here for quite another thing:
To take you, as it were, beneath my wing
And tell you what to look for, what to fear,
When *Cambridge* welcomes you this coming year.'
'Gosh,'

    Perry cried,

           'it's certain, do you think?'
'As sure as keen men rise and slack men sink
You shall go up to *Sydney Selwyn College*.
But Wisdom,'

      added *Grott*,

           'is more than Knowledge.
You have to be For Life and not Against . . .'
(The dialogue from here on I've condensed.)
'. . . And pay attention always to one man;
A man the like of whom, since Time began,
Has not been seen; a man Misrepresented,
But whose Achievement can't be circumvented

By such sophisticated forms of treason
As cleverness or wit or common reason.
The prophet *F. R. Looseleaf*'s who I mean:
My hero and, I hope, yours, *Peregrine*.'
'Gosh, yes!'

       squeaked *Prykke*,

              'I've read *The Great Pursuit*
And not a word of it could I refute.
I'm staggered by the potent observations
That crowd the pages of *Regurgitations*.
Life's Full Creative Force is what he's for . . .'
They drivelled on for half an hour or more
While *Grott* got through a fair-sized cask of sherry –
And even slipped a glass or two to *Perry*.
'Good (gosh) bye, Shir, and thanksh for all you've done.'
'Good luck,'

       gruffed *Grott*, as if to his own son:
His final words of interest to the plot,
So let's say goodbye too to *Graham Grott*
And send him off to sort out wigs and noses
For further dialogues and daring poses
Suggesting divers well-known personalities
At different times in various localities –
A pluralist approach whose guiding factor's
The fact that we could not afford more actors.

Book Two

BUT anyway, to *Cambridge*. Revelation!
Completely beyond every expectation
Revolved in *Perry Prykke*'s most fevered dreams.
The place reduced his *Mum* to muted screams
And tears of joy when she, her Consort driving,
At last attained the *Canaan* of her striving
And parked her Son with those picked to inherit
The *Earth* or else to win it by sheer merit –
A gang of pampered kids and brash young hustlers
Who talk one tongue, like cattle-kings and rustlers.
But *Peregrine* paid no heed to such things:
Instead, his narrow soul grew narrow wings.
His fund of verve might well have been exiguous
But still his revelry was unambiguous.
Though no one yet had taught him to drink deep
He stumbled as if stunned or half asleep.
He hardly spent a single moment sober
That frosty-cold and crystalline *October*,
But cycled dazedly 'twixt Hall and Lecture
Intoxicated by the architecture
And how the trees extended brittle glass
Unleaving limbs above the fog-soaked grass
(As lustrous as a cat-skin from *Siam*)
That joined the Colleges and lined the *Cam*,
Beneath whose icy surface lay concealed,
Like tools of war beneath a battlefield,
Corroded bike-frames, clapped-out batsman's boxes
And one or two cadavers of drowned coxes
Tossed in with hearty laughter at *Bump Suppers*
Or else some other orgy, e.g. *Cuppers*.
The rank, the razzmatazz, the rigmarole!
Right from the start *Prykke* swallowed that stuff whole.
He loved his little gown and wore it always.
It followed him through cloister-courts and hallways.
He wore his gown to town and to the toilet,
And if he chanced to soil it he would boil it.

On application long if in mind meagre,
Our Freshman was as pure of heart and eager
As any trainee monk in ancient *Lhasa.*
You never *saw* a *tabula* more *rasa.*
The first great influence to be impressed
Upon this bland, receptive palimpsest
Was one as drastic as it was dramatic:
It left our *Perry* limp and yet ecstatic.
Who else but *F. R. Looseleaf,* outlaw don,
Proud put-upon lay priest and paragon?
Young *Perry Prykke* found *Looseleaf's* merest seminar
As shattering as gin and bitter lemon are
To someone in the grip of hepatitis,
Or volleyball to people with arthritis.
This man had grandeur. Gritty, grim, persuasive,
Irascible, inflexible, abrasive,
He faced four-square his foes on every side
And told them what *Canute* once told the tide.
'We see that, far from evil or Satanic,
The Force of Life in *Lawrence* is Organic.
I needn't add,'

             he added,

                      'that, for *Lawrence,*
The Sex theme is no matter for abhorrence
As *Snow* or *Annan* might be apt to think,
But something more akin to meat and drink.
Against their cheap ideas of what's Enlightening
Lawrentian Desire might *well* seem frightening.
For what else is his fruitfulness, of course,
But Felt Life in its Full Creative Force?'
To malleable *Perry* this was caviar.
Now *this,* he thought, is what concern and savvy are.
At *Looseleaf's* lectures *Prykke* would sit and scribble
The whole kaboodle down without a quibble,
Then talk it over afterwards with one
Who'd done precisely that which he had done:
A comely girl called CYNTHIA DEVINE.
Ah, would the powers of *Mendelssohn* were mine!
For I would write down now a row of notes,
Which notes, when played, would, as a bubble floats,

Waft perfect pictures of her to your eye –
Or do I mean your ear? A saint would cry
To think that he must spend his life without her.
Fair *Cynthia* had something *sweet* about her.
God knows I'm less than willing to digress.
The thought already puts me in distress
That *Perry*, if I ramble at this rate
Will never even get to graduate.
But still I'm bound – and just to be judicious,
No more than that – to say she was *delicious.*
Her eyes were tubs of liquid innocence
Devoid of guile, deprived of all defence;
Her nose was built and bobbed by *Pisanello*
Or some equivalent *Renaissance* fellow;
Her skin, peach yoghurt, bloomed against the air,
Contested in food-value by her hair –
A crowning glory falling like the night
To kiss her waistline, which was very slight.
Extremities below were brief but neat.
Her skirt was plaid, and fastened at the pleat
By means of a symbolic safety-pin –
Thin armour for the charms that lay within.
Above, her tiny booblets swam before her
Like desperate hamsters drowning in angora . . .
But there, my whole description has been physical.
I fear I've missed her aura, which was *quizzical.*
When *Cynthia Devine* looked at the World
Her mouth was open and her toes were curled
For sheer anticipation of its yielding
The secrets it had spent her lifetime shielding.
She was a question mark, a walking query,
A pint-sized *Amundsen* or *Admiral Peary.*
Sweet *Cynth* was all For Life, For Creativity:
And *Perry* – well, he shared the same proclivity.
And so, coeval like the Sol and Gel
Whose two simplicities make up a Cell,
These youngsters were as one in their propensities:
Untutored spirits fused by twin intensities.
Together in the Stacks, the twain would garner
Apt quotes for essays about *Silas Marner,*

Or hand-in-hand make notes on *Sons and Lovers*
Until that tattered *Penguin* lost its covers.
Behind a sported Oak in early *May*
They sat to read, and then, one day, they lay.
'For Life and not Against it!'

                          the lad cried.

'For Life!'

                 she moaned, recumbent by his side.
The tender warmth was too much for our *Perry*:
He lost his head, and *Cynthia* her cherry.
Let's leave them to their bliss, in blossom-fall,
When *Cambridge* lawns adopt a muslin shawl;
When bluebells choking daisies in the meadows
Run crazier than *Thomas Lovell Beddoes*,
And Callowness takes up the alto sax;
When punts can barely move along the Backs
And pretty backs are bare inside the punts.
For even in *Elysium*, just once
Does First Love come, like mumps or German measles –
And meanwhile, with a mighty roar of diesels,
Somebody was arriving at the Station
To whom we should devote our concentration.
His name was broadcast by a neon sign
On top of his top hat. It said Doc Stein.
A placard on his back asked, 'Tired? Tense?'
And answered, 'Take my Culture cure. Ten cents.'
His frock coat was stuffed full of fluent speeches
Stuffed full in turn with such unusual features
As tags in every tongue, alive and dead:
Trinitro-Ruritanian, Infra-Red,
Low-Temperature Etruscan, Serb, Seismography,
Deoxyribose, X-ray Crystallography,
The signs a cockroach makes to greet its mother
And *Barthes* and *Lévi-Strauss* to greet each other.
'The Lapse',

             spake *Stein*,

                        'of Culture in the West
We know to be (a spectroscopic test
Was carried out last week at *MIT*,
By seven leading brains including me)

A function of Verbality's decay.
If Culture-Norms subsist in what we say,
Our Complex Sentences, like strings of genes –
Those Blueprints which themselves become Machines –
Contain the Codes for Structures of Cognition.
It Is No Accident that the attrition
Of our Linguistic Formulae takes place
Within the context of a Fall from Grace
By all that *Europe*'s Thinkers have erected.
The preconceptions *Heidegger* rejected
Were taken up by *Max Planck, Edward Teller,*
Hans Keller, Alfred Deller, Uri Geller . . .'
Doc Stein could keep it up like that for ages
And gently raise the stakes by easy stages
Until his ravished audience (ah, Youth!)
Were utterly convinced he told the Truth.
While winding up towards his grand finale
He ranted and waxed goggle-eyed like *Dali.*
While speaking what might well have been *Illyrian*
He blasted off in flames for the *Empyrean.*
'The longings represented by *Karl Kraus*
We know to have recurred in *Mickey Mouse*!
Krafft-Ebing, Kundt and *Kitasato* shared
A pH number times B-flat all squared!
The pulsing Neutron Star is nothing less,
It may well be, than just a game of Chess
At which, perhaps, a dog can beat a Don
By humming *Tosca* through a cyclotron!
We do not know! We only know that Violence
Has finally reduced our speech to Silence!
Dumbfounded, we are waiting for a Sign!
All tongues are still! Except, of course, for mine!'
Bedazzled, *Perry* raced away to plant a
Review of what he'd just sat through in *Granta* –
Of which he had become, by sheer hard graft,
The engine, the propeller and the shaft.
His admiration now was all for *Stein,*
But *Looseleaf* quickly got him back in line.
'We see in Stein, prolixly ineffectual,
The typical *New Statesman* intellectual.

His shallow cosmopolitan loquacity
(Both aiding and abetting that mendacity
The foolish take to be what's cultivated)
Is just what *D. H. Lawrence* always hated:
That *Lawrence* who, himself supremely apt
For penetrating cultures yet untapped
By arid, quantifying sociologists,
Perceived instinctively that all apologists
For Learning in the abstract – cold induction –
Were *ipso facto* agents of destruction.
I don't think I need add, I think you know,
That *Stein* has taken cocktails with *Lord Snow*
And has been heard – he's proud of it! – to plan an
Encroachment against Values with *Lord Annan.*'
Since *Perry* believed everything he heard
He fell for this, too, every single word,
And modified his writings in the light of it
By saying *both* these pundits had the right of it.
Nor did his handy knack of seeing double
At this stage get him into any trouble,
Because a point of pride with every Don
Is not to know a thing of what goes on
In Student Life, and hold it in derision –
A system known as Personal Supervision.
'The locus of our Structure perhaps maps
Lawrentian Verbality's collapse,'
Wrote *Perry Prykke*, agog with more ideas
(Exactly two) than he had had in years,
'We do not know the cube of the square root
Because organic languages are mute.'
The plodding yet prolific literatus
Puffed up with intellectual afflatus;
The lover of the cutest girl in *Girton*
(Which put him on a par with *Richard Burton*,
Since *Cambridge* birds are very hard to get);
Brave *Perry* was without a doubt all set
To start out on a glorious career
Of telling people what they longed to hear.
For *Prykke* was pliant in the first degree –
Which quicker spirits could already see,

And soon the *Tripos* papers made it clearer.
The Dons, half cut as usual on *Madeira*,
In lonely rooms gave pencilled approbation
To *Perry*'s faithful recapitulation
Of what each one had taught as the True Creed.
The awkward fact that *Prykke* also agreed
With everybody else, they didn't spot.
And so a *First Degree* was what he got.
Hail Graduation Day! O time of times!
When *Great St Mary*'s showers down her chimes
On those who throng the lawn of *Regent House*
To be at last rewarded. Not for nous,
But for their luck in having caught the bus
That runs express from the *Eleven Plus*,
Careering past those poor souls in the Poly –
Or else for simply having had the lolly.
Starred First? A Third? Who cares? You're still BA!
Yes, *everybody* gets a prize today!
Great bleating herds of woolly graduands
In joky hats and white bow ties and bands!
And somewhere in the middle, the grave *Perry*
Attends his *Cynthia* like an equerry.
And now we see, in search of him, his *Mum*,
Who's just arrived, and, far from stricken dumb,
She's raving with delight at all this pap.
And now she's caught a glimpse of *Perry*'s cap!
'It's got a little tassle!'
                                    With a howl
She sinks into that sea of robe and cowl,
And lying on the grass enjoys full measure
The culmination of erotic pleasure –
A sight on which the Dons turn anxious eyes
But fail, I needn't add, to recognize.
Let's leave her there and listen to her clever
Descendant pledge his fealty forever.
'Gosh, *Cynth*, I wish I didn't have to leave.'
'Ah, *Heathcliff*, dearest darling, do not grieve.'
For *Cynth* was staying on to do Research
On where the *Brontës* used to sit in church.

Did all the sisters squeeze into one pew?
If *Branwell* came they must have needed two.
Her thesis really would be *most* exciting –
And three or even four years in the writing.
'Please promise, *Heathcliff*, as you value me
That you will be For Life, as I'm for thee.'
'For Life,'
         he vowed, but Life is a long time
For young men scarcely even in their prime:
A fact to which my reference must be glancing –
The plot is in a fret to be advancing.
That *Perry Prykke* had not put in in vain
His precious time on *Granta* was now plain.
The waves of tempting offers never halted
To ply his pen in papers more exalted.
But of these *London*-postmarked exhortations
It was the briefest gave him fibrillations –
Just such a note's been known to give far hardier
Recipients than *Perry* tachycardia.
'Please see me when you come to town,' it said.
The signature read IAN HAMMERHEAD.
The famous editor they called the 00
.7 *Bond* of literary *Soho*!
The *TLS*'s frozen-eyed Enforcer
Who thought that poetry went wrong with *Chaucer*!
For *Perry* not to heed that fearsome call
Would mean to gamble nothing, yet lose all.
(He wanted, with his Destiny ahead of him,
Nobody else enjoying it instead of him.)
The gage was down, the battle-flag unfurled!
The prize? *The London Literary World*!
And so *Prykke* left the *Varsity* behind,
Full certain, in what served him for a mind,
That somewhere Southward, far beyond the *Fen*,
His Fate awaited him, in the *Great Wen*.

Book Three

Now *Hammerhead* infests, as all know well,
A pub in *Greek Street* called the GATES OF HELL,
And thither *Perry* bent his guileless step,
Astonished (while pretending to be hep)
At all the true-to-life fold-out displays
Of Doxies in the doors and alleyways
Extending him an open invitation
To some form, he assumed, of Penetration –
Though other variations of seduction
Appeared to put the emphasis on Suction.
He reached the *Gates of Hell* shocked to the core,
Breathed in, breathed out, and pushed the double door.
Good Heavens! Were this mob of odds and sods
His fondly cherished Literary gods?
Huge *Irish* navvies lounged about befuddled
Or else in softly spoken groups sat huddled
Preoccupied with clocks and bits of fuse –
It seemed a strange Headquarters for the *Muse*.
Blue clouds of cigarette smoke surged and plumed,
Then suddenly from out of them there loomed
The stony countenance of *Hammerhead*.
'You've taken your time getting here,'

                                    it said.

'Expect you'd like to write for the *Review*.
You might just do it, in a year or two.
But as for now, I'll have to dash your hopes.
You look like you might need to learn the ropes.
The first great principle you'll have to watch
Is, I take bitter with my double scotch.'
'Gosh, Sir,'

            cringed *Prykke*,

                              'I'm sorry to be rude:
It's just that, as you see, I'm not too clued
Er, up, as yet, on Literary ways.
I must look like I'm in some sort of daze.'
'There isn't any need to call me "Sir"

Or anything like that. I much prefer
To be addressed as Chief, or Number One.
But anyway, to business. We've begun
With our First Law. The Second's just as sound:
It's Nearly Always Time For The Next Round.'
'Gosh, Sir – er, Chief – I must apologize . . .'
'Forget about it, kid. I sympathize.
Hell, everyone in this dodge starts off raw:
It's just that some are less so, others more.
Now keep your lip well buttoned while I speak.
At least a hundred Novels every week
Engulf the *TLS* and must be judged –
A *Herculean* task that can't be fudged.
I need a writer with your fresh young style . . .'
(As well, he didn't say, as your dumb smile)
'. . . to grapple with this *Sisyphean* job.'
'Gosh, Number One,'

                    said *Perry* with a sob
Of gratitude, while sinking to his knees.
'You'll find that I'm an easy man to please,'
Said *Hammerhead*, his eyelids thin with scorn.
'Just take this pile of Fiction and don't fawn:
I'm more than happy if you merely grovel.
The one on top's the new *Mag Scrabble* novel.
It's all about two sisters who write books.
One's gifted, and the other's got no looks.
Lead off with that. With any luck, you'll hate it.
In which case don't be reticent – berate it.'
With *Hammerhead* beside him (a black Nemesis
Exhaustively familiar with the premises),
Our *Perry* (by now smashed out of his mind)
Was thereupon led off like *Samson* blind
To meet – or if not that, at least palpate –
The Great Names lying hazily in wait
Like fabled dreadnoughts in the *Jutland* fog.
As damply frog-encrusted as *King Log*
They hulked towards him from the gloom crepuscular.
This one, for instance – hirsute, squat and muscular –
Was *Hammerhead*'s most formidable pal:
The poet-mountaineer, L. L. EL AL.

El Al, although he scarcely scraped the sky,
Looked any man directly in the eye,
No matter if the man were *James Arness*.
The secret? It lay in his mode of dress.
Equipped with crampons, coils of nylon rope
And ever-ready ice-axe, he could cope
By night or day with climbing from your base
To plant his gallant flag in your *North Face* –
A prelude to deploying his capacity
For unrestrained rhetorical pugnacity,
Selecting verbs according to velocity
And nouns for scatalogical ferocity.
To *Prykke*, the prick of pitons in his chest,
Plus painful pick-axe prongs poked through his vest,
Spelt *finis* to his *savoir faire*. He froze –
With *El Al*'s famous beard stuck up his nose.
'Now hear me good. The big trick of this game,'
El Al announced,

    'is Build Yourself A Name.
And when you do, don't fritter it away:
Just screw the bums a century a day
For anything you write, no matter what.
Like, *Late Night Line-Up*? Forty quid a shot:
Plus helicopter fare, another fifty.
A hundred for the evening if you're nifty.
So far this year – that's Fiscal '68 –
I've earned five thou a quarter, steady rate.
My agent's agent sets the tax aside
For when I write my book on Suicide –
A treatise on the Artist's Alienation
In Business-Oriented Civilization.'
The next to bulk *Dantesquely* from the mist
Was *Hammerhead*'s death-dealing Satirist,
The man who made the hits for *Mr Big*:
Prykke caught his breath, for this was *Edward Pygge* –
Laconic in trench coat and felt fedora
Like *Dana Andrews* dreaming about *Laura*.
The poet *Walter Waiter* shook *Prykke*'s hand.
Wise *Waiter*'s cross it was to understand

The motives of all men. He thereby earned
A brand that fiercely festered, foully burned:
The fell renown of being a Nice Guy.
(The chump had never even learned to lie.)
Against him leaned the gentle *Gavin Suet*,
As finely lined and wind-tanned as *James Stewart*.
Below them *Alan Brownjug*, looking up,
Was catching all their spilled beer in a cup.
And here was *Colin Fluck*, the Aesthetician,
Profoundly silent in the Stork Position:
A witness for the creed that Art is Life –
Which is absurd, like saying Man is Wife.
And there was *Big John Gross*, the Man of Learning,
Who kept his massive mental motor turning
By feeding it some colourless, *Slavonic*
Extractive lightly qualified with tonic.
To go away, or else to stay behind?
Big John could never quite make up his mind
On that or any point, and kept contriving
To half depart while only half arriving.
And there was *Richard Bierstein*, rich in jest –
Whose task it is empirically to test
The thousand different kinds and strengths of ale
Great Britain's countless pubs have got on sale.
(The job's like tasting wine, except much greater
Amounts are swallowed and you get home later.)
Prykke gazed in speechless fright as *Bierstein* drank,
Rolled over like the *Bismarck*, heaved and sank –
A spout of steaming bubbles and low moans
Revealing where he'd gone to *Davy Jones*.
Lost in the fumes, heads intermingled hairily.
Lost in the hair, unsmiling eyes watched warily.
These were the *Belfast* poets – all called *Seamus* –
Of whom the leading light was SEAMUS FEAMUS,
Who even now attacked his midday meal:
Two slabs of peat around a conger eel.
'White spoors of cockle,'
                                        Feamus mumbled,
                                                                'plumb
Tight mounds brine-splashed with goat-frost. Futtled, numb,

I slop the dunt melt of the scurfing bog's
Black molars to the shred-hung mandrake. Dogs
Like spirochetes torment my afterbirth . . .'
Warmed by the joke, his cronies quaked with mirth.
And there the dandy formalist *John Fop*
(Whose clothes leave *Kojak* looking like a cop)
Stood talking shop with *Trotskyite James Flint*
(Who like a *Conrad* Outcast looked clean skint –
For though *Flint* had, as *Fop* had, a white suit on,
Flint's looked like it belonged to *Robert Newton*.)
And this smooth-looking lad was MARVIN GRABB,
Who seemed a drowsy victim of *Queen Mab*,
But was in fact the televisual host
Of shows that sliced the Arts like buttered toast
And served them up bedecked with marmalade –
Throughout which blithe proceedings he displayed
A bonhomie tenacious as alfalfa.
He marked the Works of Art all out of alpha,
Bestowing many pluses and few minuses
Through perfect teeth, though less than perfect sinuses.
And still they came, like damned souls to the *Styx*,
Aflicker like short candles with long wicks,
Aflutter like the air above hot streets –
Tomorrow's *Byron* and the latest *Keats*,
The future *Browning* and the brand-new *Shelley*,
And JELLY-ROLL ('Just Call Me Jelly') BELLY!
Of *Belly Prykke* had never seen the likes:
He stared at him as *Twist* stared at *Bill Sikes*.
For *Belly* was an avatar, a magus,
A blazing apparition like *Las Vegas*.
His suit was made from twenty different leathers,
His coat from forty different kinds of feathers.
Around his stetson ran a clockwork train.
He sang and danced as if he were in pain.

'Oh *Perry*, baby, welcome to the band!
I'd like to shake your lily-white wet hand!
You've got the kind of walnut-shell rear end
I once was prone to look for in a friend!

'That's *prone*, you get me? Yeah, and supine too.
But when they made it legal, I was through.
The Gay Scene nowadays is just for hicks.
The current trend is – get your kicks with chicks!

'I taught *Dick Jiggle* how to strut his stuff.
Man, when *I* learned the trade, the trade was rough!
To get the world of Showbiz by the Nuts
The thing you gotta have's a lotta guts.

'So stick with *Uncle Jelly*, Perry lad!
The Know-Alls laughed when I went out with *Trad*.
But this time round I've really struck it rich.
I stuck it out and came back in with *Kitsch*!'

On neon platform shoes whose perspex heels
Had mice inside them running round in wheels,
Exuding charismatic amps and watts
Fat *Belly* set a course for *Ronnie Scott*'s,
While *Perry* tottered onward through the gunge
To meet the Scottish poet DOUGLAS DUNGE,
A moralizing bard of wide remark –
And HUGO HARSFRIED lunged out of the dark.
Of these we will hear further, by-and-by.
But now a dozey glaze was in *Prykke*'s eye:
He ordered drinks all round and signed the cheque,
Coughed, crumpled at the midriff, hit the deck
And went to sleep in mingled pain and bliss
To dream of fickle Fame, her flagrant kiss.

Book Four

As Autumn darkness deepened in the City
The Novelists kept at it without pity.
Poor *Perry* toiled away as a Reviewer
And felt as if he drowned in horse manure.
His minuscule bedsit in *Notting Hill*
Grew insulated from the Winter chill
With brightly wrappered volumes beyond numbering,
While in amongst them *Peregrine* sat slumbering
Or else rapt in the life-consuming craft
Of shifting the new books before him aft
By reading them and typing up his thoughts –
An endless fusillade of short reports.
He hedged his praise, he modified his blame,
And wondered how he'd ever Make His Name:
However could one hope to be autonomous
While labouring so hard to stay anonymous?
(For in those days, you might just bring to mind,
The *TLS* reviews were all unsigned:
Which meant that clapped-out hack and clueless tyro
Could each drag down a few bob with a biro
And academics knife each other politely –
So long as no one ventured to write *brightly*.)
Imagine, then, *Prykke*'s joy when a commanding
Soft crackle from the phone out on the landing
Subpoenaed him to *Langham Place*. The caller?
The Kingpin of the *Listener*, KLAUS MAULER!
Despite his name, *Klaus Mauler* was a *Scot*.
Of *Scots* in *London* Life, there are a lot;
And *Welsh*, and *Ulstermen*, and, yes, *Australians*,
Hungarians, *Bavarians*, *Westphalians*,
Tanned types called *Popadom* and *Papadopoulos* –
There's everyone except the native populace.
But that's another subject in itself,
So for the nonce we'll leave it on the shelf
And stick with this one dominant Big Brother –
Who seemed to *Peregrine* much like his Mother,

Though looking even more robustly built.
A purist, *Klaus* wore naught beneath his kilt
Except a knobbly stick to beat his staff with
As well as separate the wheat from chaff with
Among his crew of academic hacks,
Who bore, upon their shoulders, shins and backs,
The marks of his *Olympian* disfavour
Delivered like a forehand from *Rod Laver.*
'I've seen your writings in the *TLS*:
They're undergraduate pretentiousness,'
Drawled *Mauler* from behind a massive desk –
And *Perry*'s bowel performed an arabesque.
'I won't stand for your puerile mewlings here.
I'm not as tolerant as I appear.
I'm offering you a golden opportunity
To pull your tiny weight in this community
By covering the Literary Scene.
It doesn't matter too much that you're green
So long as you can spell and use good grammar.
But if you can't, I'll see you get the hammer
The way your predecessors did, the turds.
Your fee will be one pound a thousand words.'
'Er, gosh, Sir, are you sure you mean a pound?'
'Good *God* no, *Prykke*, my mind must be unsound.
I meant to tell you seventeen and six.
The larger sum is for *Professor Rix* –
Who earns the bonus for his seniority
And lively air of erudite Authority.
It will be years before you reach the station
Of him who wrote *Yeats and Humiliation.*
Till you've a book to challenge that great Don with
The smaller sum is plenty to go on with.'
Proud *Prykke* was overjoyed, for, as you know,
At that time, which was several years ago,
You still bent over if you dropped a shilling.
And think of the prestige! Was *Perry* willing?
You bet your life he was! And just that night
The *Soho* bards were scheduled to recite
Their poems at a Show in *Bedford Square.*
The Book Binge it was called. They'd *all* be there –

Dunge, Fop, Fluck, Harsfried, Hammerhead, the lot!
Just think what *Cynth* would say, or *Graham Grott*!
Ah, Creativity, the mystic riddle of it!
And *Perry* would be slap bang in the middle of it!
From *Mauler*'s office *Perry* walked on air
And down the corridor towards the stair,
But as he passed a doorway his sweet dreams
Were put to flight by sudden piercing screams.
He poked his head inside and gagged with shock.
A man was stretched across a whipping-block
While *Mauler*'s cruel shillelagh rose and fell
Like some sadistic metronome in *Hell*!
As knotted shoulders writhed beneath the knouting
Prykke recognized the face that did the shouting.
Those spectacles, that plumply curving cheek,
Belonged to *Mauler*'s sidekick, *Derwent Meek*!
The yells went on. *Prykke*'s flabbergasted jaw
Yawned like a Right Whale's plankton-straining maw.
He'd heard that *Mauler* gave *Meek* a rough ride,
But *this* came close to being homicide:
The *Inquisition* under *Torquemada*
Could not have put the screws on any harder.
Prykke gumshoed off unsteady on his legs,
His First Class brain reduced to scrambled eggs,
But calmed himself by sensibly recalling
The voluntary aspect of *Meek*'s Mauling.
For such assaults, *Prykke* knew, *Meek* tolerated
In hopes that he would one day be instated
At *Mauler*'s desk as undisputed Editor.
The helpless prey was just another predator!
And as for *Mauler*, Chief of Secret Police –
Tous les grands hommes ont toujours du caprice.

Book Five

THE *Book Binge* galvanized the *Bloomsbury* night
With booming drums and waterfalls of light,
With sawdust, fairy floss and mirror-halls
And wooden clowns who swallow ping-pong balls.
A hubble-bubble *Babel-Bacchanal,*
A *bal masqué* like *Schumann*'s Carnaval,
The *Book Binge* was a three-ring Wing-a-Ding,
A *Gutenberg-Galactic* Happening –
A glowing Pleasure Garden out of *Bosch*
On which *Prykke*'s only comment could be
                                                            'Gosh'.
For here were dodgem cars, with Authors driving;
And next to them a pool, with dolphins diving;
And here were tests of strength, and bells were ringing;
And further on was *'Jelly' Belly* singing.
What games! What pipes and timbrels! What a bash!
And – here's the best bit – all of it was gash!
A dish-fit-for-a-king done to a turn,
The thing was Subsidized from stem to stern!
Charles Ozbuns of the State Arts Hand-out Panel
Had hatched the notion in his Proper Channel
In order that the Literary cliques
Who all year long intrigue and play no-speaks
Should reconcile their various activities
In one enormous outburst of Festivities.
While strident barkers bruited the attractions
Of all the different gangs, cabals and factions –
Mild Mandarins and manic Agitproppers,
Frail Struldbrugs and frenetic Teenyboppers,
Crazed New Departurists and crisp Grammarians,
Wet Apollonians and wild Aquarians –
The public flowed between the rows of tents
From Thence to Whence and Hence again to Thence.
'Neath fizzing naphtha flares, 'midst hoot of tooters,
The *mob. vulg.* milled around like bands of looters.

They jammed a booth to hear some bard recite.
They emptied it again to gain respite.
They crammed the Helter-Skelter to its summit
And rode the Roller Coaster like a plummet.
And here a row of SLAVE-GIRL NOVELISTS,
Bejewelled and chained together at the wrists,
Were belly-dancing high above the rabble –
And prominent among them was *Mag Scrabble*.
Her swerving navel plugged with a carnelian
She rippled like the skin of a chameleon
Compelled to crawl across a length of tartan –
The sight would have aroused lust in a *Spartan*.
The target for a dozen camera crews,
Tall on a gilded rostrum stood TED THEWS.
Impressively he read rhymed tales of woe
About some kind of psychopathic crow.
'Crow eats my eyeballs and spits out the pips.
Crow pecks my nose off and rips off my lips.
I like it, but I must say my face falls
When Crow declares an interest in my . . .' Calls
Of 'Genius!' went up from every side
And all agreed *Thews* should be deified,
For anyone who looked like saying no
The poet's sister flattened with one blow.
And here with muscles like the *Tyrant Gessler*'s
That pair of LIBERATED WOMEN WRESTLERS
Greer Garstleigh and *Kate Millsbomb* wrenched like plumbers
The necks and knees and elbows of all comers –
Their victims lay around on the *tatami*
Karate-chopped like slices of salami.
The atmosphere was carefree, even feckless,
But in one tent the tone was far less reckless:
For there sat the admirers, fit though few,
Of *Hammerhead*'s grim crew from the *Review*.
The aspect of the first bard to address them
Could scarcely fail to heavily impress them:
Frail *Hugo Harsfried*, Minimalist Poet!
His flaxen hair, as long as care could grow it,
Gleamed lustrously as *Jennifer O'Neill*'s,
And all the rest of him, from head to heels,

Bespoke a hypersensitive fragility
Extended to a willowy ductility –
A grail-pale male Madonna by *Rossetti*
As slender as a lightweight *Olivetti*.

'I touch your skin. You look at me askance.
We're lying sideways on, as if in *France*.
Hot talent stains my cortex like graffiti.
We're floating upside down. We're in *Tahiti*.'

This poem, first of fifteen of its kind,
Outstandingly evinced, to *Perry*'s mind,
Both Lyric Force and Technical Austerity.
What else did that add up to but Sincerity?
A photon-stream incisive as a razor,
The *Harsfried* Lyricism was a laser,
A source of light the night could not expunge.
And then he passed the torch to *Douglas Dunge*.

'Wa hae the noo, ye ken? Och aye, ye'll nae
McComprehend a mickle word I say.
I could na' give a bugger for a' that.
I dinna' hae the time for social chat.
Och, if ye canna' listen, ye can look.
Ye should hae gone and bought the bluidy book.'

Admired by all and understood by none
Dour *Dunge* kept going like a *Gatling* Gun
With infinite supplies of ammunition,
Or else a power station fired by fission.
He would have read until the Sun went *Nova*.
He could have maundered on till *Hell* froze over.
But suddenly his drone went dead as mutton
As if some giant hand had pushed a button.
The Headline Act was restless in the wings.
The time had long since come for bigger things.
Dismissing *Dunge* with ill-concealed rage
Hunched *Hammerhead* in person took the stage.
'I kick you in the ankle,'
                                    he read grimly,

Looked up, looked down again, and added,

'Dimly . . .'

His gritted voice was more intense than loud.
'. . . I see you limp away into the crowd.'
At this point there took place a lengthy pause
For which, it soon turned out, there was good cause:
A hard-won truth should not be lightly said.
'It's time to stop pretending we aren't dead.'
And that was the whole poem. It was plenty.
One little lyric did the work of twenty.
He looked into the audience, defying
The women in it not to burst out crying
With mingled fear and gratitude. Their eyes
Were full of tears, their breasts of heaving sighs,
A few rows from the back, some stricken mite
Expired with passion and dropped out of sight.
Her wrists were chafed, her corpse was carried off,
But no one present dared so much as cough,
For *Hammerhead* was slackening his jaw
A millimetre. That meant there was more.
'The last rose petal left broke off and fluttered
To settle softly on your knee,'

he muttered.

He paused, and cast his hard glance round a room
Devoid of sound as *Tutankhamun*'s tomb.
'Somewhere in *Luxembourg*, a lorry crashed.'
The next line flew for years before it smashed
As hard as a harpoon into a seal.
'Those knickers you were wearing looked like steel.'
The audience erupted in a standing
Ovation sounding like the *Concorde* landing.
To say that *Perry Prykke*, applauding wildly,
Had been impressed would be to put it mildly –
Since had not these three poets demonstrated
The truth of what *Doc Stein* had always stated?
For here was Language Tending Towards Zero!
The Poet as the Enigmatic Hero!
'Gosh,'

     Perry sighed, composing in his noodle
A fine old pot-pourri of flip flapdoodle

Concerning the forthcoming Moratorium
When poetry would be as rare as Thorium.
To change the mood, *Jeff Nuttcase* and *Bob Jobbing*
Came storming in, blind drunk from apple-bobbing –
Their fruit-caked hair and cider-soaked apparel
Suggesting they had half drowned in the barrel.
Their selfless task to represent the legions
Of Mute Inglorious *Miltons* in the Regions,
They lashed out like a brace of *Bovver Boys*
And made no end of Democratic noise –
Thus manifesting Radical derision
For *Hammerhead*'s aesthetic of Precision.
Delivered as an incoherent shout
Their slogan was

        'Establishment Pigs Out'
(A bit steep, since *Charles Ozbuns*'s accounts
Bore witness to the staggering amounts
That both these rebels had received in Grants.)
'Right lads,'

      growled *Hammerhead*,

                  'Let's have their pants.'
The signal had been given for a Rumble,
And instantly the tent was all a-tumble.
The two teams clashed as heavy-shod as Squaddies.
The injured air was full of flailing bodies.
Emitting cries as cryptic as the *Kabbalah*'s
They flew around in furious parabolas
Like hungry beggars after spilled piastres –
A Pandemonium of Poetasters.
Rock Horrorball rushed in with whirling fists
To join *Nuttcase* and *Jobbing* in the lists,
Tripped over the recumbent form of *Fluck*
And vanished like a football in the ruck.
With cries no longer modern at *Culloden*,
Dunge rendered *Nuttcase* notably less sodden
By kicking him immensely in the scrotum –
Whereat he stuck his tongue out like a totem,
Disgorging such a quantity of grog
The smell of it got in your eyes like smog.

In no time *Jobbing* also was a wreck,
For *Hammerhead* had written him a cheque –
As rubber as a truncheon and as ruthless,
It bounced so hard it left its victim toothless.
The hugger-mugger raged on unabated –
From bad to worse the mayhem escalated.
The tent pegs gave as if they had been rotten.
The guy ropes snapped as if they had been cotton.
Its central pole knocked sideways by a boot,
The canvas settled like a parachute –
But even when entrapped in swathes of wrapping
The writhing combatants continued scrapping.
A fish too tiny for the trawling mesh,
Prykke worked a passage through the threshing flesh.
He tunnelled through the heap from gap to gap
And traced the tent's hem till he found the flap.
He strode away, alert in every sense,
As if his thoughts encompassed Continents.
He reeled up *Oxford Street* and past *Hyde Park*,
His shining eyes twin diamonds in the dark.
He ate, when he got home to *Pembridge Crescent*,
A cold pork pie and felt he dined on pheasant.
He wrote, in prose appropriately cryptic,
Of Poetry approaching its Ecliptic.

Book Six

WHEN *Perry*'s Piece appeared, Success was clamorous.
Prykke's Keen Approach abruptly became glamorous.
Nobody else of his age was so sedulous,
Nobody else of *any* age so credulous.
Poseurs would praise themselves and he'd believe them!
Tired reputations sagged, he'd help retrieve them!
While all concerned adored what *Perry* said
About themselves, they never of course read
The plaudits which he might rain on a rival –
A fact that was the key to his survival.
Survive? But he did more than that. He flourished.
No longer looking wan and undernourished,
He fattened on that magic food, Renown –
The Dish You Know Will Never Let You Down.
Prykke's eager parents bought ten copies each
Of all he wrote, and anyone in reach
Was forced to take a gander, even strangers.
Sweet *Cynthia* wrote warning of the dangers
Inherent in the promptings of Ambition.
Too late, because the next Phase of the Mission
Was under way. A call from TERRY TOWELLING!
A call that set *Prykke*'s mental sirens howling –
The kind of call at which your bloodstream freezes.
To write for the *Observer*! Holy *Jesus*!
'Um um um um um um um um um um,'
Said *Towelling*. After which he seemed struck dumb
While waiting for a new thought to occur.
'Er er er er er er er er er er . . .'
Poor *Perry* stared in wonder at the blower.
Did Entropy mean telephones ran slower?
He soon would know – and so be less censorious –
That *Terry Towelling*'s phone calls are notorious.
To kill the time the point takes to be reached
(The same time *Nixon* takes to be impeached)
You carry on with what it is you're at –
With cooking, eating, sleeping, things like that –

And end the conversation fed and rested.
They say one famous critic, when requested
To do a job he failed to find amusing,
Amused his mistress three times while refusing.
'Um um, we need the younger person's view –
The view, that is, of er, someone like you –
On subjects like the ah, the *ICA*
Would um, you er, um care to? We ah, pay.'
'Gosh,'
      Prykke replied,
                    'I know. I'm deeply flattered.
We must treat Rebel Art as if it mattered:
I know that from *Doc Stein* and from *El Al.*
I'll go this very evening to the *Mall.*'
The *ICA* in those days, than yourselves,
Would sooner have played host to gnomes and elves.
It crawled with lethal, Radicalized viruses
All standardized like figures on papyruses,
Conferring the name 'poetry' on verses
Which didn't even make the grade as curses.
Shrill children vainly sought the tricky balance
Between what we'll agree to call their Talents
And Fame's demand that Art should be unique
By daubing pictures weird as they were weak,
While woaded pantaloons in dung-caked cerements
Were footling with theatrical Experiments
In which they were allowed to Improvise –
Which, in effect, means talk a pack of lies,
Since actors, when they plumb their recollection
Find little in there worth the resurrection
Except a load of trouper's time-worn gimmickry,
Outdated dialogue and mouldy mimicry.
But all of this, it must be said in fairness,
Was organized to Further our Awareness
And not, as you might hazard, to exploit us.
The hero at the helm was MICHAEL KOITUS.
A natural, with his soothing *Oxbridge* tones,
For mentioning large sums down telephones,
Keen *Koitus*, most industrious of bosses,
Precisely supervised the place's losses.

He never rested easy, always pondering
Forever more ambitious ways of squandering
The massive public funds which he was showered with.
The garden he was planted in and flowered with
Was *Swinging London* – now, alas, no more.
But Now means Later. This was still Before,
When books came out about the Power of Play
And *Koitus* held uninterrupted sway.
The *ICA* was jammed when *Perry* got there.
So who was *there*, you're asking? Who was *not* there!
What churl would dare withhold a contribution
Towards the soaring costs of Revolution?
Cool *Koitus* suavely spoke some prolegomena
To set the context for the night's phenomena.
'Our records show that in a single year
We've made a hundred thousand. Disappear.
The *Philistines* say, "Money down the drain."
But take a look at what we stand to gain.
Pauline and *Poogy Scheissenhaus* have sent,
From *Baader-Meinhof Studios* in *Ghent*,
A flushing suite of white ceramic Art
With film-loops of an anaconda's fart.
We've had a *Warhol* premiere, "Hot Crap".
And *Haiku Yamashita* the Mad Jap
Has played a conga drum for fifteen hours
With one foot while the other arranged flowers.
There's all of that, and then there's coming soon
The *Peking People's Puppeteers' Platoon*
To fill our stage once more with their red flags
And captivate our kiddies with their gags
About the contradictions of Imperialism
Laid bare by dialectical materialism.
And then that ballet group who dance in Scuba
Equipment called the *Rubber Freaks for Cuba*
Are back, and then somebody takes a mudbath,
Or – wait a second – maybe it's a bloodbath . . .
Well, anyway, there's plenty on our plate.
But let's kick off the show. It's getting late.'
He exited. The first act on the bill
Came trotting on. O atavistic thrill!

Who else but BRIAN GOUGH and HENRI PATTEN,
A double act beneath a sheet of satin
Complete with cardboard head and frayed rope tail?
The Panto Horse from *Liverpool*! Can't fail.
From each end of the horse lines emanated
Alternately until its case was stated.

'We are a pair of poets from the Mersey.'
'We never had no nanny or no nursie.'
'Our mothers wouldn't let books in the house.'
'We found out how to write from talking *Scouse*.'
'That's what makes all our poems easy listening.'
'The scrubbers hear us read with knickers glistening.'
'These are the only rhymes we've ever tried.'
'It's taken us so long we've nearly died.'
'We'd rather type things straight on to the stencil.'
'Than sit around for days and suck a pencil.'
'The intellectual thing's been done before.'
'We also think there should be no more war.'
'Nobody didn't ought to be too clever.'
'And everyone should stay eighteen forever.'

The Horse took several bows and off it pranced.
The crowd went mad while Perry sat entranced.
Now *this* was Life, by Intellect unvitiated:
The forceful Candour of the uninitiated.
For here was nothing underhand or stealthy –
Just simple, vibrant Strength, robust and healthy.
Prykke started to make notes, but then a roll
Of kettle drums which thrilled him to the soul
Announced the advent of a gorgeous creature
Sartorially superb in every feature.
Those doe-skin bowling shoes! That pink carnation!
That shy acknowledgement of adulation!
A national treasure like the Wall of *Hadrian*,
Who else but Rebel Poet MITCH L. ADRIAN!

'*Bill Blake*, they try to shoot you in *My Lai*,
But some of us refuse to let you die.

Bill Blake, they try to poison you in *Laos*,
But you reduce their crazy plans to chaos.
Bill Blake, they try to mine you in *Haiphong*,
But you outwit them like the *Viet Cong*.
Bill Blake, the whole *Strategic Air Command*
Could never bomb the pen out of your hand.
Bill Blake, you stand for thinking with the balls
The thoughts that melt their prison bars and walls.
Bill Blake, you know what's real, you know what's true,
And I know when I write that I am you.'

And so the last *Narodnik* took his leave.
Full well might his applauding public grieve:
To be without him meant to be bereft
Of everything that Humanized the Left.
The next act was the undisputed Queen
Of *London*'s Revolutionary Scene,
A protegée of CREEPING GEORGE McDEATH.
Her name was ANNA PEST. *Prykke* caught his breath.
He'd heard she was a knockout, but by Crikey!
La Pest was an assault course for the psyche:
A sight to stop a centaur in mid-gallop –
A newborn *Venus* served up in a scallop.
For *Anna* was no kewpie-doll like *Cynthia*
But something much more statue-on-a-plinthier.
A girl built like a *Grecian* Caryatid,
Except not even slightly chipped or battered.
The absolutely other thing, in fact:
Meticulously, exquisitely, Stacked.
That *Pest* was Mannequin as well as Poet –
You needn't have been *Sherlock Holmes* to know it.
For one so sensitive as well as sinuous
Why shouldn't the two callings be continuous?
She once appeared, stretched out full length, in *Vogue*,
To underline an elegy by *Logue* –
Ensuring that his lines remained unread,
Since everybody looked at her instead.
'The monster, Sex, was present at my christening . . .'
She huskily began. *Prykke* wasn't listening.

She read for some considerable time
Concoctions free of rhythm, metre, rhyme
Or any metaphors save inexact ones.
One found that when one finally had hacked one's
Way through to what she meant, the sense had perished.
No matter, for already *Perry* cherished
(Fixated on the way her eyelids fluttered)
Each flaring imbecility she uttered.
Her long harangue at last came to a close.
Fond *Prykke*, along with all those present, rose
To greet her clinching statement with applause.
'... *America*, you rape me with your wars.'
As *Prykke* tracked *Anna*'s exit with a glance
Made glaucous by his meditative trance,
He would have sunk into a deep paralysis
Except an uproar which defied analysis –
Drums, tubas, trumpets, rattles, tambourines –
Announced one of the all-time top routines
Since *Torquemada* put away his fetters:
Yes, *Creeping George McDeath*, Sick Man of Letters!
The art of *Creeping George* is so horrific it
Has seldom even got an 'X' Certificate.
Crushed bones and blood and brain-pulp are the stuff of it.
The necrophiles can't seem to get enough of it.
The *Muse*, in *Creeping George*'s view, wears black
Stiletto jackboots and a rubber mac,
While *Creeping George* himself wears snakeskin ties –
And doesn't always wait till the snake dies.

'The blood has soaked the bone which hides the stone
The rat excreted in the telephone.
Fellating stone and bone I taste the blood
Which laps around my pelvis like a flood.
I feel a painful pressure in my groin
On either side of which I have a loin.
My loins are groined, my stone's a bloody bone:
I'll have to learn to leave myself alone.'

Cheers. Total tumult. Nothing could cap that.
As *Creeping George* slid off to feed his bat

And slid back on for umpteen curtain calls,
Pale *Perry* sat enchanted in the stalls.
'But aren't you *Perry Prykke*?'

                        breathed *Anna Pest*,
A butterfly come suddenly to rest
Exotically on *Prykke*'s astonished shoulder.
'It's funny – I'd expected someone older.
I worship the ripe wisdom of your work.
A critic of one's Art who's not a berk
Is someone to be valued. There's a party.
I'll take you to it in my *Maserati*.'
'Er, gosh, Miss *Pest*, I worship *your* work too.
I'm interested in everything you do.
This party, though. I haven't been invited . . .'
A V-12 engine piercingly ignited
And all the rest of *Perry*'s words were drowned
By shattering catastrophes of sound.
They hurtled through the midnight side by side,
Young *Perry Prykke* beside himself with pride
And *Anna Pest* superb as the aurora.
Avanti! Gangway! *Tora Tora Tora*!

Book Seven

THE MARCHIONESS OF PROPERLITTLE-RAYVER
Had never taken on a venture braver
Than victualling the Literary World.
The party wasn't thrown so much as hurled.
Her modest residence in *Holland Park*
Was packed with different species, like the *Ark*:
They jammed it to the crystal chandeliers,
They scraped against the frames of the *Vermeers*.
The *Marchioness*'s forebears made their hay
By keeping hungry citizens at bay,
Discouraging requests for gifts of food
With measures firm and often downright rude.
Spilt milk. The current title-holder, though
(Though otherwise no glad hand with the dough)
Was willing to unlatch the family hampers
And hand around the scampi and the champers
To people with Artistic reputations –
The plain-clothes peerage of Communications.
'I'm glad young *Anna*,'
                          barked the *Marchioness*,
'Unearthed you. I did not know your address.
Some people here are going mad to meet you.
Some people here have said they'd like to *eat* you,
So how could you be less of an intruder?
You just leave *Anna* talking to *Neruda*
And go and chat to that man on the sofa.
He ought to come to you, but he's a loafer.'
The gentleman so blithely indicated
Turned out to be a bard *Prykke* venerated
As harbouring a mind almost *Miltonic*,
A talent *Keatsian*, a soul *Byronic*.
That shirt, that glass of scotch, that shining skull;
Our lad was being welcomed by BOB LULL!
'I've had your pieces brought to my attention,'
Croaked *Lull*.
                  'I found it strange that you should mention

422

My own name in connection with *Racine,*
Donne, Dante, Shakespeare, Marlowe, Kydd and *Greene*:
I think perhaps just *Shakespeare* would have done.
But that aside, I've recently begun
A blank verse, five-act Version of "*Tom Sawyer*"
Bipolarized in terms of Paranoia,
In which I view the plain white light of *Twain*
Refracted through the prisms of my pain.
I never knew what words like Rough or Raw meant
Until I bared my poor mind to this torment.
My brain's on fire, my enemies grow vicious:
The time could scarcely be more unpropitious
For launching a new venture in Our Trade.
Yes, Mr *Prykke*, I'm asking for your aid.'
'Gosh, Mr *Lull*, in any way I can
I'll do my best to help you with your plan.
I'm so surprised I don't know what to say.
I'll go and read "*Tom Sawyer*" right away.'
'No, Mr *Prykke*, that's just a tiny part
Of what I want to alter in my Art.
The place I want your help is in an area
Of which perhaps you might be somewhat warier:
The business I began some years ago
(And whose results so far I'm sure you know)
Of smashing up my work in angry fits
Until it's strewn around in little bits,
Or 'Sonnets' as they're kindly called by *Faber* –
Who undertake the monumental labour
Of marketing the stuff as something new
To fans who've seen it all before, like you.'
'Gosh, Mr *Lull*, I have to disagree.
Your sonnet-cycles all sound fresh to me.
Tart, erudite, elliptical, persuasive,
Your *Faustian* persona's all-pervasive.
Exploring cobwebbed corridors of Time
You never let your forms lapse into rhyme
But leave them all unfinished, like reality –
An Iso-Spatial Synchronous Modality.'
(From *Yvor Frye*, or was it *Northrop Winters*,
Young *Perry* picked these phrases up like splinters.)

'I thank you, Mr *Prykke*, for your support.
It's possible that I was overwrought.
It's true indeed that better minds than mine
Have scrutinized my Sonnets line by line
And found in them the toughness of the *Tetrarch*,
The bloom of *Brahms*, the purity of *Petrarch*.
Thrust close against the glare of my creations
Perhaps I'm blinded by their scintillations.
Old *Michelangelo*, I can't help feeling,
Had that same problem with the *Sistine Ceiling*.
It's hard to see one's own extent *in toto*.
There *Proust* would have agreed with me, and *Giotto* . . .
But modesty forbids that I expand
Much further on that theme, you understand?
So let's just say that my mature fertility
Could use assistance from your young agility.
I've put my output through the mincer once.
Before the fine edge of my talent blunts
I'd like to see if I can do it twice.
The challenge grips my forehead like a vice:
I want your help – I hope you won't refuse –
To turn my Sonnets into Clerihews.'
'Gosh, Sir, what makes you think I'm qualified –
A scholar so untested, so untried –
For this, the biggest job I've ever faced?'
'You just',

         creaked *Lull*,

                        'need scissors and some paste.'
Still gaping, *Prykke* was led away by *Anna*
To find his Fame was all around the manor.
He got on first-name terms with *Kingsley Kong*,
While *Norman Moonbase* taught him a rude song
About how *Tony Godspell* was a gremlin
Assigned to ruin *Penguins* by the *Kremlin*.
In no time these notorious Right-Wingers
Were known to *Perry Prykke* as '*Norm*' and '*Kingers*'.
Green Berets briefed to win with utmost urgency
His heart and mind and counter his insurgency,
They dived right in and did not dilly-dally:
Would *Prykke* attend a *Bertorelli* Rally?

Just try and stop him! *Tuesday* then? *Prykke* nodded,
Struck mute. As if he needed to be prodded!
For at that famous kayf in *Charlotte Street*
The elite *Fascists* weekly meet to eat
And plan their latest last-ditch, Doomwatch caper –
White Guards unleashing tigers of Black Paper.
And there you find the clever *Bernard Beaver* –
The fervid, fevered, fulvid True Believer –
Who blows on *Nixon*'s coal to the last flicker
And backs the *Pentagon* through thick and thicker,
While zany *Wildwind Wagtail* shouts approval
And calls for *Arthur Balfour*'s prompt removal.
(On being told that *Balfour* is long dead,
Mad *Wagtail* rolls up little balls of bread
And shies them at the waitresses like pebbles,
Convinced that he is executing rebels.)
JOHN BRAINWAVE then contributes his opinions
On what should be the fate of *Mao*'s minions.
'The students should be killed. They should be dead.
You hear me? I said "dead". Hear what I said?
They should be stood against a wall and shot.
Not just a few. Not most. I mean the lot.'
Then *Moonbase* sings a song, *Kong* does a mime,
And everyone pays heed to *Tony Time*,
Who peels his lips back from his teeth like scrolls
And with a blue-blood's tortured drawl unrolls
An extract from the history long as *Rome*'s
Contained in *Tony Time's Twelve Teeming Tomes*.
This coven of Cold Warriors and Hawks
Can boast the membership of *Philip Lawks*,
Who sometimes travels *South* to sit about in it
While sipping strong brown ale and saying nowt in it:
For *Lawks* in *London*'s just another tourist,
Of all dour *Northern* tourists he's the dourest,
Though some say that at home he's far less dull –
And there they call him DON JUAN IN HULL.
Imagining such eminent companions
Exchanging quips like ricochets in canyons,
Prykke gaped in awe. The gape became a gasp.
The Literary World was in his grasp!

And so, with one hand spilling pink champagne
And by the other hauled on like a train,
Our *Perry* cannoned vaguely through the cumulus
Of household names from tumulus to tumulus.
His eyes with Famous Faces were regaled
Until his heart ran hot and almost failed:
For here the old High-Born and new Self-Made
Homogenized into a Hit Parade.
The bright lights of the 'Thirties never dwindle
And here was one before him, *Stephen Spindle*,
Avowing he thought *Perry* wrote prose finer
Than *Christopher* and *Wystan* wrote in *China*.
And *Frankie Mode*, Ubiquitous Professor
Just passing through from *Dallas* to *Odessa*,
Stood weightless before *Perry* like a ghost –
His body somewhere near the *Danish* coast.
Assuring purring *Perry* that his pieces
In acumen were wealthier than *Croesus*,
Mode faded inward from the edges eerily,
And where he was, a jet stream whistled wearily.
Suave editors pressed forward to make offers
That started elbow-deep inside their coffers –
The days were done, it seemed, when *Prykke* reviewed
A novel just to flog the thing for food.
Now *Clara Tomahawk* and *N. T. Thweet*
Stood toe to toe before him to compete
For opportunities to print his writing –
A cut-throat contest fully as exciting
As all the speedway pile-ups in *Ben Hur*.
Without procrastination or demur,
Pissed *Prykke* was gaily saying Yes to each of them
When *Anna* quickly whirled him out of reach of them
To meet the publisher, WEE GEORGIE WIDE,
Who ushered him paternally aside
And got him to agree to write a Book –
The most decisive step *Prykke* ever took.
His bug eyes straying constantly to *Anna*,
Wide's mouth evoked an avalanche of manna
Engulfing *Prykke* so deep no one would find him
Once *Tightenbelt and Buckledown* had signed him.

'Mine boy, you are the likeliest new challenger
I'm seeing come along since *J. D. Salinger.*
You got a style on you like *Norman Mailer,*'
Wide whispered, and pale *Prykke* grew even paler,
Bedizened by the flattery *Wide* uttered –
The furthest up he'd ever yet been buttered.
'You stick mit *Georgie*, kid. I'll see you right.
I tell you vot. Veal clinch the deal tonight.
Most boys I vont for nine years. Sometimes ten.
For you, I'll say eleven. Got a pen?'
The documents came out, *Prykke*'s name went on,
The deal was sealed with *Moët & Chandon* –
Enough to make the average supertanker
Bend double at the bows and drag its anchor.
Our friend's last recollection of the gathering
Was *Anna*'s tongue luxuriously lathering
His ear lobe and her perfumed voice implying
The time was ripe for young folk to be hieing
Them home to slide beneath a cosy quilt.
And so, without the smallest trace of guilt –
For when is feeling *that* good ever bad? –
Our lad was off to *Anna*'s *Park Lane* pad.
I'll have to draw a veil on its appointments,
Its incense and its essences and ointments,
The tapestries and inlays and enamels,
The skins and furs from reptiles and from mammals.
Let's just content ourselves with merely noting
Our sobbing hero felt that he was floating
Towards the outer limits of exoticism
Excoriated by her wild eroticism –
Sensations so outlandish *Perry* thought
She'd have to go to jail if she was caught.
Adrift in rich pavilions and pagodas
He breathed unnerving, fluctuating odours:
Astringent tangs compounded of *Chanel*
And oysters lying helpless in the shell.
He touched an orb of amber rubbed with silk,
He tasted avocados pulped in milk.
She taught him things that felt as nice as flying
And even nicer things that hurt like dying.

Of *Cynthia*, the Love he'd left behind,
In *Perry*'s mind the memory declined –
A bonbon overwhelmed by a bonanza.
Yes, *Anna Pest* was an extravaganza.

Book Eight

THE high point of *Prykke*'s time on Earth had come.
We'll savour it a moment. *Perry*'s *Mum*,
On learning that her Son's path to Success
By now involved an actual *Marchioness*,
Erupted in a fugue of exultation
She had to be brought down from by sedation.
Not only willingly but even meekly
All monthly magazines and every weekly
Accepted anything *Prykke* thought as Topical:
Young *Peregrine* was so hot he was tropical.
By night you'd hear him laying down the law
On all the Radios from 1 to 4
With special emphasis, of course, on 3,
Where *Creeping George McDeath* would frequently
Inveigle him to do a solemn summary
Of all the latest Literary mummery.
And *Philip Phrog*, key man of *Kritiks' Kworum*,
Roped *Prykke* into that game of cockalorum
Where pundits crammed with intellectual calories
From books and plays and cinemas and galleries
Scrum down like front-row forwards with their tongues out
Around a microphone and shout their lungs out.
And thus *Prykke* joined Steam Radio's tight team
Of people primed to Talk on Any Theme,
A *mafia* of men with minds like swords
As well as some extremely brainy broads –
And truth to tell our lad found nothing easier
Than hanging on the lips of *Lady Freesia*
Or trading witticisms with *Mag Scrabble*
Or letting *Margerina Latchkey* babble.
The more that *Perry* made himself available
The more he found his Keen Approach was saleable,
And if he sometimes flannelled . . . well, you know:
A *beau mentir qui vient de loin*, not so?
On Television, too, our *Perry* bloomed.
He bloomed? He boomed, he roared, he soared, he zoomed!

He showed a gift for popularized gab
Which rivalled even that of *Marvin Grabb*,
Whose show it was that he appeared on most –
Preceded by a build-up from his host.
'And with us in the studio once more
Is *Perry Prykke* the critic, and I'm sure
That you won't – I know I won't – find it dull
To hear what he's been doing with *Bob Lull*,
The man who wants to make his poems smaller.
A poem is, I'm certain you recall, a,
Well, smallish piece of writing which has got
Er, rhythm – or, in *Lull*'s case, which has not.'
'Gosh, thank you, *Marv*. I'm glad to say that *Bob*
Has given me a free hand on this job,
Including open access to his diaries.
I should be soon completing my inquiries
And hope to get clear pictures of the state
Of mental agony we know the Great
Have always manifested throughout history.
We might just have the answer to the mystery.'
'That's marvellous, *Perry*. More from him next time,
But now we're due to see a famous mime.
It's *Haiku Yamashita* from *Japan*.
A mime is someone, usually a man,
Who doesn't need his voice to tell you things.
And then, for jazz fans, "*Jelly*" *Belly* sings!'
His prominence endorsed by *Private Eye* –
Who mentioned him in every second lie
And printed bits cut out from what he said
Sent in by dolts whose lips moved when they read –
Prykke seemed to be poised at the apogee
Of every single ladder, heap or tree:
He even found his name used by *Bron Wan*
(An infant who can't grasp that Youth is gone)
To spark the kind of envy-ridden rumour
Where want of truth's offset by want of humour.
It lacked, however, one last accolade
To show how utterly he'd made the grade.
But finally that happened, in *The Times*:
A lovingly assembled set of rhymes

Entitled, *To a Young Man Almost There*:
An Old Man's Tribute – by LORD TEDDYBEAR.

'I cast a wise old eye upon young *Prykke*
And feel that once again I ride my bike
Towards some nameless, adolescent thrill
Recumbent at the foot of *Rosslyn Hill*.

'Ah me, the joy of Starting Out again!
Of taking tea with well-informed young men
(Supposing they still do that nowadays)
Who loll about dispensing blame and praise!

'To look on Literature as some fresh church
Discovered behind screens of larch and birch!
To say of it, "How finely bricked and plastered!"
And hear it murmur back, "You fey old bastard!"

'It must be wonderful to be Beginning,
To lay the basis for a whole new inning.
Monumentum requiris? Look around.
I think my clockwork panda's overwound.

'So square the marble slab to build your edifice
Young *Prykke*! But different Endings lie ahead of us,
For I have got it made while you must quarry it,
And that is why I am the *Poet Laureate*.'

The *Prykke* renown seemed limitless, unbounded,
Its heights unreachable, its depths unsounded.
He gave himself a lifetime to enjoy it,
All unawares the thing that would destroy it
Was even then, and by his own endeavour,
Collecting strength to wreck his name forever.
It was the Book, the Book it was to blame:
The Book that should have reinforced his fame
But punctured it instead and brought it crashing –
Pink flames of hydrogen profusely splashing –
With incandescent girders to Disaster.
The plaudits which had made his heart beat faster

Had given him a sense of his own worth.
A brand-new *Perry Prykke* had come to birth:
A *Prykke* who dared to qualify his praise
Of writers with the odd paternal phrase
Suggesting So-and-So, though near perfection,
Had minor faults requiring some correction.
Though *Hammerhead, Prykke* wrote, dwarfed *Baudelaire,*
He ought to make appearances less rare;
Though *Mitch L. Adrian* had joined the Greats
He still had several things to learn from *Yeats*;
Though *Harsfried* was at one with the Eternal
He lacked sufficient nut around the kernel;
Doug Dunge could learn a thing or two from *Browning*
And *Churchill College* take a tip from *Downing* –
Doc Stein should be, like *Looseleaf,* for Felt Life
(A dictum which cut both ways, like a knife:
For *Looseleaf* ought to grant *Stein* more respect
Concerning the Collapse of Intellect).
The Book was called *Loose Laurels.* It was bold,
And one brave statement made your blood run cold.
Intrepid *Prykke* said *Lull,* by just a skerrick,
Fell short of being totally *Homeric*!
Aware that not in Fame but in Authority
Is housed the only true Superiority,
Dim *Perry* must have thought a show of rigour
Would help him cut a more distinguished figure.
If that was his idea, he quickly rued it.
The people who were in the book reviewed it!
And what they found was something worse than witticisms,
Squibs, epigrams or wisecracks. They found CRITICISMS!
Restrictions placed upon their giant stature!
Irreverent gibes wrapped up in nomenclature!
A crawling bum they'd picked out of the gutter!
They'd known him when his mouth would not melt butter!
And here he was, the two-faced little sod,
Excreting on their stuff like he was *God*!

Book Nine

THE Notices hit *Prykke* like heart attacks.
He staggered from the blows of *El Al*'s axe,
While *Hammerhead*'s sharp biro pierced his lung;
By *Harsfried* in the *Statesman* he was hung,
Cut down, cut up, rolled flat and then cremated;
By *Creeping George McDeath* he was castrated.
As *N. T. Thweet* took time and space to mount a
Retaliatory air-strike in *Encounter*,
Mitch Adrian said *Prykke* was in the pay
Of both the *FBI* and *CIA*,
While *Kong* claimed *Prykke* received a monthly fee
From both the *TUC* and *KGB*.
Bob Lull attacked him with the family sabre.
Doug Dunge took careful aim and tossed a caber.
Doc Stein joined in, insisting all that stuff
About the Verbal Holocaust was guff.
He couldn't think where *Perry* must have read it.
It wasn't in *Stein*'s books. He'd never said it.
No, *Stein* had just been quoting *Leopardi*,
Or *Tristan Corbière* or *Thomas Hardy*,
Or maybe – ah yes, that was it – *Franz Werfel*.
Deplorable. *Prykke* should have been more careful.
(For *Stein*, you see, could hear the ticking clock,
And knew that *Perry*'s time was nigh. The *Doc*,
Though pretty swift already at contriving
To climb on board a bandwagon arriving,
Is so quick climbing *off* it's breath-bereaving
Should that same vehicle show signs of leaving.)
What better time for *Perry*'s *Mum* to send
A tear-stained telegram from *Audley End*?
'Please don't come here for *Xmas*. Go to *Rome*.
Why not try *Tokyo*? But *don't come home*.
We're moving out to stay at your *Aunt Nina*'s.
The neighbours here are laughing like hyenas.'
His brilliant future blasted in the bud,
Prykke's name in *Bertorelli*'s was now Mud.

Served hand and foot by coolie, cooled by punkah,
The *Tuesday Fascists* lunching in their bunker
Dropped hints it might be on the whole more pleasant
If *Perry* could contrive not to be present.
The buzz from *Soho* said that *Hammerhead*
Was grooming someone younger in *Prykke*'s stead
Who might get right what *Perry* had got wrong –
A clever son of *Kingsley*'s called *Kid Kong*.
The ICA called *Perry* a Defeatist,
A Category-Mongering Elitist –
Acceptance was what Art was all about,
And that was why they had to kick him out.
Phil Phrog and *Creeping George* and *Marvin Grabb*
No longer seemed so keen to send a cab
And haul him off to *BH* or *TC*.
Prykke was as *infra dig* as *Simon Dee*,
A Has-been of the Airwaves and the Screens –
And similarly of the Magazines,
Since neither *Towelling, Tomahawk* nor *Mauler*
Nor *Thweet* was any more a morning caller
To ask him for a quick piece on *Max Weber*
Or some duff poet canonized by *Faber* –
And *Frankie Mode* wrote briefly from *Brazil*
Advising *Prykke* with ill-concealed ill will
The '*Modish Masters*' Series would not need
That book which he was planning on *Lou Reed* –
While *Wide*, to put the cap on the attainder,
Consigned '*Loose Laurels*' wholesale to remainder –
A bargain bookworms warily inspected,
Rejecting it as if it were infected.
Deducing *Prykke* had lapsed into disfavour
The *Marchioness of Properlittle-Rayver*
Endorsed the literati's verdict massively
By simply lying back and acting passively.
She spent no time composing scorn to pour on him,
Since all she had to do was shut the door on him
And instantly his status was no higher
Than somewhere between polecat and pariah.
She slammed it. Far away, *Prykke* heard it boom
And knew that she had sealed his social doom.

For *Perry*-About-Town the end had come.
Beau Prykke was *Acherontis pabulum*.
Would everyone deny him in his need?
Would even *Anna* laugh to see him bleed?
From *Notting Hill* the long mile to *Park Lane*
He stumbled in the early morning rain,
Afraid in his chill heart she'd ceased to care.
She had indeed. She wasn't even there.
She'd been involved with *Harsfried* for a week:
They were out together dancing, *chic* to *chic*.
It was the last, dark hour before the dawn.
Poor *Perry* reached his room completely shorn
Of all his erstwhile appetite for living.
The Literary World is unforgiving,
That much he knew. There could be no way back.
He felt the pressure at his waist go slack
And saw his belt half-hitched around a beam.
He watched himself like someone in a dream
Construct a scaffold largely from *Larousse*
Encyclopedias and tie the noose.
He kicked off from a stack of *Livres de Poche*.
The last word that he ever heard was,
                                                    'Gosh.'

Book Ten

THE evil tidings coiled and thinly curled
And drifted through the Literary World.
Obituaries stressed the victim's Youth,
The risks attendant on the Search for Truth.
The *Guardian* had something signed by *Stein*
Connecting *Prykke*'s demise to Our Decline.
'The Overriding Need for an Alliance
Persists between the Cultures Art and Science.
Will Music make the Relevant Connection?
Until it does, we all must face infection.
A few will die, like *Prykke*, like *Gaudier*,
Like *Mandelstam, Camus* and *Hemingway*,
Like *Mayakovsky, Jackson Pollock, Lorca* . . .'
He printed it again in the *New Yorker*.
Sere *Looseleaf* wrote a letter no one saw
To some review that died before the war.
'In placing self-destructive insecurity
Beside the dying *Lawrence*'s maturity,
We cannot help but find *Prykke*'s flight of panic
Against Life. Uncreative. Inorganic.'
El Al brought out his book on Suicide –
A publishing success for *Georgie Wide*
Which helped him to offset the *Perry* flop.
For *Perry*'s Mother, life came to a stop:
The rest of it is no concern of mine.
No more is *Dr Cynthia Devine*,
Who's now at *Lady Margaret Hall* and lost in
Composing *A New Reading of Jane Austen*.
The Wake for *Perry* in the *Gates of Hell*
Went off, so legend tells us, pretty well.
A score or so of literati came
Of whom a handful still recalled his name
And three of those had heard the tragic news.
All present went like camels through the booze
And presently the booze all went through them.
It joined the cigarette butts, scum and phlegm

That choked the white-tiled gutters in the bog.
It trickled through, then tunnelled like a trog
The sodden furlongs to the sewage farm,
And there was scoured and filtered free of harm
Before they spread it thin to be sucked high
By *London*'s fitful Sun into the sky
In proper time to reimburse the rain
And so in due course tumble down again
To meet the *Thames* and with the turning tide
Revolve into an eddy, boil and slide
From bridge to bridge and Pool to Estuary
And so on, ever *Eastward*, to the Sea.
A tenuous memento of our *Perry*
Finessed to bubbles by the Channel Ferry.
A distant memory of beer and whisky
Disintegrating in the *Bay of Biscay*.

And so our story ends. Its simple moral
Is one with which I'm certain few will quarrel.
The Literary World is you and I:
We change from day to day or else we die.
The Innocent should stay the way they are:
For them, to live means following their Star.
The one thing they must do is trust in Fate.
The one thing they must not, *manipulate*.
For that, they just aren't built to stand the pace –
So if we break their hearts, it's no disgrace.
It's just a shame. And *that*'s what he was like.

'The good die young'
hic jacet
PERRY PRYKKE.